WE

ARE

DATA

ALGORITHMS

AND THE MAKING

OF OUR DIGITAL SELVES

JOHN CHENEY-LIPPOLD

NEW YORK UNIVERSITY PRESS NEW YORK

NEW YORK UNIVERSITY PRESS
New York
www.nyupress.org

© 2017 by New York University
All rights reserved

References to Internet websites (URLs) were accurate at the time of writing. Neither the author nor New York University Press is responsible for URLs that may have expired or changed since the manuscript was prepared.

ISBN: 978-1-4798-5759-3

For Library of Congress Cataloging-in-Publication data, please contact the Library of Congress.

New York University Press books are printed on acid-free paper, and their binding materials are chosen for strength and durability. We strive to use environmentally responsible suppliers and materials to the greatest extent possible in publishing our books.

Manufactured in the United States of America

10 9 8 7 6 5 4 3 2 1

Also available as an ebook

W E

A R E

D A T A

To Mamana Bibi and Mark Hemmings

Contents

Preface

Are you famous?

Celebrities are our contemporary era's royalty, the icons for how life ought (or ought not) to be lived. They and their scrupulously manicured personae are stand-ins for success, beauty, desire, and opulence. Yet celebrity life can appear, at least to the plebeian outside, as a golden prison, a structurally gorgeous, superficially rewarding, but essentially intolerable clink. The idea of the "right to privacy," coined back in the late nineteenth century, actually arose to address celebrity toils within this prison.[1] Newspaper photographers were climbing onto tree branches, peering into high-society homes, and taking pictures of big-money soirees so as to give noncelebrity readers a glimpse into this beau monde. Our contemporary conception of privacy was born in response to these intrusions.

For those of us on the outside looking in, our noncelebrity identity and relation to privacy may seem much simpler. Or is it? How can one really be sure one *is*—or *is not*—a celebrity? It's easy enough to do a quick test to prove it. Go to google.co.uk (note: not google.com), and search for your name. Then, scroll to the bottom of the results page. Do you see the phrase "Some results may have been removed under data protection law in Europe" (figure P.1)? The answer to this question—whether this caveat appears or not—will tell you how Google, or more precisely Google's algorithms, have categorized and thus defined you.

If you encounter this phrase, it is an algorithmic indication that Google doesn't consider you noteworthy enough to deserve the golden prison—you are not a celebrity, in the sense that the public has no right

Some results may have been removed under data protection law in Europe. Learn more

FIGURE P.1. When searching for your name on Google within the European Union, the phrase "Some results may have been removed under data protection law in Europe" appears if you are not a Google celebrity. Source: www.google.co.uk.

to know your personal details. You are just an ordinary human being. And this unadorned humanity grants you something quite valuable: you can request what European Union courts have called "the right to be forgotten."

In 2014, Google was forced by EU courts to allow its European users the "right to be forgotten." Since May of that year, individuals can now submit a take-down request of European search results that are "inadequate, irrelevant or no longer relevant, or excessive in relation to those purposes and in the light of the time that has elapsed."[2] An avalanche of hundreds of thousands of requests followed—some from people with legitimate grievances, others from those attempting to purge references to various kinds of criminal convictions.[3]

In response, Google quietly introduced a new feature that automates part of this take-down process. In a letter to the European Union's data-protection authorities, Google's global privacy counsel, Peter Fleischer, explained that since "most name queries are for famous people and such searches are very rarely affected by a removal, due to the role played by these persons in public life, we have made a pragmatic choice not to show this notice by default for known celebrities or public figures."[4] In other words, whether the phrase appears or not reflects Google's determination of whether you are a regular person who can request the removal of certain search results or a celebrity who presumably just has to lump it when it comes to privacy.

This "pragmatic choice" is algorithmic—an automatic, data-based division between "celebrities or public figures" and the rest of us. Yet the EU legal opinion did not define who counts as a public figure. Google gets to make it up as it goes. The exact method by which it does this is unknown, hidden behind the computational curtain. *Washington Post* legal blogger Stewart Baker, who first brought this algorithmic assessment to public attention, found that Google believed pop singer Rihanna to be "Google famous" but Robyn Rihanna Fenty (the singer's legal name) "not."[5] The distinction is intriguing because it shows a gap, a separation that exists primarily at the level of knowledge. In this case, Google isn't really assessing "fame." Google is creating its own, proprietary version of it.

Of course, fame, much like Google fame, has always been a creation. Film studies scholar Richard Dyer detailed this point many decades ago: who becomes a flesh-and-blood celebrity, or in his words, embodies a "star image," is neither a random nor meritocratic occurrence. "A star image is made out of media texts that can be grouped together as promotion, publicity, films, and commentaries/criticism."[6] A star is not born. A star's image is meticulously made and remade according to, in Dyer's case, Hollywood.[7]

Suitably, the site of any star's making is also a site of power. In the case of Hollywood and other mass-media industries, this power facilitates profit. But of equal importance is how these industries simultaneously produce what cultural theorist Graeme Turner calls the "raw material" of our identity.[8] Our aspirations, desires, and expectations of life are influenced, in some way, by the star images we all encounter. To be in control of these images is to control how a social body understands itself. Or who is on the screen or onstage (and who isn't) concretizes the epistemic possibilities of who we can imagine ourselves to be.[9]

But Google's celebrity is functionally different. When Google determines your fame, it is not trying to package you as a "star image," nor is it producing "raw material" for cultural consumption. Rather, it is automatically fulfilling a legal mandate to facilitate European Union personal information take-down requests. And it is through this functional difference that Google has structurally transformed the very idea of fame itself. By developing an algorithmic metric that serves as a data-based stand-in for celebrity, Google created an entirely new index for who legally has the "right to be forgotten" (noncelebrities) and who doesn't (celebrities).

In short, Google's algorithmic index is an emergent way of thinking about what a celebrity is in our contemporary, data-rich communications environment. And in doing so, this emergent index fundamentally reworks our ideas around identity. In the present day of ubiquitous surveillance, who we are is not only what we think we are. Who we are is what our data is made to say about us.

Through Google's extensive database network, celebrities are a different form of "star" and thus produce another kind of "raw material" for who we are seen to be online. And in this difference is where the line between celebrities and "the rest of us" begins to blur. A Google celebrity may not be an actual celebrity. Rather, a Google celebrity is someone whose data is algorithmically authenticated as such. And while Google users might not grace the covers of magazines, they do produce an unprecedented amount of information about themselves, their desires, and their patterns of life. This data is a different type of raw material according to a different kind of industry—what media scholar Joseph Turrow calls the "new advertising industry" and WikiLeaks described as the "global mass surveillance industry."[10]

That is to say, "Google famous" may not equal famous, but "Google famous" influences which search results get censored and which lives are deemed available for public consumption. It orders the discourses of, and access to, personal privacy rights. And it inaugurates a new future for what it means to be a celebrity or public figure. But unlike the media-industry networks that painstakingly curate the raw materials of a star image, Google uses an algorithmic category of celebrity based entirely on interpretations of data.

Twentieth-century scientific positivism demands that we let data speak for itself. Following this mantra, wherever data tells us to go, we will find truth. But the data that Google uses to categorize people and assign status of identity does not speak; it is evaluated and ordered by a powerful corporation in order to avoid legal culpability. Indeed, scholars Lisa Gitelman and Virginia Jackson argue data doesn't speak but is spoken for.[11] Data does not naturally appear in the wild. Rather, it is collected by humans, manipulated by researchers, and ultimately massaged by theoreticians to explain a phenomenon. Who speaks for data, then, wields the extraordinary power to frame how we come to understand ourselves and our place in the world.

To participate in today's digitally networked world is to produce an impressive amount of data. From those who post personal details on Facebook to others who simply carry their cell phone with them to and from work, we leave traces of our lives in ways we never would expect. And as this data funnels into an expansive nexus of corporate and state databases, we are clearly not the ones who interpret what it means.

In the following introductory chapter, I begin to etch out what it means to be made "of data." Algorithmic interpretations about data of our web surfing, data of our faces, and even data about our friendships set new, distinct terms for identity online. And it is through these terms that our algorithmic identities are crafted—terms in which race is described by ones and zeros and emotions defined by templates of data.

We Are Data is about how algorithms assemble, and control, our datafied selves and our algorithmic futures. It's about how algorithms make our data speak as if we were a man, woman, Santa Claus, citizen, Asian, and/or wealthy. And it's also about how these algorithmically produced categories replace the politicized language of race, gender, and class with a proprietary vocabulary that speaks *for* us—to marketers, political campaigns, government dragnets, and others—whether we know about it, like it, or not. The knowledge that shapes both the world and ourselves online is increasingly being built by algorithms, data, and the logics therein.

INTRODUCTION

We are "well filled with data" in today's networked society.[1] If you don't believe me, open your computer and roam the web for five minutes. In a period of time only slightly longer than the average television commercial break, you will have generated, through your web activity, an identity that is likely separate from the person who you thought you were. In a database far, far away, you have been assigned a gender, ethnicity, class, age, education level, and potentially the status of parent with x number of children. Maybe you were labeled a U.S. citizen or a foreigner. There's even a slight chance you were identified as a terrorist by the U.S. National Security Agency.

This situation is simultaneously scary and intriguing. It's scary because of the very real power that such classifications hold: having a SIM card match the data signature of a suspected terrorist can put someone at the receiving end of a drone missile strike. Having Internet metadata that identifies a user as a foreigner means she may lose the right to privacy normally afforded to U.S. citizens. And it's intriguing because there's something gallingly, almost comically presumptuous about such categorizations. Who would have thought class status could be algorithmically understood? How can something as precise as citizenship be allocated without displaying one's passport? And how audacious is it to suggest that something even less precise, like ethnicity, could be authoritatively assigned without someone having the decency to ask?

We live in a world of ubiquitous networked communication, a world where the technologies that constitute the Internet are so woven into the fabrics of our daily lives that, for most of us, existence without them seems unimaginable.[2] We also live in a world of ubiquitous surveillance, a world where these same technologies have helped spawn an impressive network of governmental, commercial, and unaffiliated infrastructures of mass observation and control.[3]

Today, most of what we do in this world has at least the *capacity* to be observed, recorded, analyzed, and stored in a databank. As software developer Maciej Ceglowski explains, "The proximate reasons for the culture of total surveillance is clear. Storage is cheap enough that we can keep everything. Computers are fast enough to examine this information, both in real time and retrospectively. Our daily activities are mediated with software that can easily be configured to record and report everything it sees upstream."[4] A simple web search from even the most unsophisticated of smart phones generates a lengthy record of new data. This includes your initial search term, the location of your phone, the time and day when you searched, what terms you searched for before/after, your phone's operating system, your phone's IP address, and even what apps you installed on your phone. Add onto this list everything else you do with that phone, everything else you do on your computer, and everything else that might be recorded about your life by surveilling agents.

This resulting aggregation of our lives' data founds the discursive terrain of our digital environments. We live in what legal scholar Frank Pasquale has termed a "black box society," where algorithms determine the contours of our world without us knowing. Within this society, "a predictive analytics firm may score someone as a 'high cost' or 'unreliable' worker, yet never tell her about the decision."[5] What "high cost" and "unreliable" mean is up to the algorithms' authors. It's an output that we feel only as we wait for a job interview that will never come. In the case of identity online, it is this categorical output that speaks for you—not you, yourself.

Indeed, you are rarely "you" online. "We are data" is not a claim that we, individually, are data. Rather, we are temporary members of different emergent categories, like "high cost" or "celebrity," from this book's preface, according to our data. The future of identity online is how we negotiate this emergence. Accordingly, the arguments in this book deliberately attend to the level of the category itself, not the "you" of the user.

Through various modes of algorithmic processing, our data is assigned categorical meaning without our direct participation, knowledge, or often acquiescence. As Pasquale puts it, "the values and prerogatives that the encoded rules enact are hidden within black boxes."[6] Which is to say that our social identities, when algorithmically understood, are really not social at all. From behind the black box, they remain private and proprietary. Yet when employed in marketing, political campaigns, and even NSA data analytics, their discursive contents realign our present and futures online.

Who we are in this world is much more than a straightforward declaration of self-identification or intended performance. Who we are, following Internet researcher Greg Elmer's work on "profiling machines," is also a declaration by our data as interpreted by algorithms.[7] We are ourselves, plus layers upon additional layers of what I have previously referred to as algorithmic identities.[8]

Algorithmic interpretations like Google's "celebrity" identify us in the exclusive vernacular of whoever is doing the identifying. For the purposes of my analysis, these algorithmic categorizations adhere to what philosopher Antoinette Rouvroy calls "algorithmic governmentality"—a logic that "simply ignores the embodied individuals it affects and has as its sole 'subject' a 'statistical body'. . . . In such a governmental context, the subjective singularities of individuals, their personal psychological motivations or intentions do not matter."[9] Who we are in the face of algorithmic interpretation is who we are computationally calculated to be. And like being an algorithmic celebrity and/or unreliable, when our embodied individualities get ignored, we increasingly lose control not just over life but over how life itself is defined.

This loss is compounded by the fact that our online selves, to borrow the overused phraseology of pop psychology, is a schizophrenic phenomenon. We are likely made a thousand times over in the course of just one day. Who we are is composed of an almost innumerable collection of interpretive layers, of hundreds of different companies and agencies identifying us in thousands of competing ways. At this very moment, Google may algorithmically think I'm male, whereas digital advertising company Quantcast could say I'm female, and web-analytic firm Alexa might be unsure. Who is right? Well, nobody really.

Stable, singular truth of identity, also known as authenticity, is truly a relic of the past. Our contemporary conception of authenticity, as argued by feminist scholar Sarah Banet-Weiser, has become malleable, even ambivalent. What used to be sold to us as "authentic," like the marketed promise of a corporate brand, is now read as polysemic multiplicity.[10] Google's, Quantcast's, and Alexa's interpretations of my data are necessarily contradictory because they each speak about me from their own, proprietary scripts. Each is ambivalent about who I am, interpreting me according to their individual algorithmic logics.

But in the algorithmic identifications of our gender, unreliability, or celebrity status, we are given little recourse. We most often have no way to say "no!" or "yes, but . . ." Nor can we really know who we are online, as our algorithmic identities change by the input: minute by minute and byte by byte.

In other words, online you are not who you think you are. Indeed, one of the key consequences of our algorithmic identities is how they recast the politics around identity into the exclusive, private parlance of capital or state power. If you have a Google account, go into your "Settings for Google Ads" to see what Google infers your age and gender to be (www.google.com/ads/preferences). These gender and age formulations are not based on your voluntary identification, physical performance, or amount of times you have revolved around the sun. Instead, Google's assignments of your gender and age come from the collection of web pages you have visited over the course of your Google career.

And whether you recognize it or not, these identifications affect our lives. Your search results and advertisements will be subsequently gendered and aged. Websites will take the fact that you went to a certain site as evidence of your identity as, say, a middle-aged man. And on-line news editors may then see your visit as proof that the site's new campaign aimed at middle-aged-men-centered content is succeeding. The different layers of who we are online, and what who we are means, is decided for us by advertisers, marketers, and governments. And all these categorical identities are functionally unconcerned with what, given your own history and sense of self, makes you *you*.

Theorists Geoffrey Bowker and Susan Leigh Star write that "classifi-cation systems are often sites of political and social struggles, but these sites are difficult to approach. Politically and socially charged agendas are often first presented as purely technical and they are difficult even to see."[11] The process of classification itself is a demarcation of power, an organization of knowledge and life that frames the conditions of possibilities of those who are classified. When Google calls you a man or celebrity, this is not an empty, insignificant assessment. It is a struc-turing of the world on terms favorable to the classifier, be it as a mem-ber of a market segment for profit or as a categorized public figure to avoid the legal morass of European privacy law.

We witness this favorable structuring in legal scholar C. Edwin Bak-er's concept of "corruption" that "occurs when segmentation reflects the steering mechanisms of bureaucratic power or money rather than the group's needs and values."[12] Consider, for example, how your own gender identity interfaces with the complexities of your lived experi-ence. When Google analyzes your browsing data and assigns you to one of two distinct gender categories (only "male" or "female"), your al-gorithmic gender may well contradict your own identity, needs, and values. Google's gender is a gender of profitable convenience. It's a cat-egory for marketing that cares little whether you really are a certain gender, so long as you surf/purchase/act like that gender.

Google's category, moreover, speaks with a univocality that flattens out the nuance and variety of the lived experience of gender. And that corrupt category, says Baker, "undermines both common discourse and self-governing group life."[13] More comprehensively, an algorithmic gender's corrupt univocality substitutes for the reflexive interplay implicit in gender's social constructionism.

As an example, I could identify and perform as a man, while Google thinks I'm a woman (this is true). Or I could be in my thirties, possess a driver's license to prove it, but Google could think I'm sixty-five (this is also true). In these examples, I am not merely listing instances of misrecognition or error on the part of an algorithm. Machines are, and have been, "wrong" a lot of the time—often more than the techno-enthusiasts among us would like to admit. Even the most expensive computer software can crash, and biometric technologies routinely fail despite their touted infallibility. The point of this example, rather, is to highlight the epistemological and ontological division between my gender and how Google defines and operationalizes my algorithmic gender.

And precisely because Google's gender is Google's, not mine, I am unable to offer a critique of that gender, nor can I practice what we might refer to as a first-order gendered politics that queries what Google's gender means, how it distributes resources, and how it comes to define our algorithmic identities. Here I offer an alternative to political economist Oscar Gandy's claim that "because identity is formed through direct and mediated interaction with others, individuals are never free to develop precisely as they would wish."[14] When identity is formed without our conscious interaction with others, we are never free to develop—nor do we know how to develop. What an algorithmic gender signifies is something largely illegible to us, although it remains increasingly efficacious for those who are using our data to market, surveil, or control us.

Of course, interpretations of data have always mediated identity, whether it be through the applications of census records, econometrics, and even IQ test results. From philosopher Ian Hacking's work on statistics "making up people" to the cyberculture studies of media theorist Mark Poster's "database discourses," the nominal underpinning of "we are data" is hardly an unprecedented phenomenon.[15]

What *is* new about the categories that constitute us online is that they are unknown, often proprietary, and ultimately—as we'll later see—modulatory: Google's own interpretation of gender, faithful to nothing but patterns of data, can be dynamically redefined according to the latest gendered data.

These categories also operate at—and generate—different temporalities. As a general rule, Gandy reminds us that "the use of predictive models based on historical data is inherently conservative. Their use tends to reproduce and reinforce assessments and decisions made in the past."[16] This type of categorization delimits possibility. It shuts down potential difference for the sake of these historical models. It constructs what digital media theorist Wendy Hui Kyong Chun has called "programmed visions" that "extrapolate the future—or, more precisely, a future—based on the past."[17]

However, the myriad flows of ubiquitous surveillance reorient these visions. For companies like Google, algorithms extrapolate not just a future but a present based on the present: of near real-time search queries, web browsing, GPS location, and metadata records.[18] This change in temporality reframes the conservatism of categorical knowledge to something more versatile, similar to what geographer Louise Amoore's calls a "data derivative"—"a specific form of abstraction that distinctively correlates more conventional state collection of data with emergent and unfolding futures."[19]

When algorithms process near real-time data, they produce dynamic, pattern-based abstractions that become the new, actionable indices for identity itself. These abstractions may be invested not in extrapolating a certain future or enacting a singular norm but in producing the most efficacious categorical identity according to available data and algorithmic prowess.

Correspondingly, in an online world of endlessly overhauled algorithmic knowledge, Google's misrecognition of my gender and age isn't an error. It's a reconfiguration, a freshly minted algorithmic truth that cares little about being authentic but cares a lot about being an effective metric for classification. In this world, there is no fidelity to notions of our individual history and self-assessment.

As philosopher Alexander Galloway observes about the video game *Civilization III*, "the modeling of history in computer code . . . can only ever be a reductive exercise of capture and transcoding," whereas "'history' . . . is precisely the opposite of history . . . because the diachronic details of lived life are replaced by the synchronic homogeneity of code pure and simple."[20] The complexity of our individual histories cannot be losslessly translated into a neat, digital format. Likewise, our self-assessments come from layers upon layers of subjective valuations, all of which are utterly unintelligible as ones and zeros.

In this algorithmic reality, there is instead a dependency on something else, a data-based model of what it means to be 'famous,' 'not famous,' 'man,' 'woman,' 'gay,' 'straight,' 'old,' 'young,' 'African American,' 'Hispanic,' 'Caucasian,' 'Asian,' 'other,' 'Democrat,' 'Republican,' 'citizen,' 'foreigner,' 'terrorist,' or 'college educated.' I offset all of these algorithmically produced categories with an unattractive use of quotation marks precisely because they are not what they say they are. Like the sardonic use of air quotes to emphasize an ironic untruth, each quotation-marked classification is an algorithmic caricature of the category it purportedly represents. These algorithmic caricatures, or what I call *measurable types*, have their own histories, logics, and rationales. But these histories, logics, and rationales are necessarily different from our own. Google's 'gender' is not immediately about gender as a regime of power but about 'gender' as a marketing category of commercial expedience.

Crucially, algorithmic categories do not substitute for their non-quotation-marked peers but rather function—sometimes in concert, sometimes in tension—with them as an additional layer of identity. I might be a man, but I am *also* a 'woman.' In my day-to-day life, I might be a boring professor. But if Google determines I'm a 'celebrity,' I lose the right to be forgotten. In this layered approach, I must attend to both the offline and the online, as both have impact on my life, and both bleed into each other. This collapse subsequently disallows any clean conceptual separation between life as data and life as life.

And given this layered interaction, our algorithmic identities will certainly impact us in ways that vary according to our own social locations "offline," which are likewise determined by classifications that are often not of one's choosing but which operate according to different dynamics from their algorithmic counterparts. Similarly, to the extent that one's online and offline identities align or misalign, the effects of this interface will vary according to the relative status assigned to each category and one's own power to contest or capitalize on it.

All of which is to say, companies like Google use their algorithms and our data to produce a dynamic world of knowledge that has, and will continue to have, extraordinary power over our present and futures. And as we also continue to be well filled with data, this algorithmic logic produces not just the world but us. *We Are Data* aims to extend the scholastic lineage that connects the social construction of knowledge with the layers upon layers of technical, quotation-marked constructions of knowledge—a union where essential truths do not and cannot exist.

ON DATA'S TERMS

Algorithmic agents make us and make the knowledges that compose us, but they do so on their own terms. And one of the primary terms of an algorithm is that everything is represented as data. When we are made of data, we are not ourselves in terms of atoms. Rather, we are who we are *in terms of data*. This is digitization, the term that MIT Media Lab founder Nicholas Negroponte employs to talk about the material conversion of "atoms to bits."[21] It is also biomedia, the "informatic recontextualization of biological components and processes" of philosopher Eugene Thacker.[22] And it is ultimately datafication: the transformation of part, if not most, of our lives into computable data.[23]

Importantly, the "we" of "we are data" is not a uniform totality but is marked by an array of both privileging and marginalizing difference.

As digital theorist Tyler Reigeluth reminds us, we need to see digital technology "in continuity with 'previous' or existing social, political and economic structures, and not only in terms of change, revolution or novelty."[24] And as *all* data is burdened by this structural baggage, any interpretive classification of datafied life necessarily orders and organizes the world in the shadows of those structures' effects.

It is significant to note that these shadows have, for centuries, proliferated across the datafied world. From the state's use of DNA to support claims of "authentic" racial character (to reference the work of critical scholars like Kim Tallbear and Alondra Nelson) to now-debunked histories of phrenology, hegemonic forms of empiricism have long buttressed the "corrupted" identification of race to make sense of, and thus validate, dominant classifications of identity.[25] More recently, surveillance theorist Simone Browne's concept of "digital epidermalization" reminds us that algorithmic interpretations of race corrupt as well: "the exercise of power cast by the disembodied gaze of certain surveillance technologies . . . can be employed to do the work of alienating the subject by producing a truth about the racial body and one's identity (or identities) despite the subject's claims."[26]

Indeed, all algorithmic interpretations produce their own corrupted truths—not just about race—in ways particular to their technological capacity and programmed direction. Digital media scholar Lev Manovich defines this as "transcoding," or how cultural concepts, when brought onto the data/algorithm ontology of the computer, must follow the "established conventions of the computer's organization of data."[27] To perceive the world on data's terms is to recognize how "the logic of a computer can be expected to significantly influence the traditional cultural logic of media."[28] We are not simply well filled of data but made of data that is interpreted, conferred truth, and disseminated for motives of profit, organization, and/or control. The resulting classifications become the discursive terrain from which we, and others, compose our digital selves.

Consider two seemingly separate, but algorithmically connected, examples. If I smile, a computer doesn't see a cheerful man like a human

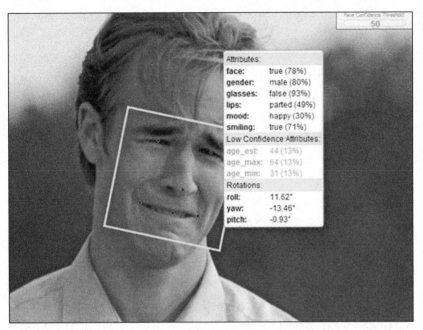

FIGURE I.1. Face.com's software analyzed photos according to a predefined set of attributes: 'face,' 'gender,' 'glasses,' 'lips,' 'mood,' 'smiling,' and 'age.' Source: Kenneth Butler, "New Face.com Tool Can Guess Your Age, Determine Gender and Mood [Hands-On]," *Laptopmag*, April 2, 2012, http://blog.laptopmag.com.

would. A computer can "see" my smile only upon interpreting the discrete pixels forming the shapes believed to be my 'eyes.'[29] It then crops, rotates, and scales the image to produce a standardized 'face.' Next, it encodes that modified image, using several algorithmic filters according to prototypical 'smiling' photos, into a single number that evaluates me as either 'smiling' or 'not smiling.'[30] Voilà, a data-'smile.'

In July 2011, this type of technology is exactly what the facial-recognition company Face.com unveiled with its innovative facial-analytics software that detects "moods and key facial expressions" in digital photographs.[31] Not limited to 'smiling,' Face.com claimed that its algorithms would be able to evaluate a 'face's' 'mood,' from 'surprised' to 'angry,' from 'sad' to 'neutral' (figure I.1). Even 'kissing' is available as a facial category, where a 'face' can have 'lips' that are 'parted,' 'kissing,' or 'sealed.'

All of these descriptive states are accompanied by an associated confidence percentage, the statistical certainty that the 'face' the machine sees is, in fact, interpreting the correct 'emotion.' Our data-'smiles' are only smiling if Face.com's algorithms statistically say so. Quite unsurprisingly, Face.com's recognition technology was purchased in 2012 for an estimated $80 million by the owner of the largest repository of photographs on the planet, Facebook.[32]

Emotions have become datafied. But unlike the computational wizardry of turning "atoms into bits," our emotions are not understood only as atoms. Like identity, they're a complex, culturally situated, and materially incoherent experience that technically overwhelms that which is computable. Defining 'emotion' via algorithm is an interpretation of the world that ushers us into a distinct suite of knowledge, one that orders and understands the ineffable chaos of our world as operational bits of data.[33]

But as noted earlier, when we are made of data, we are not just represented but also regulated by data. And not all data is treated alike. Face.com's algorithms, for example, are not infallible truth tellers. Like latent spirits, our data might be present but remain unseen. By this, I mean the computer encounters us and represents us in pixel (or data) form but fails to recognize us. There might be a face in an image that we, feeble humans, can visually attest is there. But there isn't a data-'face.'

This kind of nonrecognition may occur because computers are unable to identify every particularity and dimension that the world has to offer.[34] Despite attempts otherwise, notably by proponents of the field of digital philosophy, it's quite difficult to assume and represent the entire world according to ones or zeros.[35] What is "seen" and "not seen" is more than a technological phenomenon or limitation but an algorithmic consequence shaped by history: who is empowered to look, what is made visible, and what is made invisible?

Like digital epidermalization, the algorithms that facilitate facial recognition—following the work of surveillance scholar Kelly Gates—are burdened with a politics, a programmed rule set that administers the designated identity of a 'face.'[36] An algorithm might disadvantage some data while privileging others, through either technological failure and/or an innate bias of the algorithm's authors. What can be seen is what can be made intelligible, and what can be intelligible determines who we can be.

To repurpose René Descartes' dictum "I think, therefore I am," if we are made of data, but our data is not "seen," do we exist?[37] Or to less clichédly relate this to computer science, we are encountering a world where "negation as failure" becomes the central mode of existence: "not p can be inferred if every possible proof of p fails."[38] "Not p" is unknowable—it can only be assumed when every alternative is shown to be unsuccessful.

This type of (unintended) negation is precisely what happened in a piece of viral media that made its rounds in late 2009. In the YouTube video "HP Computers Are Racist," two people are shown speaking into a new, HP Mediasmart computer with an embedded motion-tracking and facial-recognition camera. These individuals, identified as "Black Desi" Cryer and "White Wanda" Zamen, are employees at an unnamed Texas retail store. The video (figure I.2) begins with Cryer introducing himself and the technology and explicitly stating his race and the issue at hand with the computer: "I'm black. . . . I think my blackness is interfering with the computer's ability to follow me."[39]

Indeed, the facial-recognition software seems unable to identify Cryer's black face. He asks his white coworker Zamen to pop into frame. The absurdity of the video begins when the camera almost immediately recognizes Zamen, zooming in and following her as she floats around the screen. Cryer, who narrates through all of this, visually reintroduces himself within the camera's view and instantly breaks the facial-recognition software: the frame stops following Zamen, and the camera moves back to its default position.

And the worst part is I bought one for Christmas.

FIGURE I.2. Desi Cryer and Wanda Zamen appear in the 2009 YouTube video "HP Computers Are Racist." Source: Wanda Zamen, "HP Computers Are Racist," YouTube.com, December 10, 2009.

The undisguised immediacy of the computer's identification/non-identification based on skin color provides a powerful example of the embedded digital epidermalization within HP's software.[40] Whiteness was legible to the machine; blackness was not. In fact, not only was Cryer's blackness illegible, but it also spoiled Zamen's experience, halting the software that was attentively recognizing and tracking whiteness.

HP responded to the video with a brief statement on its website: "We are working with our partners to learn more. The technology we use is built on standard algorithms that measure the difference in intensity of contrast between the eyes and the upper cheek and nose. We believe that the camera might have difficulty 'seeing' contrast in conditions where there is insufficient foreground lighting."[41] This response is compelling for many reasons, not least of which is the technically descriptive explication of why the problem occurred in the first place. HP talks about the algorithm's difficulty in "seeing" the contrast of eyes, upper cheek, and nose due to "insufficient foreground lighting." Importantly, computers don't see; they compute.[42] And while the metaphor of "seeing" functions as a physical, and near-universally accessible, analogy for the nonvisual algorithmic processing that calculates HSV (hue, saturation, value) contrast, the metaphor's imprecision runs up against the sharp edge of power.[43]

When feminist theorist Donna Haraway writes that the "'eyes' made available in modern technological sciences shatter any idea of passive vision," she points squarely to the impossibility for neutral sight.[44] "Difficulty 'seeing'" is not just the consequence of bad eyesight. To "see" is itself an act saturated in politics, writes visual culture scholar Nicholas Mirzoeff, a manifestation that "sutures authority to power and renders this association 'natural.'"[45]

Nevertheless, HP employs the sense of sight to emphasize its camera's presumed baseline neutrality. And this neutrality is then believed to let HP off the hook. According to the company's account, HP computers weren't racist; they were merely technologically/optically limited. The computer failed to recognize blackness not because of the latter's history or cultural encoding but because of a simple, resolvable lighting problem. Doubling down on the ruse of postracial optimism, HP argued that its computers would surely "see" the various hues of racial difference once this technical problem was addressed.

Cryer and Zamen's experience with HP's technology gracefully intersects the seemingly discrete fields of humanities and social science with the more hard-science approaches of computer science and engineering. Here, it becomes even more apparent, citing digital media theorist Beth Coleman, that "what used to be a matter of flesh and blood is now highly abstracted data. Race has been made information."[46] And while unintentional, the racial dimension of HP's algorithm disadvantaged dark-skinned users. Cryer jokes at the end of the video, "I bought one of these for Christmas. . . . I hope my wife doesn't see this video."[47] Full use of HP's computer was denied to users with darker bodies—a distinction based not on traditional, prejudicial racism but on a functionalist decision that put values on HSV contrast, not skin color.[48]

This functionalist decision wrapped the human body with a new, racialized layer. In the preceding case, 'face,' and thus 'race,' is represented in the digital language of HSV contrast. Waning may be the days of unadorned racist stereotypes and "one-drop" rules, for HP's 'race' is not black and brown versus white but intelligible versus unintelligible data.[49] It's a graphical template that faces either fit or frustrate. The corruption implicit in HP's classification is not rooted in explicit racial bias, and yet the classification nonetheless reflects and reinforces what digital scholar Lisa Nakamura calls a "digital racial formation" that reifies whiteness as normal and blackness as abnormal.[50]

The pattern that authenticates White Wanda's 'face' but denies Black Desi's is not white because it enjoys playing golf and listening to Jimmy Buffett. It's 'white' thanks to a politics of computation that clearly culls from the traces of its offline predecessor: we can only imagine that Cryer would not have had any issue if the HP engineering team and its beta testers were majority dark-skinned. But the realities of the U.S. tech industry forbid that possibility: in 2012, citing U.S. Department of Labor Statistics, Silicon Valley's ten largest companies employed only 6 percent Hispanic and 4 percent black workers. Those numbers are quickly halved to 3 percent and 1 percent, respectively, when we consider only those who hold executive and top-managerial positions.[51]

The unspoken and unintentional presumption of whiteness in HP's facial-recognition technology exemplifies white privilege as more than societal advantage. It embeds seemingly neutral technological and infrastructural projects with (often white-supremacist) racial logics at their most ground level.[52] Accordingly, when whiteness is operationalized as the norm, and thus as the default, the possibility for a universally consistent "we" as data is disrupted.

But while a face cannot be perfectly transcoded into 'face,' neither can users' offline positionalities. Even if "we" is not a homogeneous entity, the asymmetries of the we do not perfectly overlap the asymmetries of the 'we.' More simply put, HP's algorithm might be unable to recognize a white user with a dark tan but could easily authenticate a black user with lighter skin. It is on the terms of data, and how racial differences are converted into data, that recognition occurs—not the essentializing terms of racialization itself.

DATA WARS AND DATAVEILLANCE

Of course, who we are as data draws from much more than our names and our faces. But a user's mundane datafied behavior—an email, a GPS location, or a visit to sports site ESPN.com—is quite meaningless in and of itself. It is when this data becomes aggregated, tethered together and operationalized, that we, as data, become worthwhile. If that same user also goes to tech blog Arstechnica.com, home-repair site Homedepot.com, and jejune men's magazine Maxim.com, that quick tour around the Internet can become quite meaningful. It might even suggest that this user is 92 percent confidently 'male.'

Our datafied lives, when aggregated and transcoded into quotation-marked categories, increasingly define who we are and who we can be. But to make sense of this aggregation requires a new definition of 'man,' one based on website visits instead of performance or self-identification. In this case, a user is a 'man' according to how closely 'his' data stacks up to preexisting models of 'man.' These models are what I call measurable types, or interpretations of data that stand in as digital containers of categorical meaning. And in order for companies or governments to construct these measurable types, they need a lot of our data.

It was 2007, and the "Data Wars" had just begun.[53] Actually, the exact day was Friday, April 13, and search supergiant Google had just acquired targeted-advertising supergiant DoubleClick for $3.1 billion in cash, ushering in a massive agglomeration of data between Google's search information and DoubleClick's user-tracked marketing data. Rumors that Microsoft and Yahoo! were planning to scoop Google preceded the deal, and the eventual purchase, valued at twenty times DoubleClick's annual revenue, achieved what we could indulgently call a coup "d'ata" for Google.

With this announcement, data itself had become a business, maybe even the central commodity for digital capital.[54] Prior to the deal, Google had access only to my email and search history. Now, blessed by DoubleClick's extensive network, Google also would know which pages I visited, how often I visited them, how long I stayed on those pages when I did, and which pages I went to before and after visiting a certain site. This aggregated data would end up making Google "staggering" amounts of money.[55]

More structurally, by purchasing DoubleClick, Google had woven an Internet-wide surveillance network. This "surveillant assemblage" conjoined the various, decentralized vestiges of data about us and our online behaviors—things we might not care about and/or things we might not even share with our closest confidant—and funneled their flows into Google's own private databases.[56] Today, Google records data from more than a billion Google users, more than three billion search queries a day, more than 425 million Gmail accounts, and traffic from an estimated one million websites, including almost half of the ten thousand most visited.[57]

Indeed, in 2007, one could focus on the potential dangers of how this data could be used—and some did. The acquisition's announcement was met with immediate resistance. Advocacy groups including the Center for Digital Democracy appealed to the U.S. Federal Trade Commission and European Union to stop the merger on grounds of privacy and anticompetition. Marc Rotenberg, executive director of the Electronic Privacy Information Center, testified in a Senate hearing against the acquisition. Even Microsoft, in an ironic postscript to its famed 2001 *United States v. Microsoft* antitrust case, critiqued the proposed merger because it "raise[d] serious competition and privacy concerns."[58]

But the Data Wars were already in full swing. Four months later, Microsoft went on to spend a whopping $6.3 billion to buy digital-marketing parent company aQuantive. In the interim, Yahoo! had purchased two companies at a more sober price. Full ownership of ad exchange Right Media and advertising network Blue Lithium had set the company back a cool $1.15 billion. Clearly, these "wars" weren't about companies spending more than $10 billion just to invade your privacy. For Google, Microsoft, and Yahoo!, this was about a new type of market dominance: collecting enough data to grow from mere search engines into much more profitable advertising behemoths, capable of providing query results next to exactly defined commercial propaganda.[59] They wanted to be sovereigns over what digital humanist Frédéric Kaplan later called linguistic capitalism, or the commodification of our textual lives.[60]

With all this available data, Google, Microsoft, and Yahoo! could found and fund their own proprietary digital kingdoms at the same time. Yes, we were being surveilled, but this grand aggregation of data wasn't the surveillance of Orwell's "Big Brother" or the FBI's COINTELPRO. Nor did it resemble the kind of two-hundred-year-old portmanteau that paired the French word *sur*, meaning "on/over," with the even Frenchier word *vellier*, meaning "watch." Surveillance in this frame prompts docility: populations are seen as spatially underneath power, both observed and manipulated by a larger, towering, and eternally vigilant entity.

The surveillance embedded in the technical structure of these billion-dollar acquisitions is subtler, more mundane, yet ever more extensive in reach. Google is "watching" us, but we're also voluntarily logging into Google's servers, quickly and wantonly accepting terms of service agreements that relinquish our formal rights to privacy. This is a type of surveillance, surely, but it's also something different. It's what computer scientist Roger Clarke calls dataveillance, "the systematic monitoring of people's actions or communications through the application of information technology" that reconfigures the character of surveillance and its subjects.[61]

For thinkers like Clarke, the introduction of information technology into the surveilling relationship fundamentally changes both what is being watched and how that watched object is perceived. It is our data that is being watched, not our selves. And when dataveillance observes, saves, pattern analyzes, and uses our own data to profile us, its relationship to liberal theories of privacy becomes muddled. The data that Google, Microsoft, and Yahoo! collect is sometimes encrypted, usually anonymized, and mostly "not personally identifiable," leading some privacy theorists to argue "no harm, no foul" if such data cannot be tracked back to an individual, discrete, personally nameable self.[62]

But what dataveillers know about me is not just a catalogue of different data elements. These elements must be aggregated, cross-referenced, and algorithmically analyzed to produce knowledges about my life that, while not discernible at face value, can then be used by marketers, political campaigns, spy agencies, big-data researchers, and even police departments.[63] As we'll learn in the coming pages, Google's dataveillance creates the datafied templates, or measurable types, for what it means to be an 'old' 'man.' Web-audience measurement company Quantcast constructs the datafied idea of users who are 'Hispanic.' And the NSA uses its incredible government dragnet to pattern analyze who is a 'terrorist.'

These productions of life are the hidden stakes of the Data Wars, the consequences of which go well beyond Google (or Microsoft or Yahoo!) as a unique institution and its role in the general erosion of privacy online.

For example, take the trend toward "predictive policing" in U.S. police departments. In this techno-enthused strategy, police departments use crime statistics to generate maps highlighting five-hundred-by-five-hundred-square-foot areas (one city block) where crimes are likely to occur.[64] A block might be "high crime" at two a.m. on a Friday but "low crime" at two p.m. on a Tuesday. Or we could think like the Chicago Police Department (CPD) in 2013 and channel this logic—*Minority Report*-style—in order to assign "criminality" not to blocks but to people.[65]

Criminology research finds that behavioral traits—like being a victim of a previous shooting, having an arrest record, or being friends with others who are similarly affected by crime—are closely correlated with being either a perpetrator or a victim of a violent crime.[66] Researchers have thus theorized that if you or your associates have experience with the criminal justice system and/or crime, you're more likely to experience the criminal justice system and/or crime. At face value, this assumption is quite obvious. Crime and incarceration are structural issues that affect communities, not individual people; they are not random occurrences.[67]

What is more noteworthy is how this algorithmic assessment led the CPD to create a "heat list" of four hundred 'at-risk' individuals, an algorithmic category populated by both 'victims' and 'offenders.' To be algorithmically identified as 'at risk' means that you will physically receive a visit from Chicago's "finest." And to be visited by Chicago's "finest" means you will actually be at risk: a CPD officer will "[warn] those on the heat list individually that further criminal activity, even for the most petty offenses, will result in the full force of the law being brought down on them."[68]

Here, we encounter two foundational interpretations that establish the measurable type of 'at risk.' One, there's an explicit value judgment that social connections themselves are the most efficacious indicators of 'at-risk' behavior. And two, there's an implicit value judgment about what data is available, and eventually used, in processing. It is impossible to divorce the CPD's "heat map" from centuries of preceding racist and classist policing practices, as those who are assigned by the department to be 'at risk' are unlikely to be affluent whites from Chicago's Gold Coast neighborhood. The data used to generate 'at risk' is not representative of a universal population and thus does not treat all populations equally. Nevertheless, to have someone knock on your door because your data is seen to be 'at risk' reaffirms some of the worst fears we might have about this new, datafied world: our data is spoken for louder than we can speak, and it is spoken for on its own terms.

One of these terms is what I have been calling the measurable type. This concept appropriates the sociological design of an "ideal type," or what social theorist Max Weber defines as "the one-sided accentuation of one or more points of view . . . arranged according to those one-sidedly emphasized viewpoints into a unified analytical construct."[69] Measurable types like 'at risk' are actionable analytical constructs of classificatory meaning, based exclusively on what is available to measure. When "we are data," we are indebted to both how our lives are datafied and how that data is algorithmically interpreted.

Communication scholar Tarleton Gillespie writes that algorithms "are not barometers of the social. They produce hieroglyphs: shaped by the tool by which they are carved, requiring of priestly interpretation, they tell powerful but often mythological stories—usually in the service of the gods."[70] We can think of a measurable type like 'at risk' as a hieroglyph, not a truth of identity but a priestly interpretation. It is not simply an officer who decides our fate in any given encounter with the police. Rather, it's an algorithmic interpretation of our own, datafied social networks that enacts police suspicion.

This brings us back to Pasquale's *Black Box Society*. In a diagram of web surveillance, we encounter the metaphor of "one-way mirrors," in which Internet users remain ignorant of how their data is used while site owners are privileged with near-universal access to that data.[71] Our algorithmic identities are similarly made behind a one-way mirror: it is largely impossible to know what our 'gender' is, how 'old' we are, and possibly if we're 'at risk' (as well as what all of those measurable types actually mean). But there are nonetheless powerful effects to this algorithmic unidirectionality. One effect is that while we know ourselves and exist as beings in highly politicized worlds, we don't know ourselves as beings in highly politicized algorithmic worlds. In most instances of algorithmic identification, we are seen, assessed, and labeled through algorithmic eyes, but our reaction is often available only to be obliquely felt. Like a sudden draft of air from an unseen window, we may very well feel we are being watched but never see what sees.

Accordingly, our own algorithmic sight can never be complete. Instead, it is an impaired sight plus an added *else*. This concept of the else is unquantifiable. Like scopaesthesia, we are affected by the thought, we know that something else is going on, but we're not exactly sure what it may be. We can't really understand how we're talked about. We can't really experience, directly and knowingly, what our algorithmic identities are. But they're there regardless, and their epistemic corruption alerts us to their presence.

Our algorithmic identities emerge from a constant interplay between our data and algorithms interpreting that data. This dynamism echoes a larger argument, best detailed in philosopher Judith Butler's work around gender performativity, that rejects any stable truth of identity.[72] What we call gender, and what we can call identity at large, is derived from our own particular performance of gender—and not an attachment to some totalizing essentialism around, for example, what it means to be a man. Queer theorist J. Halberstam locates this gender performativity within an algorithmic logic: it is a "learned, imitative behavior that can be processed so well that it comes to look natural."[73]

Gender's naturality is a processed output, one that necessarily changes over time to accommodate new behaviors. What becomes prototypically masculine at the moment is contingent on what men are doing right now. Gender—and, I propose, identity at large—is a processed construct; it "has a technology."[74]

Online, this axiom of performative power shifts from a largely theoretical argument to one that is squarely empirical. Data about who we are becomes more important than who we *really* are or who we may choose to be. We intentionally perform our data when we fill out our name, date of birth, and gender when buying plane tickets online: those pieces of data allow the U.S. government to identify who is traveling from Caracas to Atlanta. And we unintentionally perform our data when we buy food at the grocery store, use our cell phone to invite a friend to dinner, or even just move around our neighborhood (our phone's internal GPS alerts our mobile carrier, Facebook, and our other mobile applications where we are, at what time we are there, how long we stay, and potentially who we are with). Our data is constantly being "watched" by, or in media scholar Mark Andrejevic's words, "interacts" with, algorithmic machines.[75]

But in this uncertainty, we can also find incredible possibility. When identity is made in terms of data, the antiessentialism of measurable-type meaning lets us play with its instability. Google does not discipline us back into being a "good 'man,'" nor do we know what the discursive parameters of Google's 'man' are. Similarly, we can confound the CPD's 'at risk' algorithm by managing not who we are friends with but how those friendships get datafied. In the coming chapters, we'll further explore the logic of algorithmic identification, its operation, and how we can play, experiment, and ultimately resist it.

OUR ALGORITHMIC IDENTITIES

Our algorithmic identities are based on near-real-time interpretations of data. And as we produce more and more pieces of data, these interpretations must necessarily change—the foundry of who we are online lacks epistemic stability. For example, an individual previously not on the Chicago Police Department's radar might become 'at risk' because she made new friends and put their contact information into her phone. You might have previously been unrecognizable according to HP's facial-recognition algorithm, but after the purchase of a new office lamp, you now have a 'face.' And as a user surfs from one site to another online, that user might change from being 92 percent 'male' to 88 percent 'male' within a few seconds. What the world looks like to you today, and who you are seen to be this afternoon, is constructed from the datafied scraps of what you did last night.

This type of dynamism of categorical membership sets the stage for what philosopher Gilles Deleuze has called the "societies of control." In these societies, control regulates its subjects with constant contact to power, whereby structures of constraint move according to "ultrarapid forms of free-floating control."[76] This constraint makes and remakes itself, a process Deleuze describes as modulation: "like a self-deforming cast that will continuously change from one moment to the other, or like a sieve whose mesh will transmute from point to point."[77] As subjects to algorithmic interpretation, who we are also changes "from point to point," moving from 'woman' to 'man' or 'old' to 'young.'

But because these measurable types are also made exclusively from data, new data necessarily changes what defines 'old woman' and 'young man,' as well. Not only does your algorithmic identity readjust when you visit a new website, but the measurable types that are used to compose you modulate as well. "We are data" means that our data, produced in accelerating quantities and with increasing intimacy, is not just data but constitutive material for interpretative, structuring, and ultimately modulatory classifications.

Theorist Tiziana Terranova traces these dynamic algorithmic productions in terms of what she calls "network power." A company like Google doesn't talk to a specific person. Google listens to and talks to that person's data, the subindividual units that we can think of as dividuals: "the decomposition of individuals into data clouds subject to automated integration and disintegration."[78] We are automatically integrated/disintegrated according to the needs of whoever possesses these clouds. For Terranova, when individuals are replaced by dividuals, the categories of identity that we normally think of as politically owned by us, like gender, race, and citizenship (what she calls "macrostates"), become nonlinearly connected to an endless array of algorithmic meaning, like web use and behavior data (what she calls "microstates").[79] In other words, we produce the dividual, microstate data that Google uses to make our algorithmic, macrostate templates. And these macrostates are the conceptual forebears to what I have been referring to as measurable types.

More directly, as Alexander Galloway writes, "on the Internet there is no reason to know the name of a particular user, only to know what that user likes, where they shop, where they live, and so on. The clustering of descriptive information around a specific user becomes sufficient to explain the identity of that user."[80] Our individualities as users may be quite insignificant. Rather, what our dividualities can be algorithmically made say is how we are now seen.

Furthermore, much like "there is no reason to know" a user's name so long as that user is sufficiently profiled, any enduring identity of 'man' itself is similarly ignored. As new, descriptive information (microstates) for what makes a 'man' changes, the resulting measurable type (macrostate) realigns 'man' in accordance. Galloway defines his concept of "protocol" in a parallel way: "an algorithm, a proscription for structure whose form of appearance may be any number of different diagrams or shapes."[81]

When 'gender' is made through different diagrams and shapes according to flows of near-real-time data, 'gender' ceases to be a stable referent of identity. A user might be 92 percent 'male' at 9:30 p.m. But eight hours later, at 5:30 a.m., after spending the evening asleep and visiting no new sites, that user could now be 88 percent 'male.' What 'man' looks like today and who 'men' are seen to be later this afternoon are also constructed from the datafied scraps of what 'men' did last night. When who we are is made from shifting founts of measurable-type meaning, the network power of algorithmic machines, citing Galloway and philosopher Eugene Thacker, "set[s] the terms within which practices may possibly occur."[82] This mode of shifting algorithmic identity is what I have previously called *soft biopolitics*, which I will describe further in chapter 2.[83]

In the preceding analysis of user profiling, I'm not referring to critiques of personalization technologies like those spelled out in legal scholar Cass Sunstein's *Republic.com 2.0* or author Eli Pariser's *The Filter Bubble*, in which data profiles construct self-affirming echo chambers of targeted advertisements and content according to one's presumed identity, political affiliation, or interests.[84] I'm instead describing a form of control that is much more indirect and unapparent. It's a form that moves the goal posts of what is and what is not true, algorithmically regulating discursive construction largely beyond our gaze and most often without our comprehension.

These profiling algorithms continuously redefine the "knowledge" element in philosopher Michel Foucault's power/knowledge doublet.[85]

They measure and react to streams of available data, diligently following users' new datafied, microstate tendencies all while those users remain largely unaware of their formative role in macrostate construction. More to the point, algorithms delimit the discursive substrates that determine what can and cannot be said, dynamically modifying what Judith Butler calls the "limits of acceptable speech."[86] With ubiquitous surveillance, a macrostate like Google's 'gender' is constantly made and remade, updated based on the infinite fount of new microstate inputs coming from our datafied lives.

And with hundreds of other companies similarly assigning each of us different 'genders,' 'races,' and even 'classes,' there is no single, static sense of us but rather an untold number of competing, modulating interpretations of data that make up who we are.

When profiling algorithms interpret and reinterpret our data, the resulting macrostate emergence comes to define and redefine the conditions of possibility of who we are seen to be online: a Google 'woman,' a CPD 'at risk,' and potentially an HP 'white,' ad infinitum. And as our measurable-type identities shift according to changes in data, and those measurable types dynamically adapt to these changes as well, we encounter an algorithmic version of what artist Mary Flanagan calls "creatures of code," a "virtual body" for which "information has taken over," all while that body's "racial, aged, and sexual categories . . . are constructed as personality features rather than historical or culturally specific categories."[87]

Here, an 'at-risk white woman' is not necessarily an at-risk white woman reared in the structural particularities of that subject position. 'At-risk white woman' is instead a template of datafied performances, a "feature" as opposed to a set of historically or culturally grounded subjective experiences. The gap between these two interpretive modes emphasizes the disempowering asymmetry, quoting digital theorist Anna Watkins Fisher, between how we "use" and how we are "used."[88]

In the book *The Googlization of Everything*, cultural historian Siva Vaidhyanathan writes that while the Internet giant may proclaim users' control over their use of the system, "as long as control over our personal information and profiles is granted at the pleasure of Google and similar companies, such choices mean very little. There is simply no consistency, reciprocity, or accountability in the system."[89] The one-sidedness of algorithmic identification normalizes this inconsistency at every datafied step.

We Are Data is an attempt to continue a long analytical tradition that interrogates how the terms of information become the terms of our emergent subjectivity. This theoretical move isn't to displace the corporeal from our understanding of ourselves, to be posthuman or a cyborg in such a way that erases the body or affirms a neodualism of mind and body. Rather, I want to explore how companies, governments, and researchers use algorithms to augment our already-posthuman selves with layers upon additional layers of new, datafied identifications.

Our algorithmic identities are made through data and only data. It is a process that gleans from databases; it reads our behaviors as data, our social ties as data, and our bodies as data. And it conditions our present and futures on the basis of a dynamic interpretation of that reading. When media theorist Friedrich Kittler writes in *Discourse Networks* that technologies actively produce the discourses that we as subjects speak and are made through, he's pointing to what I argue is the kernel of algorithmic identity.[90] What is new, though, is how these very discourses are now composed from a near-real-time, dynamic terrain of statistics and commonality models—not from life's subjective experience and the conflicts therein.

And here we encounter the political rub of "we are data": we lack the vocabulary needed to enact a politics around our algorithmic identities. To repurpose a phrase from the field of computer science, we lose expressive power.[91] To think politically about algorithmic 'race,' 'gender,' and 'class' is to attach a politics onto something that is both predominantly unknowable and changes without our knowing. We can't think about 'gender' in the same way as we think about gender. We can't talk about 'race' in the same way either. But what we can do is appreciate the changes that happen when categorical definitions are reconfigured through an algorithmic locum.

Measurable types of identity like Google's 'gender' or the CPD's 'at risk' are dispersed, dividuated, and saved across a range of databases in many different countries. But more importantly, they are also ever changing, dependent on flows of available data. They are what we can think of as "just-in-time" identities that are made, ad hoc, in an ongoing conversation between our data and the various algorithms that process it.[92] To revise the web-surfing exercise that began this chapter, a simple five-minute sojourn across the online universe fails to construct for us a single identity. It rather assigns us an unstable, multivariate set of modulating identifications.

Paired with other instances of algorithmic processing (facial-recognition technologies, semantic analyses of my writing on my Facebook wall or Twitter feed, a history of purchases on my credit card, etc.), I am utterly overdetermined, made and remade every time I make a datafied move. Through my data alone, I have entered into even more conversations about who I am and what who I am means, conversations that happen without my knowledge and with many more participants involved than most of us could imagine.

To make the world according to algorithm is, to paraphrase one of historian Melvin Kranzberg's laws of technology, neither good nor bad nor neutral.[93] But it is new and thus nascent and unperfected. It's a world of unfastening, temporary subject arrangements that allows a user to be, for example, 23 percent confidently 'woman' and 84 percent confidently 'man' at the same time. Categories of identity of any sort, quotation-marked or not, might not be superficial, but they also aren't impossibly profound. As we move "point to point," the daisy chain of modulation does as well, requiring a buoyancy to categorical meaning and identity as life's changes alter their discursive contents.

But our algorithmic identities are not a recasting of our single, offline self into a digital self. This type of work has already been well documented by sociologist David Lyon, in his work on data doubles, or what legal scholar Daniel Solove dubs a "digital dossier."[94] Instead, we should locate our algorithmic identities in the spirit of how data sociologist Evelyn Ruppert theorizes her database subject: "the subject is made up of unique combinations of distributed transactional metrics that reveal who they are and their capacities, problems and needs."[95] When "we are data," we become fluidly responsive to these datafied transactions, unsettled like a sailor lost at sea who is slowly lobbed to and fro by the water's silent undulations. Rather than seeing our online identities as aberration or misidentification, I propose we acknowledge that they merely signal a great diversity of who we are and can be, even as different technologies of power desperately try to wrangle us into preexisting boxes of identity.

METHODOLOGY

The research that grounds this book comes from years of investigatory work around an object of study that remains difficult to pin down. The process by which algorithms produce knowledge about us is both unwieldy and often impossible to know. The companies, governments, and researchers that collect, evaluate, and algorithmically interpret our data are agents invested in keeping their interpretations secret. Google's 'gender' and 'age' algorithms are proprietary, as are HP's 'face' and Face.com's 'emotions.'

In response to this methodological limit, I rely on a series of empirical examples to demonstrate the theoretical schematic by which we are made of data. This patchwork, cultural studies approach attempts to identify how different algorithmic logics produce the knowledge by which we live our digital lives. As information technologies increasingly datafy the world and its inhabitants, what our data comes to mean is determined by neither a person nor (as yet) a global, universal "master algorithm," such that "all knowledge—past, present, and future—can be derived from data by a single, universal learning algorithm."[96]

Rather, we are pushed and pulled by different interpretations of our data through different algorithmic instructions. And how those interpretations are made and how those interpretations change according to new data mean that any algorithmic object of study is a moving target. New technologies, new algorithms, and especially new cultural implementations of algorithmic judgment confound any notion of a single "algorithm."

The theoretical arguments that this book makes are not claims about algorithms at large. Rather, they are attempts to show how data about us is used to produce new versions of the world—versions that might differ greatly from their nonalgorithmic counterparts. For this reason, I move from example to example, measurable type to measurable type, in order to paint a fuller picture of how "we are data."

CHAPTER OVERVIEW

This book has two intersecting purposes. First is to understand how algorithms transcode concepts like gender, race, class, and even citizenship into quantitative, measurable-type forms. Second is to recognize how these measurable types reconfigure our conceptions of control and power in a digitally networked world. The political battles that surround structures of patriarchy, white supremacy, and capitalism writ large must necessarily attend to the terms of algorithm.

In other words, while HP's facial-recognition cameras might promote asymmetrical usages across racial lines, an algorithmic 'race' complicates this asymmetry. HP's response is indicative of this complication, in that HSV contrast, not skin color, shared history, or even DNA, stands in for the concept of race. We're talking about HP's construction of a 'white' 'face,' not White Wanda's white body. But we're talking about whiteness nonetheless. Race is incessantly being made and remade, and we must focus on how digital technology also makes and remakes 'race' on algorithmic terms.

Explicating the terms that underpin this making/remaking is the ultimate goal of the book. In the following pages, we'll talk about jazz, terrorists, HP being racist (again), marketing, the NSA, citizenship, and even Santa Claus. The shift to the data/algorithm ontology of the computer conceptually moves identity past explicit, policed boundaries that require negation and exclusivity (either male or female, at risk or not, black or white).

This move lays the foundations for a plane of smoothness, an open set of possibilities where we play on the limits of established truth. Algorithmic identity doesn't declare that you are just 'male' or 'female.' Statistical confidence and probability, even the chance that this book will spontaneously combust, can never be 100 percent anything. Rather, you're likely to be 92 percent confidently 'male' and 32 percent confidently 'female.' Algorithmic 'race' and 'gender' isn't about being a white man. It's about being a 'Caucasian' 'man' with a confidence measure of 87 percent. In algorithmic identity, we confirm the inorganic realities of Donna Haraway's cyborg, one who is "not afraid of permanently partial identities and contradictory standpoints."[97]

Chapter 1. Categorization: Making Data Useful

In order to compute something like 'woman' or 'smiling,' one needs to first make data useful. In chapter 1, I describe the how-to of algorithmic knowledge production. This how-to centers on how computers create categories through patterns in data, which then construct algorithmically transcoded ideas about the world that I call measurable types. Algorithms are neither magical nor mysterious. Instead, they make data useful through a very intricate but, I promise, also very interesting constellation of different technologies (like metadata or marimbas) that then create different algorithmic identifications (like 'terrorist' or 'John Coltrane').

Chapter 2. Control: Algorithm Is Gonna Get You

Measurable types are much more than descriptive containers for algorithmic meaning. They also play formative roles in how life and knowledge is controlled. With the aid of Gilles Deleuze's concept of modulation, I theorize how the deluges of data we produce online help enact a form of control. This type of control substitutes the strongly worded, hard-coded prohibitory "no!" of traditional modes of power in exchange for what some scholars have called "control without control"—and that I call soft biopolitics. These soft biopolitics describe how our algorithmic identities can regulate life without our direct participation or realization.

Chapter 3. Subjectivity: Who Do They Think You Are?

Soft-biopolitical measurable types structure our lives' conditions of possibilities every time we buy a plane ticket, cross a border, or translate a document on Google Translate. While we are ceaselessly made subject to different arrangements of algorithmic knowledges, these *datafied subject relations* are foreign to our most immediate experiences. We are not individuals online; we are dividuals. And without the philosophical anchor of the individual to think alongside, we are often at a loss in how we interpret ourselves as users. This chapter explores how algorithms make us subject in ways unique to online, algorithmic life.

Chapter 4. Privacy: Wanted Dead or Alive

How does one practice privacy in a world where not only is almost everything surveilled but that surveillance is rarely, if ever, felt? I evaluate privacy's legacy and outline its origins in the nineteenth-century phrase "right to be let alone," in order to bring that history into conversation with the exigencies of our contemporary era. I argue that privacy cannot just be about whether you have a password on your email or whether there are doors on a bathroom stall. Privacy must be a practical response to the lived restriction and control implicit in ubiquitous surveillance. In this way, I theorize a *dividual privacy* that focuses especially on how the freedom in being "let alone" might translate to a datafied, algorithmic world.

Conclusion: Ghosts in the Machine

At the end of the book, I return to my central arguments: online we are made, read, interpreted, and intelligible according to data. Our world, and the knowledge that gives it its meaning, is increasingly a datafied world. We are subsequently understood in the datafied terms of dynamic, soft-coded, and modulating measurable types. The contemporary encounters we have with ubiquitous surveillance suggest a new relationship to power that I term soft biopolitics. And the resulting ubiquity and emergent configurations of these different types of knowledge force us to rethink how subjectivity functions and what it is that privacy can practically defend.

1

CATEGORIZATION

Making Data Useful

This, the ability to take real-world phenomena and make them something a microchip can understand, is, I think, the most important skill anyone can have this day. Like you use sentences to tell a story to a person, you use algorithms to tell a story to a computer.

—Christian Rudder, founder of OkCupid[1]

"We kill people based on metadata."[2]

Metadata is data about data. It's data about where you are, from where you send a text message, and to where that message is sent. It's data that identifies what time and day you sent an email, the subject of that email, and even the type of device you used to send it. It's data that flows openly through cell and fiber-optic networks, easily plucked from the ether and connected together. And it's data about you that, when processed, is algorithmically spoken for in ways you probably wouldn't want it to speak.

In the quotation that begins this chapter, former NSA chief Gen. Michael Hayden alerts us to how metadata can be spoken for "as if" it was produced by a 'terrorist.' That is, one's metadata can be compared against a preexisting pattern, a "signature" in the parlance of the U.S. intelligence community. And if that metadata fits within this "signature" of a 'terrorist' template, one might find oneself at the receiving end of a Predator drone strike.

This data-based attack is a "signature strike," a strike that requires no "target identification" but rather an identification of "groups of men who bear certain signatures, or defining characteristics associated with terrorist activity, but whose identities aren't known."[3] With this in mind, we might choose to revise Hayden's remarks to be a bit more specific: "we call people 'terrorists' based on metadata. The U.S.'s War on Terror does the rest."

At the onset of the U.S.'s drone program in the early 2000s, strikes were "targeted." Intelligence officials identified suspected individuals through their voice, their name, or on-the-ground reconnaissance. Then, a drone operator would launch a missile down onto where that individual was believed to be. But in 2008, and following Pentagon frustration with the constraints imposed by the Pakistani state's military policy, the U.S. loosened its wartime drone guidelines. Now, a terrorist isn't just who the U.S. claims is a terrorist but also who the U.S. considers a data-based 'terrorist.' While the U.S. doesn't publicly differentiate between its "targeted" and "signature" strikes, one likely consequence of this shift was a spike in the frequency of drone attacks: there were 49 strikes during the five years between 2004 and 2008 and 372 during the seven years between 2009 and 2015.[4]

This loosening of legal restriction reindexed terrorist into 'terrorist': "a pre-identified 'signature' of behavior that the U.S. links to militant activity."[5] Since 2008, the U.S. government has launched what were billed as "precision" drone attacks against not just individual people but patterns in data—cell-phone and satellite data that looked "as if" it was a target that the U.S. wanted to kill, that is, a 'terrorist.'[6] Foreseeably, this "as if" mode of identification was not the same as "as."

And hundreds of civilians have since died as a probable result. Journalist Tom Engelhardt proposes that "the obliterated wedding party may be the true signature strike of the post-9/11 era of American warmaking, the strike that should, but never will, remind Americans that the war on terror was and remains, in distant lands, a war of terror."[7] The unintentional targeting of wedding parties, where individuals (and their cell phones) congregate outside city centers, producing data "as if" it was a terrorist meeting, reifies a level of permanent uncertainty in the geographic areas where these strikes happen. Even those who are not on a U.S. "kill list" live the potential to be identified "as if" they were—a precariousness of life that is terrorizing in and of itself.[8]

This operationalizing of 'terrorist' as an algorithmically processed categorization of metadata reframes who we are in terms of data. In our internetworked world, our datafied selves are tethered together, pattern analyzed, and assigned identities like 'terrorist' without attention to our own, historical particularities. As media scholar Mark Andrejevic writes, "such logic, like the signature strike, isn't interested in biographical profiles and backstories, it does not deal in desires or motivations: it is post-narratival in the sense conjured up by [Ian] Bogost as one of the virtues of Object Oriented Ontology: 'the abandonment of anthropocentric narrative coherence in favor of worldly detail.'"[9]

Yet even without an anthropocentric narrative, we are still narrativized when our data is algorithmically spoken for. We are strategically fictionalized, as philosopher Hans Vaihinger writes in his 1911 book *The Philosophy of "As If"*: "the purpose of the world of ideas as a whole is not the portrayal of reality . . . but to provide us with an instrument for finding our way about more easily in this world."[10] Importantly, those who use our data to create these ideas have the power to tell our "as if" stories for us. They "find" not "our way" but *their* way.

In this "as if" story of discovery, it is data that drives the plot. As Hayden described, "our species was putting more of its knowledge out there in ones and zeroes than it ever had at any time in its existence. In other words, we were putting human knowledge out there in a form that was susceptible to signals intelligence."[11] In a world inundated with data, traditional analyses fail to capture the rich, "worldly detail" of an NSA wiretap.[12] Indeed, through this big-data perspective, to make sense of such vast quantities of data functionally requires the move from "targeted" to "signature." Paring down the datafied world into "as if" 'terrorist' patterns is perceived as the logical next step.

Of course, the now-commonplace acceptance that the world is increasingly "data driven" might miss out on the fact that a 'terrorist' still looks and sounds very similar to whom the U.S. government has historically declared to be a terrorist. Both are most likely located in the Middle East and its neighbors. Both most likely speak Arabic or Urdu. Both most likely are not white. And both most likely practice Islam.

The discursive construction of terrorism in the U.S. draws from what Arab and Muslim American studies scholar Evelyn Alsultany describes as its Orientalist "baggage."[13] And this baggage also encounters, in the words of queer theorist Jasbir Puar and new-media scholar Amit S. Rai, the intersection of the racial and sexual "uncanny" of the "terrorist-monster."[14] Subsequently, the rhetoric of a monstrous other, one that designates the terrorist subject as a subject that deserves violence, flows easily into President Barack Obama's routine defense of his own drone program: "let's kill the people who are trying to kill us."[15]

This othered monstrosity both defines contemporary U.S. enemyship and expands the conditions for who can be considered a terrorist. Here, the truism of "one man's terrorist is another man's freedom fighter" is reinforced by the fact that this identification is always made on terms favorable to the classifier's geopolitical needs.[16] So when the allocation of "terrorist" passes through the figure of the terrorist-monster, that is, one whose death is a priori justified, the already-dehumanizing protocol regulating aerial, "targeted" assassinations can be further dehumanized. Presently, a terrorist needs only to be a data "signature," not a human being.

As an anonymous U.S. official told the *Wall Street Journal* in 2012, "You don't necessarily need to know the guy's name. You don't have to have a 10-sheet dossier on him. But you have to know the activities this person has been engaged in."[17] Absent a legal requirement to target a single, identifiable individual, the ontological status of "target" is technologically rerouted. Rather than being a more adept or accurate processing feature, the U.S.'s 'terrorist' is merely a datafied object of simple, strategic convenience. It's a functionalist category appropriate to the growing data-based logic of the NSA.

Rephrased in these functionalist terms, the loaded question of "who is a terrorist?" is answered in the logical vernacular of engineering. As Phil Zimmermann, creator of encryption software PGP, described, "The problem is mathematicians, scientists, engineers—they'll find ways to turn these problems into engineering problems, because if you turn them into engineering problems then you can solve them. . . . The NSA has an incredible capability to turn things into engineering problems."[18] Knowledge about who we are is constructed according to what ethicist

Luciano Floridi refers to as the "small patterns" in data, or what political theorist Stephen Collier would call "patterns of correlation," that extend the limits of conventional knowledge.[19] The NSA's 'terrorist' doesn't replace the concept of terrorist but adds onto it yet another layer. The classificatory family of terrorist must also include its algorithmic cousins.

THE 'NEEDLE' IN THE 'HAYSTACK'

Philosopher Grégoire Chamayou has deftly outlined this shift to algorithmic knowledge in his investigation of NSA history, writing on the various ways a 'terrorist' signature can be defined—much like the different ways and reasons that someone is called a terrorist. For example, using a method called graph matching, a "pattern graph" is modeled in order to compare subsets of a larger graph, an "input graph." If elements in an input graph find near equivalence with a pattern graph, those elements are classified accordingly.[20] Or, following Chamayou and with attention to figure 1.1, "If Bill and Ted live at the same address, rent a truck, visit a sensitive location and buy some ammonium nitrate fertilizer (known to be used for growing potatoes but also for the production of home-made bombs), they would exhibit a behavioural pattern that corresponds to that of a terrorist signature, and the algorithm designed to process this data would then sound the alarm."[21]

We might better understand this method in terms of one of the U.S. intelligence community's favorite metaphors: the needle in a haystack. As former deputy attorney general James Cole argued, "if you're looking for the needle in the haystack, you have to have the entire haystack to look through."[22] But there is no actual haystack. Rather, the haystack is the "observed activity" of the input graph, a technological construction according to the array of political decisions that determine what and whose activity is observed—and how that activity comes to be datafied.

Similarly, there is no such thing as a needle, either. While there may be a group of people who intend to commit an act of violence against

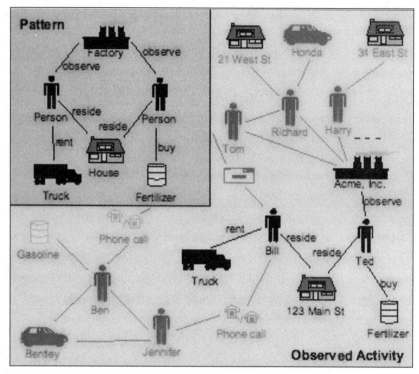

FIGURE 1.1. A graph showing the "pattern" of a 'terrorist' and the "observed activity" of available data. Source: Seth Greenblatt, Thayne Coffman, and Sherry Marcus, "Behavioral Network Analysis for Terrorist Detection," in *Emergent Information Technologies and Enabling Policies for Counter Terrorism*, ed. Robert L. Popp and John Yen (Hoboken, NJ: Wiley–IEEE, 2006), 334.

U.S. soldiers or citizens, that intention cannot be "found" like a physical needle. Rather, the needle must be constructed. To do so, the NSA aggregates an "as if" set of datafied elements. Then, it uses that set to parse the constructed haystack (data set) in order to find something that statistically resembles its patterned equivalence. For the aforementioned hypothetical 'terrorist,' that needle looks like data about two people, who reside in the same house, buy fertilizer, rent a truck, and observe the same factory. In this way, it's not a needle that U.S. government looks for; it's a datafied representation of that 'needle.'

'Needle' is a new technical construction that facilitates algorithmic analyses of the datafied world. Much like the social constructions of gender, race, sexuality, and terrorist, the datafied world is not lying in wait to be discovered. Rather, it's epistemologically fabricated. And because these constructions—of who counts as a terrorist or what it means to be a man—are legitimated through institutions like the state, media, medicine, and culture at large, they are also politicized and thus, in the words of legal scholar C. Edwin Baker, "corrupt."[23] They are "inventions," to use social theorist Nikolas Rose's term, born in contemporary relations of power and logics of classification and thus not authentic versions of who we think we might be.[24]

We return to Chamayou: "The entire [U.S. government] project rested on the premise that 'terrorist signatures' actually existed. Yet this premise did not hold up. The conclusion was inevitable: 'The one thing predictable about predictive data mining for terrorism is that it would be consistently wrong.'"[25] Any single, universal model of 'terrorist' will unavoidably fail to account for the wide varieties of different terror attacks that happen around the world.

In one reading, this regularity of error might suggest abandoning use of signatures in the first place. But following the engineering logic of the NSA, it simply means the constructed signature just needs better data. As the NSA mantra went, "sniff it all," "collect it all," "know it all," "process it all," and "exploit it all."[26]

Who counts as a terrorist is certainly a construction, a classification of people or organizations that a certain state doesn't like. Likewise, a 'terrorist' is also constructed, fabricated via patterns of data that seem "as if" they were made by a terrorist. This 'terrorist,' then, serves as a construction about a construction. But unlike the indefinite, relative category of terrorist, the category of a 'terrorist' empirically exists. It's a datafied model, a material template that can be copied, changed, and ceaselessly compared.

"We are data" means we are made of these technical constructions, or what I describe as measurable types.

As noted by an array of different scholars from various disciplinary backgrounds, these datafied models are quickly becoming the primary mechanisms by which we're interpreted by computer networks, governments, and even our friends.[27] From the corporate data troves of Google to the governmental dragnets of the NSA, who we are is increasingly made through data . . . and only our data.

All the while, these algorithmic interpretations are rarely known to us. They make who we are from data we likely have no idea is being used, a denial of explicit reflexivity that suppresses the "social" component of our identity's social constructionism. But who determines where this data comes from? What data is available and what data isn't? And, most importantly, how is this data made useful?

This last question is meant to echo Google's mission statement, "to organize the world's information and make it universally accessible and useful."[28] Here, I want us to focus on what exactly it means to make something useful. A hammer is useful in breaking things but only presuming those things want and deserve to be broken. The same hammer can hurt people or serve as a prop in a play. Even a gun on a table, despite Chekov's maxim, might be nothing more than a poorly chosen centerpiece.

This chapter will continue to explore the *how* of algorithmic construction: how governments, corporations, and researchers use algorithms to make data useful. This how will begin with what I call the measurable type, a concept that emerges from a datafied "exercise of power that creates and causes to emerge new objects [categories] of knowledge and accumulates new bodies of information," to quote philosopher Michel Foucault.[29] To further define the measurable type, we will take a tour of various algorithmic examples.

We'll explore techniques of machine learning, a subset of artificial intelligence that studies how computers generate abstract models from data. We'll look at a marimba-playing robot that can be programmed to perform at 70 percent 'John Coltrane' and 30 percent 'Thelonious Monk.' And given the growing attention to big data, we'll investigate how the immense fount of data produced every minute on services like Twitter allows machine-learning algorithms to actively reconstruct the online world as we know it.

Broadly speaking, we'll look at how computers use data to make versions of things that were never really there in the first place—or, to cite Christian Rudder, founder of data-driven dating site OkCupid, "making the ineffable totally effable."[30]

DEFINING THE MEASURABLE TYPE

A 'terrorist,' be it the datafied model of an NSA "signature" strike or a graph pattern compared to "observed activity," is what I call a measurable type—a concept I am repurposing from sociologists Max Weber's and Ervin Goffman's interpretations of the "ideal type."[31] A measurable type is a data template, a nexus of different datafied elements that construct a new, transcoded interpretation of the world. These templates are most often used to assign users an identity, an algorithmic identification that compares streams of new data to existing datafied models. Categorical membership is assigned based on algorithmic fit: if one's data is spoken for "as if" it was produced by a 'terrorist,' for example, one is seen to be a terrorist. And fit is subsequently based only on what data is available to be measured, so membership—and identity at large—is based exclusively on data.

These measurable types are ultimately classifications, empirically observed and transcoded as data, that become discrete analytical models for use in profiling and/or knowledge abstraction. As computer scientist Brian Cantwell Smith writes, "to build a model is to conceive of the world in a certain delimited way."[32] The resulting datafied model is what visual theorist Johanna Drucker refers to as a data object: a "model [that] is an interpretative expression of a particular data set. More importantly, it is what the interpreter says it is at any given point in time." These data objects "can then be exported and used elsewhere or even edited," their definition dynamic, reflexive to new available data.[33]

Who we are in terms of data depends on how our data is spoken for. And in general, our data is spoken for with a language fashioned from these models. Or returning to Smith, "computers have a special dependence on these models: you write an explicit description of the model down inside the computer, in the form of a set of rules or what are called representations."[34] Measurable-type models are extant, datafied objects that determine the discursive parameters of who we can (and cannot) be. The result is an array of measurable-type categories that our data either fits within or doesn't. That subsequent fit then governs how systems of classification algorithmically authenticate us online.

For example, in an experiment from 2012, investigators at Cornell University and Facebook found that "emotional states can be transferred to others via emotional contagion, leading people to experience the same emotions without their awareness."[35] In this study, researchers took a large sample of Facebook users (about seven hundred thousand people) and learned that when 'positive' expressions were removed from a population's News Feed (no longer would you see people write things like "I really like pomegranates"), users posted less 'positive' and more 'negative' updates. Similarly, when 'negative' expressions from its population's News Feed were removed (you would stop seeing strongly worded diatribes against pomegranates), users posted more 'positive' and less 'negative' updates.

Facebook's study used a relatively straightforward word-analysis software called Linguistic Inquiry Word Count (LIWC) as its measurable-type foundation. In the 2007 version of the LIWC, the index for 'negative' and 'positive' expressions is an inventory of words, taxonomized according to preexisting emotion-rating scales.[36] These taxonomies were vetted by a panel of judges and then used in a two-year test phase of psychometric evaluation. In the final stage, LIWC researchers removed words used less than 0.005 percent of the time during preliminary testing. The result was forty-five hundred different words that were then affixed with membership to sixty-four different, statistically significant "bag of words," or measurable-type, models.

homosexual*	60	62				
honest* 12	13					
honey 31	34					
honor* 12	13	47	50			
honour* 12	13	47	50			
hope 12	13	15	20	23	25	39
hoped 12	13	15	20	23	25	38
hopef* 12	13	15	20	23	25	
hopeless*	12	16	19			
hopes 12	13	15	20	23	25	39
hoping 12	13	15	20	23	25	
horny 60	61	62				
horribl*	12	16				
horrif* 12	16	17				
horror 12	16	17				
hostil* 12	16	18				
hour* 37						
house* 51	52					
how 20	21					
how's 20	21	39				
however 45						
hug* 27	30	60	62			
human 31	36					
humans 31	36					
humiliat*	12	16	17	18		
humor* 12	13					
humour* 12	13					
hundred*	11					
hunger* 60	61	63				
hungr* 60	61	63				
hurt* 12	16	19				
husband*	31	35				

FIGURE 1.2. The Linguistic Inquiry Word Count's data set includes forty-five hundred words, arranged into sixty-four different categories. In this figure, a word with a 13 next to it is deemed 'positive,' while a 16 denotes 'negative.' Source: James W. Pennebaker, Cindy K. Chung, Molly Ireland, Amy Gonzales, and Roger J. Booth, "The Development and Psychometric Properties of LIWC2007," LIWC.net, 2007.

As an individual measurable type, 'positive expressions' is composed of 408 words including "hug," "share," and "excel*" (where "excel*" is a stem that can also be "excellence" as well as "excelling"). The measurable type of 'negative expressions' comes from a list of 499 words including "fool," "missed," and even "geek" (figure 1.2). Quite quickly we can see how problems might arise when LIWC treats a status update like "I rarely share seafood with friends #shelfish" as 28.57 percent 'positive' while reading "a bowling ball just missed striking me on the head #spared" as 9.09 percent 'negative.'

Clearly, 'positive' and 'negative' are incomplete, error-prone assignments, just like any other category or taxonomy. But after the LIWC creates the measurable type of 'positive,' it is treated as positive in the big-data studies that employ it—and in the subsequent news stories written about those studies. As a data object, it becomes the singular arbiter of what is 'positive' and 'negative' writing for its users and thus what positive and negative eventually come to mean. Referencing the work of philosopher Bernard Stiegler, the LIWC produces its own, particular "grammars" that describe not just the world but who we are seen to be.[37]

Within the LIWC dictionary, there are many other measurable types available for text analysis: 'anger,' 'sadness,' 'health,' 'sexual,' 'work,' 'leisure,' 'religion,' and even 'death.' The approximations that the LIWC uses to assess a text's traits are understandably inexhaustible. Any measurable type is necessarily incomplete, much like any attempt to represent the world in abstraction. Accordingly, a measurable type's aim is instead directed toward operability and efficiency, not representative exactness. As digital humanist Willard McCarty writes, "computers are essentially modeling machines, not knowledge jukeboxes."[38] So when "rarely" is erroneously interpreted as 'positive,' it is seen as outlier to an otherwise satisfactory model, not cause to abandon the measurable type itself.

This reindexing of categorical meaning away from the human-centered complexities of narrative, context, and history and toward measurable datafied elements within a closed set (in mathematical set theory, 'sexual' = [abortion, aids, arous*, ass, asses, bi, . . . , womb*]) casts the measurable type as a discursively contained, and empirically definable, vessel of meaning.[39] This set can open at any time, as I can add and subtract words from the dictionary to fit my own needs and interpretations. Or the LIWC team can create a new version with a revised list of classified words—like they did in the LIWC's 2015 edition. But lying there, inert and untoyed with, a data object like 'sexual' is defined as an imperfect but static relation between words and meaning.[40] The dynamism of 'sexual' discourse is momentarily lost inside the closed confines of the LIWC's measurable-type model.

Measurable-type models are datafied versions of ideal types. The ideal type, a concept inaugurated by Max Weber, is "formed by the one-sided accentuation of one or more points of view and by the synthesis of a great many diffuse, discrete, more or less present and occasionally absent concrete individual phenomena, which are arranged according to those one-sidedly emphasized viewpoints into a unified analytical construct." And, like any reputable ideal form, "in its conceptual purity, this mental construct cannot be found anywhere in reality."[41]

Fifty years later, sociologist Erving Goffman defined this ideal type as a stylistic, constructed coherence between "setting, appearance, and manner"—or, more generally, the social norms for appropriate behavior in a specific situation. Goffman offers us the example of how the life of a rich man, like Empire State Building real estate agent Roger Stevens, performatively resists the ideal type of wealthy by having "a small house, a meager office, and no letterhead stationery."[42] Stevens's deficient inconsistency challenges the one-sided ideal of affluent existence. *How delinquent.*

Goffman's ideal type thus produces a norm. And this norm is then used, in traditional ideal-type fashion, to discipline people like Stevens into comporting with that which fits their station. As sociologist Pierre Bourdieu clarifies, the performance of a certain class is attached to an endless list of cultural qualifications that define categorical identity beyond income or self-identification.[43] Being wealthy isn't just about having a sizable bank account. It's also about knowing the works of Debussy, pronouncing French words correctly, and insisting that, yes, you really do enjoy the taste of caviar.

The preceding ideal type is an essential, idealist model of what it means to be wealthy, bound together by an empowered, Weberian univocality. The measurable type of the LIWC's 'sexual' produces a similarly essential, one-sided representation. But unlike the ideal impossibility to define what it means to be wealthy, the measurable type of 'sexual' exists as a defined data object. It is programmed, recorded into a data set, and then mathematically used to calculate the percentage-value of how 'sexual' your Facebook status updates are.

But what it means to be wealthy—or even who is a 'terrorist' and what is 'sexual'—inevitably changes. Its meaning evolves according to an itinerant circuit of competing theoretical and practical claims to definition. How much money do you need to be rich in 2010 versus 2015? What new plots are 'terrorists' trying? What words have become 'sexualized' from 2007 to 2015? (Answer: words like "bisexual*," "gigolo*," and "swinger*").

The epistemological construction of any ideal-type identity cannot rely on concreteness but rather must rely on an approximation of dynamic phenomena. Philosopher Gaston Bachelard understood this as an "abstract-concrete object," an incomplete claim about the physical world that assumes that world constantly changes.[44] Measurable types are no different. Their computational models are what McCarty describes as "temporary states in a process of coming to know rather than fixed structures of knowledge."[45]

Of course, even without "fixed structures of knowledge," knowledge still retains structure. What is known is always an empowered relation, from Foucault's power/knowledge to political theorist Antonio Gramsci's work on hegemonic and counterhegemonic knowledge and to a wide array of social-constructionist epistemological critique.[46] Indeed, life is neither without structure nor naturally occurring. It is always of power.

Existing classification theory also does well to demonstrate how different taxonomic types are made up, changing, and always incomplete. Like sociologists Michael Omi and Howard Winant's work on racial formation to theorists Geoffrey Bowker and Susan Leigh Star's *Sorting Things Out*, scholarship on classification has already chronicled a discursive world constructed according to, and for, those who are in power—and how those constructions dynamically attend to power.[47] Measurable types extend this body of scholarship with the very fact that this constancy of change is definable in near real time. In the case of LIWC, 'sexual' is a list of ninety-six different words used for data analysis. When a 'sexual' word is added or removed, that change is saved, is revised as an updated data object, and thus becomes part of the new, overhauled arbiter of what's 'sexual.'

Our "thoughts, feelings, personality, and motivations," as the LIWC markets itself, are made and regulated according to a statistical analysis of our writing on the basis of these transitory, measurable-type data objects.[48] When data defines us, the complexities of our emotional and psychological lives online are flattened out for purposes of mass-scale, approximate data analysis. In a parallel move, digital theorist David M. Berry argues that "for computer scientists, it is the translation of the continuum into the discrete that marks the condition of possibility for computationality."[49] To make something operable for a computer means that something has to be transcoded into discrete, processable elements. Datafied life undergoes what science and technology scholar Sheila Jasanoff calls "the simplifying moves that are needed to convert the messy realities of people's personal attributes and behaviours into the objective, tractable language of numbers."[50]

These moves produce quantitative standards that set the classificatory standards by which we are evaluated and judged. As historian Theodore Porter writes in his *Trust in Numbers*, "numbers turn people into objects to be manipulated."[51] Most recently, the identification of "10 percent 'sexual'" refashions the social world into a clean, cardinal positivism by which a company like Facebook can conduct experiments on its unknowing user base. Earlier than that, IQ tests created a standardized, hegemonic quantitative definition of intelligence.[52] And even earlier still, the national census, citing the work of political scientist James C. Scott and historian Mae Ngai, makes up not just us but the nation-state itself through numbers.[53] "The census produces abstract space through the regularization of difference," writes gender and race theorist Grace Hong.[54] What is race, what is gender, and thus who counts as a citizen of the state—all get rewritten and standardized when histories and context are made numerical. Indeed, the lineage of the quantification of social life precedes the contemporary novelty of "we are data" by centuries.

Much like the hegemonic power that specifies what a census counts and who counts for a census, measurable types are similarly burdened with iterations upon iterations of empowered interpretations. At the origin of our data, there is always an a priori value that it has before processing. This point rehearses the long-standing argument that "'raw data' is an oxymoron."[55] The production of data is, at its genesis, encased in a web of preexisting meanings, in which data "are not given; they are made."[56] As such, anyone who employs the term "raw data" forcefully forgets from where that data came. The data that make up our measurable-type identities must have a history, and that history is anything but untouched by human interference.[57]

Like the "translation of the continuum into the discrete," when measurable types are made from our available data, the lived specificities of our own perspective, history, and context are denied by these objectifying claims of identification. This denial sits alongside feminist theorist Donna Haraway's critique of the "corporeal fetishism" of genetic research. For Haraway, the gene is a "phantom object," an abstraction of the body that "forget[s] that bodies are nodes in webs of interactions."[58] By omitting the particularities of a body, fetishistic interpretations transcode that body into an arrangement of static knowledges. The lived realities of what Haraway calls "heterogeneous relationality" are converted into "a fixed, seemingly objective thing."[59]

For example, when a body is read by biometric technology, that body is seen as an object to be measured, analyzed, and sorted according to the biometric machine's measurable-type definition of 'human,' as we saw in this book's introduction. When biometrics fail, it is precisely because one's body fails to meet the datafied standards of that 'human' template.[60]

Corporeal fetishism abstracts the body, and thus the 'human,' into a "fixed" object of data. And in that temporary fixity, the unmanageable array of worldly difference is shaved away to form an operational whole. It's an abstraction in computer science in which "a whole explanation," like the template of 'human,' "applies to a range of possible situations," like the multiplicity of bodies that count as human.[61]

As corporeal fetishism is the objectification of the body, the categorical fetishism of measurable-type identification transcodes the category into an object, as well. The whole of what is 'sexual' is applied to the near-unlimited configuration of words in the English language. And we are authorized if, and only if, our data fits within a certain, "whole explanation" data template.

ALGORITHMICALLY DEFINING THE MEASURABLE TYPE

Although there is no such thing as raw data, the cultural and political foundations that "cook" data do not losslessly translate into measurable-type outputs. While both "what is sexual?" and "who is a terrorist?" are questions embedded in norms, access to data, and assumptions of what either means, both do not share these relations of power evenly.[62] The initial, cooked quality that informs all data cannot perfectly straddle the bridge between terrorist and 'terrorist,' precisely because these two categories are speaking about two distinct things.

On the one hand, a terrorist is a loosely defined ideal of legal and political knowledge, a villainous stand-in for those who are assigned as enemies of the state. It is an edict more than an analysis, as we see in George W. Bush's notorious September 20, 2001, address to a joint session of Congress: "either you are with us, or you are with the terrorists."

On the other, a 'terrorist' is an empowered data object. It defines exactly who is considered a 'terrorist' according to available data. While a 'terrorist' quickly becomes seen as a terrorist in the eyes of an NSA analyst, its categorical definition remains distinct. An individual might commit an act deemed terroristic and is subsequently identified as a terrorist. But that individual is not a 'terrorist' if her data fails to fit within the NSA's existing data template. Who is authorized as a 'terrorist,' then, is exclusive to whose data can be measured and thus interpreted. Geoffrey Bowker agrees: "if it's not in principle measurable, or is not being measured, it doesn't exist."[63]

While the human curation of the LIWC's 'sexual' provides us a productive example of how data becomes an empirical object, some of the most interesting measurable types are curated not by humans but by algorithms. The U.S.'s 'terrorist' is exactly this: an algorithmically constructed data object. So while humans may code algorithms and define their operable data structures, the emergent meanings of algorithmic processing produce a distinct kind of measurable type. Following what anthropologist Tom Boellstorff calls "platform-agnostic theory," the rest of this chapter will stitch together a theoretical framework of algorithmic knowledge that aims to excavate this distinction without necessarily limiting its scope to a single field site or context.[64]

With the ubiquitous surveillance that coconstitutes our networked society, what is available to be measured is ever increasing. Take the current move toward what is called "big data," or what digital scholars danah boyd and Kate Crawford define as

a cultural, technological, and scholarly phenomenon that rests on the interplay of:

(1) Technology: maximizing computation power and algorithmic accuracy to gather, analyze, link, and compare large data sets.

(2) Analysis: drawing on large data sets to identify patterns in order to make economic, social, technical, and legal claims.

(3) Mythology: the widespread belief that large data sets offer a higher form of intelligence and knowledge that can generate insights that were previously impossible, with the aura of truth, objectivity, and accuracy.[65]

For purposes of this book, big data represents a shift toward an algorithmic production of knowledge that is regarded as more true, and more efficacious, than nonalgorithmic, non-big-data forms. By producing knowledge from immense scales of available data, big data generates measurable types ("insights") that might be surprising but are treated as nonetheless correct. In this way, big data is seen to be useful for the very reason that any local assessment of it (less than big) would be incomplete. Anything less is too close, too focused on a specific mode or set. Its metaphorical equivalent is not missing the forest for the trees but missing the ecosystem of the forest for the forests.

Big data needs to be analyzed at a distance, because as Franco Moretti claims, "distance, let me repeat it, is a condition of knowledge: it allows you to focus on units that are much smaller or much larger than the [singular] text."[66] Big-data practitioners like Viktor Mayer-Schönberger and Kenneth Cukier aren't really concerned with analytical rigor: "moving to a large scale changes not only the expectations of precision but the practical ability to achieve exactitude."[67] Big data is instead about understanding a new version of the world, one previously unavailable to us because in an antiquated era before digital computers and ubiquitous surveillance, we didn't have the breadth and memory to store it all.

Moretti, though, is no data scientist. He's a humanist, best known for coining the concept of "distant reading." Unlike the disciplinary English practice of "close reading," in which a section of a certain text is painstakingly parsed for its unique semantic and grammatological usage, distant reading finds utility in the inability to do a close reading of large quantities of texts.[68] One human cannot read and remember every last word of Hemingway, and she would be far less able to do the same for other U.S.-born authors from the early twentieth century. But a computer can do so very easily and efficiently. Sure, a computer may not be able to understand the subtleties in Hemingway's description of the masculine condition or the themes of love, loss, and misogyny present in his works. But then again, computers aren't reading the text for pleasure or interpretation but rather parsing which words are present, what order they are in, and with what frequency they come. This type of analysis is concerned with knowledge, not pleasure, following Moretti's controversial declaration that "knowing is not reading."[69]

Big data's resulting knowledges are algorithmically defined through what is generally referred to as data mining.[70] But to discover an a posteriori pattern in a text is just that—a pattern. As geographer Rob Kitchin offers, "it is one thing to identify patterns; it is another to explain them."[71] In the same way, when algorithmic pattern analyses produce the discursive contours of our identifications, who we are becomes an unexplainable phenomenon. Our big data-algorithmic identities are statistically ordained by correlation and nothing else.

Consider a story about a friend of mine who has worked for the better part of a decade researching cell biology. Her job requires her to spend a remarkable amount of her life online, reading scholarly journals and reports about cell development and experimental methodologies. To be current in a field like cell biology research, even in her small subspecialty of protein quality control and neurodegeneration, takes considerable effort. Her aggregated RSS feeds of scientific journals' tables of contents and Google Alerts for research-related keywords churn out new information constantly. And in the spring of 2012, she was finishing up a review of recent literature in her field, requiring even more hours reading even more articles on her computer screen.

Around this time, an online trend—"Who Does Google Think You Are?"—began to circulate on social networks like Twitter and Facebook. A new feature in each Google account had been introduced: a demographic estimate of your 'age' and 'gender.' This estimate was based largely on which websites you visited, all collected and processed by Google in order to provide a more "personalized" set of search results.

As referenced in the introduction, Google had interpreted me and my behavior quite inaccurately. I mentioned this miscalculation to my science friend over brunch one Sunday. She replied that she had seen it and that she was similarly amused by Google's guess. In "real life," my friend was a twenty-eight-year-old woman. In "Google life," she was a 'forty-five- to sixty-five'-year-old 'man.' At first, her identity seemed goofy. But after thinking according to Google's inference logic, it started to make sense. My friend's web habits were almost entirely in line with her work. She was looking at articles (largely) written by older men, was in a field dominated by old men, and was working under the supervision of old men. If you spend all your time online looking at scientific scholarly articles about cell biology, why would Google think you were anybody other than an old man?

This apparent mistakenness of gender and age is a consequence of old men getting algorithmically reconfigured into 'old' 'men.' Using the company's huge swathes of data, Google's machines had learned—in a method somewhat similar to graph patterns of who is a 'terrorist'—what it meant to be 'old' and a 'man.' And it turns out that my friend's Internet use fit into those models of behavior more significantly than into those of a 'young' 'woman.'

But Google's own methodology to create these pattern-based demographic models is black boxed, proprietary and thus kept secret. While we may never be able to know, exactly, what makes an 'old' 'man,' we can fasten together two related algorithmic instances to better understand Google's underlying logic for measurable-type construction. First, some researchers at Google publicly proposed a method to define an audience in terms of 'age' and 'gender' on the basis of a "combination of data from several different sources to compute audience reach metrics: U.S. census data, ad server logs from the ad serving network, publisher-provided self-reported demographic data, and a representative online panel."[72] Here, the proposed categories of 'old' and 'man' are based on a wide array of different data sources, including a "representative online panel," to create, as well as calibrate, different demographic measurable types.

Second, data analytic companies like San Francisco–based Alexa and Reston, Virginia–based comScore make similar demographic assessments of their own users and are much less reticent to publicly discuss their methodologies. Both rely heavily on the use of panel analyses to create the measurable types like 'age' and 'gender,' as well as 'education' and whether you do or do not 'have children.'[73] More specifically, in terms of 'gender,' both companies grouped together users who identify as men and users who identify as women and then aggregated each group's web behavior together. The most common search queries, web-browsing habits, and other online behavior in each grouping determined what became the data object of 'man' and 'woman.' The same method goes for constructing 'age,' and the same could go for any quality or identity one might conjure up.

This is what computer scientists call semi-supervised learning, in which a machine is paternally taught what it means to be a 'man' by developing an averaged web-use model of users who identify as men.[74] The subsequent index for masculine identity is not men but the datafied patterns of what users do as 'men.' And anyone who fits inside this 'male' model is likely to be categorized as a 'man.'[75] These semi-supervised algorithms produce 'truths' about the categories that compose us. But in this example, 'gender' is not lived but latent. My friend may not be a man, but her web-surfing behavior is read as 'masculine.'

Here, this univocal identification complicates previous theorizations we have about both identity and, in this case, gender. With the impossibility of raw data in mind, Google's 'gender' is surely indebted to gendered life, logic, and politics. What men do is what 'men' are subsequently interpreted to be, so the sexist overrepresentation of men in fields of science, for example, makes it unsurprising that my scientist friend is an 'old' 'man.'

But when queer theorist J. Halberstam writes of gender as "learned, imitative behavior that can be processed so well that it comes to look natural," we see how an identity like gender is dependent on reflexive disciplinarity.[76] The processed output of gender in Halberstam's formula is an output that must immediately return to the individual subject, an iterative process that continually cycles back to some perceived naturality of gendered performance.

Philosopher Judith Butler's own interpretation of gender follows closely to Halberstam's: "gender is a contemporary way of organising past and future cultural norms, a way of situating oneself in and through those norms, an active style of living one's body in the world."[77] Indeed, we can step back to consider that most categories of identity need to directly interface with their subject in order to have the desired normalizing effect. For the individual, these norms enact a disciplinary relation to recenter an ideal-type identity. As Foucault explained in his *Security, Territory, and Population* lectures,

> Disciplinary normalization [which he eventually terms "normation"] consists first of all in positing a model, an optimal mode that is constructed in terms of a certain result, and the operation of disciplinary normalization consists in trying to get people, movements, and actions to conform to this model, the normal being precisely that which can conform to this norm, and the abnormal that which is incapable of conforming to the norm. In other words, it is not the normal and the abnormal that is fundamental and primary in disciplinary normalization, it is the norm.[78]

A focus on "normation" is a focus on the norm of the model, which then gets ordained as normal. The naturalized output of gender must be in constant, disciplinary contact with this norm.

When thinking through our algorithmic identities, we can regard these norms in terms of what philosopher Ian Hacking calls "statistical reasoning": "we obtain data about a governed class whose deportment is offensive, and then attempt to alter what we guess are relevant conditions of that class in order to change the laws of statistics that the class obeys."[79] In this case, a norm then isn't "men do *x*." Rather, a norm might be a statistical representation of men's aggregated behavior—a population-level quantitative model that serves as the discursive stand-in by which men are monitored, evaluated, and eventually governed.

Importantly, as Hacking explains, this statistical reasoning requires guesswork: while a governing class disciplines a governed class in order to guide the governed toward an optimal identity, the efficacy of that discipline can be statistically interpreted only at the level of class. More specifically, the consequences of making a class less offensive to the governing is not a list of individuals who now comport themselves differently. Instead, it's an aggregated quantitative representation of the governed. The diverse instances of individual reactions to discipline are collapsed in favor of a class-level, statistical barometer of social change.

Let's return to my scientist friend. Google algorithmically assigned her a 'gender' by treating her web-surfing data as inputs. Then, Google subsequently spoke for her data according to how well it statistically stacked up to its quantitative models. But there was no human curation of 'gender,' nor was my friend an 'old' 'man' because she learned, through normation, what it meant to be an 'old' 'man.' Indeed, when we are identified according to a measurable type without our direct knowledge, the potentiality of disciplinarity is routed through what I define in chapter 2 as control—or more precisely what I describe as soft biopolitics. Here, the processed measurable type of 'gender' largely discards relations of disciplinary reflexivity. It instead reads, processes, and allocates identifications silently from behind the computational curtain.

Algorithmic measurable types follow social theorist Isaiah Berlin's likely apocryphal adage, "to understand is to perceive patterns," precisely because it is impossible for a computer to understand, much less defend, the idea of man in and of himself. While Google is obviously invested in knowing who we are as users for purposes of profiling, marketing, and profit, the knowledge that emerges from algorithmic measurable types is qualitatively different from the gendered knowledge of feminist-situated epistemologies, as seen in the work of philosopher Sandra Harding, or the diverse experiences that different women have under "white capitalist patriarchy," to quote feminist theorist bell hooks.[80]

Google cares less about "governing" a class and more about reaching a consumer, wherein a user who looks like an 'old' 'man,' surfs like an 'old' 'man,' and talks like an 'old' 'man' will be treated as an 'old' 'man.' Similarly, NSA analysts are not employed to discipline 'terrorists' according to a norm. Instead, the NSA wants to know who a 'terrorist' is so it can track their data and kill them.

And precisely because these measurable types are calculated only according to patterns of behavior—thus avoiding the normating forces of some desired, optimal identity—their datafied templates necessarily change. But unlike their nonalgorithmic peers that must wait for human intervention to recalculate each data object, the recursive quality of an algorithmic 'gender' can automatically recalibrate its discursive meaning according to a flow of new inputs.

This recalibration of 'gender' disavows traditional conventions of gender, focusing instead on the empirically available, latent attributes that define how 'man' is being performed, en masse, at each and every moment. Like theorist Tiziana Terranova's concepts of "microstate" and "macrostate" from this book's introduction, when new microstate data comes in, new macrostate 'gender' comes out.[81] Gender, much like 'gender,' dynamically develops over time, from dress to vocabulary to access to resources. But unlike gender, 'gender' is not a category that we consciously perform and personally comprehend as a political identity. 'Gender' is not something we know about or are asked about. 'Gender' instead is valued or devalued according to what 'gendered' data is algorithmically interpreted to say at that moment, expanding or shrinking its measurable-type definition like bellows filled by nascent patterns.

However, while an algorithmic 'gender' may dynamically reconfigure itself according to flurries of new data, any effective measurable-type category requires a moment of discursive respite wherein its provisory output is operationalized "as if" it was true. In this way, algorithmic processing mimics the concept of arbitrary closure introduced by cultural theorist Stuart Hall: to make any claim about oneself, or to define one's own subject position, requires a hypothetical halt to the changing nature of the world.[82] Arbitrary closure is a pause button on the dynamism of discourse, a conceptual stop to space and time in order to analyze and make assertions about who we are.

Not limited to an algorithm's output, digital computers produce arbitrary closures every time they calculate a function, a technological feature/bug inherited from the serial calculations of Alan Turing's machinic legacy. To add two plus two together means that the computer, for a brief millisecond, will conceptually focus its entire processing power on a two, then an addition sign, and then another two, eventually spitting out its output as four. But in the brief, transient moment when electronic signals signified as ones and zeros streak across a microprocessor during computation, the world is stable and closed. It is peaceful and unsullied. When these twos and four are read by the computer's processor, the machine has no idea what will come next.

When a measurable type like 'gender' moves to the algorithmic rhythm of what 'old' 'men' do, 'gender' loses an element of its assumed essentialist identity. The empowered agents that dictate the conventional, political limits of gender are not queried when Google makes a 'man.' Rather, Google's new interpretation of 'gender' reessentializes gendered behavior into a concrete object of data.

This reessentialization is similar to boyd and Crawford's description of how "Big Data stakes out new terrains of objects, methods of knowing, and definitions of social life."[83] Here, rather than posing orthodox scientific inquiries like "what data satisfy this pattern?" data analysts like those at Google ask, "what patterns satisfy this data?"[84] This turn of phrase methodologically establishes a baseline unknowingness in which patterns rise to the surface to "satisfy" data without purpose, intention, or hypothesis. The essentialism implicit in "what data satisfy this pattern?" transforms into an algorithmic, output-oriented "what patterns satisfy this data?"

The resulting 'gender' output is not a structured political identity but a pattern that can sometimes puzzle its own algorithm's authors. Indeed, as seen in the work of both communication scholar Mike Annany and anthropologist Nick Seaver, the recursive complexities built into many algorithmic instructions, coupled with the different engineers and workgroups that collectively author algorithms, make any notion of algorithmic causality difficult to diagnose.[85]

The aforementioned error in identifying my friend's 'gender' is due to this "what patterns/data satisfy this data/pattern" distinction. Google's measurable types are not trying to be their non-quotation-marked counterparts. In this way, algorithmic miscategorization is better understood as *neocategorization*. Being an 'old' 'man' might seem erroneous in our world of conventional gender and identity regimes. But my friend will likely continue as an algorithmic 'old' 'man' in accordance to her dedication to cell biology research.

In fact, it's measurable types' universality of allowable wrongness that permits them the ability to move, to reform the world into new, measured 'truths.' Consider geographer Louise Amoore's interpretation of the Foucauldian security apparatus: instead of "prevent[ing] events from happening, to 'allow nothing to escape,'" the apparatus "rather . . . 'let[s] things happen.'" These apparatuses "rely on details that are not valued as good or evil in themselves" so that what "Foucault calls details we might think of as our data elements whose value as such is only ascribed through their relations to other elements."[86] The data elements in Amoore's theorization are made from the bottom up. They are taken from what is empirically available and used in measurable-type construction.

It follows that measurable types forbid strict allegiances to what we call identity, the complex formation of histories, power relationships, and subjective experiences that make us who we are. My scientist friend may not be a man, but she's "as if" a 'man' according to her data. And unlike our identities that enjoy/suffer at least temporary consistency across time, our new, measurable-typed identities can change by the hour: later in the afternoon, my friend's data trail might suggest yet another identification.

This "as if" quality means measurable types can be found everywhere. They're our 'age' and 'genders' by Google; they're our 'positive expressions' in our writing. And they're even, as we'll see, famous 'jazz musicians.' They are the arbitrary closures that allow someone or something to say, at this moment, in this space, that you are going to be seen, evaluated, and treated like a 'woman' who is 'sad' and 'young.' And because measurable types have no timeless essence, they are wed to data: only that which can be datafied is included, as my friend can pathetically scream at her computer, "No, I'm not an old man, Google!" with no success. Measurable-type identity is beholden to algorithmic fit, not the disciplinary confines of political identity.

Measurable types are most often subterranean, protected and unavailable for critique, all while we unconsciously sway to their undulating identifications. Every time we surf the web, we are profiled with measurable types by marketing and analytic companies such as the San Francisco–based Quantcast, the San Francisco–based Alexa, and the Bellevue, Washington–based AudienceScience. We are assigned identities when we purchase a product, walk down a street monitored by CCTV cameras, or bring our phones with us on a vacation to Italy. Even that trip to the doctor last week might produce knowledge that will, for good or for bad, have a direct influence on you and others.

Google cofounder Larry Page alarmingly defended this biopolitical variety of the measurable type when he asserted, "Right now we don't data-mine healthcare data. If we did we'd probably save 100,000 lives next year."[87] In technology discourse today, there is a devotion to the measurable type, a belief that data both speaks without impediment and with a lifesaving eloquence that describes the human condition better than any doctor or scientist could have. But patterns in data aren't truth. They are constructed, algorithmically produced 'truths.'

It is the entwining of truth and 'truth' into a single core concept that this chapter will continue to disentangle. As mentioned in the introduction, the quotation-marked categories of the measurable type are in no way improved versions of what is 'man'—or, even worse, a hackneyed 'man 2.0.' While measurable types are powerful tools that capture and analyze the high-velocity tornadoes of data used to generate knowledge about populations, they do not replace their historical predecessors. Rather, they add another layer, another set of discursive meanings that we must consider when we talk about the politics around things like gender, sex, or terrorism.

MACHINES LEARNING JAZZ

Quite prodigiously, machines learn by teaching themselves based on data and algorithmic instructions. Machine learning is the "technical basis . . . used to extract information from the raw data in databases—information that is [then] expressed in a comprehensible form and can be used for a variety of purposes such as prediction and inference."[88] More colloquially, it's how computers can learn what a certain thing is, taken from a large data set, to produce newly abstracted, measurable-type meaning.

If, as we've seen, a computer can abstractly learn the patterns that make up 'gender,' 'age,' and more daringly 'terrorist,' can a computer learn something more out there, more otherworldly and less tangible, like 'jazz'? Louis Armstrong famously responded to the question "what is jazz?" with a pithy "if you still have to ask . . . shame on you."[89] Jazz has to be felt. Its sonic, genre-defining quality is less a variable of time signature, instrumentation, or strict rhythm and more a matter of culturally specific sentiment and affect.

There's also the fact that jazz as a genre, following scholars like Herman Gray and Paul Anderson, has always had direct ties to racial histories of violence and urban segregation, blackness in general, and the aesthetic dimensions of the black avant-garde that helped spark the Harlem Renaissance and the artistic movements that birthed rock and roll.[90] A computer making an 'old' 'man' might be one thing, but 'jazz' seems to be another planet. Can a computer learn the cultural politics of jazz and their profound historical connection to an aesthetic form, all while performing an instrument?

To answer this question, we turn our attention to a robot living in Georgia that can play the marimba.[91] With four mallet-hands, a long, lamp-like neck, and a softball-sized head, the robot hunches over a four-octave wooden marimba and starts to move. Its head nods to the beat, even closing its camera-lens eye to imitate both a blink and immense concentration. A human bassist sits to its left, a human keyboardist to its right. All three players improvise a song, in real time, that evolves over time. The music slows, becomes more syncopated, or even shifts keys. The robot can be programmed to play like you or to follow your lead and accompany you. And the robot can also be told to play like John Coltrane or Thelonious Monk. It even can play like a percentaged buffet of all three ('Coltrane,' 25 percent; 'Monk,' 25 percent; 'You,' 50 percent).[92]

The name of this marimba-playing automaton is Shimon, and it was designed by researchers at the Georgia Institute of Technology. Developed originally in 2007, Shimon has played with hundreds of different human performers and other computers, earning robotics accolades as well a 2010 feature on *The Colbert Report*'s "ThreatDown" segment. But unlike many of Shimon's nonrobotic marimba-playing peers, it never spent a minute in a music classroom. Instead, Shimon spent all of its time in an engineering lab, learning how to play jazz from data in a database. At Georgia Tech, Shimon majored in 'jazz,' relying on machine-learning algorithms to parse the musical solos of two jazz masters, Thelonious Monk and John Coltrane, in order to discern the pitch, rhythm patterns, and volume of each artist. With these transcoded variables in tow, programmers instructed Shimon to play the marimba like 'John Coltrane' and/or 'Thelonious Monk.'

The perceptual algorithms that create a 'John Coltrane' take an input, like hundreds of pages of transcribed improvised solos by John Coltrane, and let a computer find the commonalities in that inputted data set to then make a general, abstract claim about what John Coltrane's improvisation means.[93] Each note and rest is inputted to denote its pitch (A#5), its duration (an eighth note or a whole rest), and its volume (pianissimo or forte).

Taken as a whole, Coltrane's oeuvre teaches Shimon which melodies, syncopated rhythms, and volume changes a 'Coltrane' would likely play at a certain time. What the machine perceives is, at first, what the algorithm's authors point the machine to learn (pitch, rhythm, and volume). The clusters of meaning that the machine then perceives (Coltrane often uses syncopation, or he really likes playing in A minor) becomes the measurable type of what 'Coltrane' comes to mean.

But what makes Shimon so innovative is not just how it generates a musical measurable type from jazz data. The other half of Shimon's algorithmic soul is how it adapts to change. Our sonic environment affects how we act in the world but also how we play and conceive of music. Just think of how quickly people start walking on beat if they mistakenly pass a nearby drum circle. This is Shimon's generative side, or the "how" that allows Shimon to play not just as 50 percent 'Coltrane' and 50 percent 'Monk' but also as 25 percent 'Coltrane,' 25 percent 'Monk,' and 50 percent 'you.'

Indeed, Shimon changes its musical performances in real time, basing its playing style on new, context-aware algorithmic models.[94] Any good band member knows that the primary convention in making decent music is to modulate your playing style to fit with others. Shimon does this by thinking about 'you' as a measurable-typed subject, a musician just like 'John Coltrane' whose performance is melted down into an abstract statistical essence: the commonality patterns of your playing as defined by pitch, rhythm, and volume.

'You' is a constantly evolving rendition of self, an undoing and redoing of hidden patterns that Shimon perceives from your playing. These constantly recalibrating models of 'you' generate a new aesthetic form, one dependent on musical inputs but also reflexive to how those inputs change. To do so, Shimon relies on Hidden Markov Model statistical analyses, recording data from your playing through a piano keyboard or other MIDI-supported device (figure 1.3).[95] What makes these models fascinating is how efficiently they produce an actionable measurable

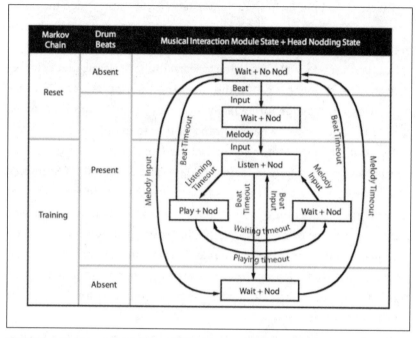

FIGURE 1.3. Shimon's Hidden Markov Model diagram describing how its learning algorithm functions. Source: Gil Weinberg, Aparna Raman, and Trishul Mallikjaruna, "Interactive Jamming with Shimon: A Social Robotic Musician," *HRI '09 Proceedings of the 4th ACM/IEEE International Conference on Human Robot Interaction*, 2009, 234.

type. After only twenty seconds of inputted (training) music, Shimon can suss out your sonic core. Shimon calculates the statistical similarities of your playing style, finding the common rhythmic, volume, and tonal patterns that might emanate from eight bars of improvisation.[96]

It should be obvious that no such essence actually exists. Instead your playing is read as a model, a probabilistic definition of how often you might play in C minor or how rarely you play the same note twice in a row. Let's say that in an eight-bar call-and-response performance, you repeatedly play the sequence G♯, D3, C♯3, B3. Shimon will keep this data in mind for its rejoinder. Maybe it will mimic the sequence you play or transpose it to its minor third in order to provide a harmonic overtone. Maybe it will play frantically between G♯ and D3 and then play sluggishly between C♯3 and B3. Or maybe it will do something else, based on the presumed but invented pattern that undergirds your playing style. What Shimon plays is up to what 'you' are, its probabilistic model, and the current value of your percentaged slider (50 percent).

Yet all of these interpretations are temporal. The patterns of a minute ago are useless; the patterns of now are what matter. Shimon's interpretation of you does not mirror a person who knows your influences and the extensive music collection you have at home. Instead, it's a memoryless musical capture of your playing at a very specific moment. That model changes as new input arrives, allowing Shimon to sense an increasing fervor in your playing, for example, and in doing so can match that new style effectively and without pause.

'Coltrane,' 'Monk,' and 'you' are all measurable types, the transcoding of individuals into mathematical musical models. As a measurable-type musician, you are an abstracted entity defined exclusively by your latest datafied actions. While 'John Coltrane' might be dead, you are definitely alive, but you are alive only according to how you play. The example of Shimon offers us an excellent insight into the real cultural work that is being done by algorithmic processing.

Shimon's algorithmic 'Coltrane' and 'Monk' are new cultural forms that are innovative, a touch random, and ultimately removed from a doctrinaire politics of what jazz is supposed to be. It instead follows what 'jazz' is and can be according to the musical liberties taken by predictive statistical modeling. This is what anthropologist Eitan Wilf has called the "stylizing of styles"—or the way that learning algorithms challenge how we understand style as an aesthetic form.[97] 'Jazz' is jazz but also not. As a measurable type, it's something divergent, peculiarly so but also anthropologically so.

So if 'jazz' can be made up of transcribed solos and MIDI-input melodies, what role does race play in this "stylizing of styles"? Or more directly, how does Thelonious Monk and John Coltrane's blackness get read by Shimon into their measurable-type definitions? The answer is in the same way that 'race' is read into HP's facial-recognition camera from this book's introduction. The impossibility of raw data means that race will always factor in. It will, at the very least, be expressed implicitly. Yet unlike the racial disparities that become apparent, almost perfectly along the discriminatory lines of the Jim Crow South, when HP ignores Black Desi while simultaneously authenticating White Wanda, there is no telltale way for Shimon to demonstrate racial difference.

As a performer, Shimon is patently nonhuman, fabricated out of plastic, wires, and microprocessors that lend themselves poorly to racial assessment or heritage-"discovering" blood-quantum tests and DNA swabs. Indeed, Shimon's suggestive postraciality unintentionally pleads with the audience to ignore the racial legacies that made jazz a genre. Read as data, 'jazz' and 'Monk' are mere patterns, not authored, musical/political acts. As such, we have to consider how algorithmic classifications profoundly disrupt what we refer to when we talk about race and legacies of blackness, as well as new forms of whitewashing and cultural appropriation. It is inescapable that Shimon reads race into part of its algorithmic assessment. But it also folds this trace of race into the manifest postraciality of a silver robot that plays jazz on the marimba at an engineering lab in Atlanta.

By collapsing the possibility for racial distinction into a univocal, robotic reading of musical performance, Shimon transcends immediate racial logics—it doesn't explicitly adhere to any notion of identity politics—and thus refuses race as a descriptor. Indeed, no algorithm nor abstraction can fully represent any experience or history. But while there is no such thing as raw data, the complexity and legacy of black identity in musical performance is flattened out by algorithmic interpretation. Race is embedded within the measurable type, but excavating or discerning it often proves impossible. Part of 'jazz's' musical identity loses its historical, racialized form.

MAKING DATA MEAN SOMETHING

The data objects that compose measurable types like 'Monk' or 'Coltrane' are not mimetic to any nondatafied category. Accordingly, the measurable type of 'man' is not a social and political identity that articulates various bodies, performances, and self-identifications into a semi-intelligible conceptual whole. The empirical identity of Google's 'man' is a set of observed patterns, literally removing from the equation what gender essentialists believe makes a man.

This is also why the category of 'man' could be called anything, really: 'users that produce apparently masculine data' or 'users who solely visit sites about sports and power tools.' Even something more technologically astute but culturally remote would work, like 'profilesegment3.' Because man is a lived, sociocultural identity, while 'man' is a data object often assigned to our behavior without our knowledge, there remains an incollapsible distinction between the two. And with this distinction in mind, there's no real reason for 'man' to be called man, other than to semantically bridge this divide.

But this construction of identity is also not new. Media scholars Joseph Turrow and Nora Draper have written about marketing's "industrial construction of audiences," in which many different industry forces converge to shape how an audience is composed, named, and managed.[98] Similarly, journalism scholar C. W. Anderson has traced how audience constructions changed when news outlets moved onto the web.[99] For institutions interested in selling products to or producing content for men or women, gender may never possesses a solid, immobile essence. But gender is still deemed a useful category that narrows consumer markets into legible, manageable segmentations.

When these categories are ushered into the world of ubiquitous dataveillance, we see digital media scholar Lev Manovich's claim that "the language of cultural interfaces is largely made up from elements of other, already familiar cultural forms" echoing an equivalent point.[100] Online, a marketer or news publisher will never be entirely sure of a user's gender identity. But 'man' serves as a semantically convenient placeholder to let clients know that 'men' might mean something, with high statistical confidence, that could possibly have gendered implications for sales, page views, or editorial decisions.

This is also the placeholding process by which anything and everything under the algorithmic 'sun' can be made into a measurable type: 'age,' 'gender,' 'income,' 'ethnicity,' 'education level,' 'number of children,' 'sexual orientation,' and even 'marital status' ('single,' 'divorced,' 'engaged,' 'relationship,' or 'swinger'). In fact, this list of categories is the same by which users were profiled when playing the game *Angry Birds* in early 2010.[101]

While you might not have known it as you swiped your finger across the screen, ordering suicidal birds to attack a never-ending encampment of cartoon pigs, Baltimore-based marketing company Millennial Media was aggregating data about your smart-phone behavior. Here, a 'swinger' is not someone who raises her hand affirmatively to the question "Are you a swinger?" It's the patterns of data, tracked and analyzed by marketers, that are the real 'swingers.'

And while Millennial Media was busy determining the complexities of users' sexual practices, they and *Angry Birds'* creators, Rovio Entertainment, were ignoring several vital security conditions that made this information vulnerable to prying eyes. Quite soon after these profile segments were launched, NSA and British intelligence agency GCHQ discovered that apps like *Angry Birds* weren't just angry. They were also "leaky," meaning their data was unencrypted and vulnerable to poaching.[102] Governmental surveillance dragnets could then piggyback onto the already-processed measurable types, capturing user data as it moved through private cell-phone networks in order to store it within their own state databases.

But the U.S. government has no idea what makes a 'swinger' or even how Millennial Media algorithmically created 'ethnicity.' For all you know, you might be a 'swinger' just because you enjoy the early frat-pack movie *Swingers* a bit too much. 'Swingers' is nothing but a suite of datafied, patterned performances that becomes a new template defining the swingers lifestyle. Such is the imperfection and inconsistency of the measurable type.

Even with this imperfection, measurable types are often seen by marketers and web-analytic companies as more efficacious than hard-coded, curated demographic data. Take the early 2000s literature surrounding "post-demographics." The move to the post-, as digital theorist Richard Rogers writes, "marks a theoretical shift from how demographics have been used 'bio-politically' (to govern bodies) to how post-demographics are employed 'info-politically,' to steer or recommend certain information to certain people."[103] For governments and marketers, strict demographic categories are increasingly perceived to be less efficacious in targeting groups, markets, and voters than previously thought. And over the years, nondemographic modes of classification, like interests, favorites, and tastes, have been elevated as the more efficacious, and profit-rewarding, vehicles of audience construction.[104]

Which is to say, even before the 2000s, advertisers had already been moving away from strict demographics-based assessments for decades. In 1964, marketing guru Daniel Yankelovich proposed constructing audiences according to what he called "segmentation analysis." The essential qualities of demographics had become too stringent, Yankelovich argued. By targeting products to men as a single group, for instance, one collapses the multiplicity of consumer types within a single, static masculine identity. "Traditional demographic methods of market segmentation," he writes, "are not likely to provide as much direction for marketing strategy as management requires."[105]

In response, marketers in the 1970s shifted their analytic focus from the world of essentialist demographics to what industry types now call "psychographics."[106] No longer were advertising workers slinging products at some mythical, universal man. They instead sought types like those defined in the famous 1979 "Values and Lifestyles" (VALS) marketing research from SRI International. Marketers were then able to divide the American consumer population according to a "detailed quantification of VALS types in terms of demographics, attitudes, regional distribution, household inventories, activities, media habits, and consumption patterns for over 700 categories."[107]

Consumer groups may have lost singular demographic specificity, but in that loss, they gained a more nuanced character. Freed from the rigid terminologies of either gender or race or class, marketers now could seek those with "high incomes," "married with few children who live in fashionable homes on small, manicured lots," and composed of "a high concentration of Asian Americans" with "advanced degrees and sophisticated tastes to match their credentials."[108]

With this cursory intersection of class, marital status, place of residence, ethnicity, education, and taste, marketing company Claritas's PRIZM NE Segmentation System aggregated the foregoing characteristics in the early 2000s to create the composite profile of "Money & Brains." This amalgamation of different behavior and identity categories quickly revealed to marketers the glaring inefficiency of targeting only men—mainly because it resulted in a loss of revenue and a waste of advertising resources. As the web-audience measurement company Quantcast explained in 2014, "when advertisers want to reach college-aged females from Texas, they aren't interested in reaching females, Texans, and college-aged people separately—they want to reach an audience with all three of those attributes."[109]

We can see in this brief account that marketers understood and practiced the much-heralded concept of intersectionality years before (largely white) critical theory.[110] Indeed, an individual's experience of gender can and must intersect with her experience of race. And we know, through these experiences and thanks to black feminist theorists like Kimberlé Crenshaw, that identity in a "single-axis framework," like "I am a man" or "I am white," says little about who we are as subjects or how we are treated by power.[111] These conceptions must also intersect with issues of class, sexuality, age, ability, and so on, and vice versa.

But even within the theoretical foundations of intersectionality, we are still unable to know or define what intersectionality looks like. Indeed, the methodological intricacy of intersectional analysis over the past several decades has provided different responses to the question, what does it mean to "intersect"? Sociologist Leslie McCall outlines three historically founded approaches. One, anticategorical complexity "deconstructs analytical categories" like race, gender, and class, as lived experience always fails to fit cleanly within these social constructs. Two, intercategorical complexity "provisionally adopt[s] existing analytical categories to document relationships of inequality." And three, intracategorical complexity "focus[es] on particular social groups at neglected points of intersection," a strategic combination of the first two approaches to understand "the process by which [categories] are produced, experienced, reproduced, and resisted in everyday life."[112] But in terms of analysis, each of these approaches to complexity forces us to ask yet another question: what exactly *is* being intersected in intersectionality?

This second question has led theorists like Jasbir Puar to reconsider intersectionality when the historicized and localized epistemologies that define our identities are taken into account. In turn, she proposes we consider identity, via philosophers Gilles Deleuze and Félix Guattari, as formed through "assemblages [that] foreground no constant but rather 'variation to variation' and hence the event-ness of identity."[113] Her resulting interpretation is that "intersectional identities and assemblages must remain as interlocutors in tension. . . . Intersectional identities are the byproducts of attempts to still and quell the perpetual motion of assemblages, to capture and reduce them, to harness their threatening mobility."[114] This by-product of identity remains in a constant dialogue with that assemblage's dynamism. In short, when accepting of intersectional complexity, we return to the impossibility of empirically pinning down what our identities mean and thus what *is* intersected.

But in terms of who we are as data, this epistemological variance is explicitly transcoded—and thus made empirical. Google's 'man' is a changing, dynamic measurable type, an algorithmic output processed from Google's own data assemblage. And given the specificity of each algorithmic script and the particularities of each company's available data pool, Google's 'man' is necessarily different from Yahoo!'s 'man,' Microsoft's 'man,' and any other 'man' that might be created. But each of these measurable types is a data object with a concrete, demonstrable definition.

In fact, we already encountered a transcoded form of intersectionality at the beginning of this chapter. Google's inference of 'gender' and 'age' operates on the same data foundation, using the same elements (what websites you visit) to connect two seemingly different categorizations. Since measurable types are based exclusively on statistical relationships to datafied phenomena, it is entirely possible for Google to identify a user's exact intersectional 'gender and age' identity on the basis of their mathematical intersection: the overlap between two different information sets.

Here we can connect two conceptually, but not necessarily theoretically, similar terms: intersection in mathematics and intersection in social theory. In mathematical set theory, if A = [1, 2, 4] and B = [1, 2, 3], then A ∩ B = [1, 2]. Or if set A has numbers 1, 2, and 4, and set B has numbers 1, 2, and 3, then the overlap/intersection of A and B is 1 and 2. But this example operates best if we think of A and B not as lists of numbers but as measurable types for 'age' and 'gender': A('45–65') = [ProductX, SiteY, SearchQueryZ] and B('man') = [Product Z, SiteY, SearchQueryZ], then A ∩ B = [SiteY, SearchQueryZ].

The preceding intersection is built on an a priori dependence on category: 'old' ∩ 'man' = ['old man']. This follows the previously cited debates around intersectional feminist cultural theory, largely the inter-categorical approach that aggregates existing categorical identities to generate a long, comma-delineated list of adjectival specifications: in nonalgorithmic life, my scientist friend is a white, straight, cis-woman in her twenties who is highly educated, has no kids, has no disabilities, and earns a decent salary. My friend's intersectional identity is available exclusively through the language of these ready-made, operationalized categories—just as 'old' ∩ 'man' relies on the a priori construction of both measurable types.

But, with the help of data-clustering algorithms, intersectional identities can also be built a posteriori. Through what is called unsupervised machine learning, researchers focus on a data set's latent attributes to identify nascent meaning. Computer scientist Zoubin Ghahramani defines it as a process in which a "machine simply receives inputs x_1, x_2, . . . , but obtains neither supervised target outputs, nor rewards from its environment. . . . In a sense, unsupervised learning can be thought of as finding patterns in the data above and beyond what would be considered pure unstructured noise."[115]

Unlike supervised and semi-supervised learning, which require human intervention to draw the initial limits for categorical identity, unsupervised learning lets those new categorical limits arise based on data's statistical proximity. In this way, we see how intersectionality might be lived on nonprefigured terms. This serves as an illustrative—but, as we'll see, superficial—alternative to the intersectional theory that Puar critiques: one in which "positioning does not precede movement but rather it is induced by it" and one that continually mistakes the "complexity of process . . . for a resultant product."[116]

This alternative is what we can very tentatively think of as a fourth, regressively postidentity approach: *protocategorical complexity*. For example, inspired by Judith Butler's theory of gender performance, some U.S. machine-learning researchers looked to unpack the intersectional essentialism implicit in closed, concretized a priori notions like 'old' and 'man':[117]

> The increasing prevalence of online social media for informal
> communication has enabled large-scale statistical modeling
> of the connection between language style and social variables,

such as gender, age, race, and geographical origin. Whether the goal of such research is to understand stylistic differences or to learn predictive models of "latent attributes," there is often an implicit assumption that linguistic choices are associated with immutable and essential categories of people. Indeed, it is possible to demonstrate strong correlations between language and such categories, enabling predictive models that are disarmingly accurate. But this leads to an oversimplified and misleading picture of how language conveys personal identity.[118]

These researchers recorded data from 14,464 individual Twitter accounts and their 9,212,118 individual tweets. Using an unsupervised-machine-learning model, they discovered twenty distinct clusters of writing styles that pointed not to a single 'gender' but to different 'genders' with unspoken but implied dimensions of race, class, and age. By avoiding the temptation to direct the clustering algorithm to look for either 'men' or 'women,' it was possible to arrive at twenty different protocategorical intersectional identities.

These twenty classifications are outputs based on patterns from immense founts of data, for which, as Chris Anderson, then-editor of *Wired*, controversially wrote, "correlation is enough." This hyperpositivistic perspective on big data perceives and thus represents the world through data and only data. It suggests, "We can stop looking for models. We can analyze the data without hypotheses about what it might show."[119] Of course, as discussed in the preceding pages, data is never "just" data. But this antihypothetical interpretation, with all its methodological baggage, has set the trajectory for big-data science itself.

Data-mining and machine-learning research is at a fever pitch. The data culled from the surveillant assemblages of our networked society has been dubbed "oil of the 21st century," while algorithmic analytics are "the combustion engine."[120] Even with powerful critiques of this hyperpositivism coming from scholars like David Ribes, Steven J. Jackson,

Kate Crawford, and Rob Kitchin, these clustering techniques are perceived as increasingly efficacious.[121]

The protocategorical is how, reciting Google's mission statement, the algorithmic world makes the logic of intersectionality useful. As a process, the categories extracted from the aforementioned Twitter data set take the form of a distinct cluster of tweets with similar lexical frequencies, read as "large-scale evidence for the existence of multiple gendered styles."[122] And these lexical frequencies are mere patterns in tweet data that "demonstrate strong correlations between language and . . . categories," suggesting both a nonacceptance of preexisting gender assignments as well as an example of the identificatory potential of a posteriori models.

By following the pattern rather than a priori taxonomies, algorithmic analytics can read some of the unique intricacies baked into 'man' and 'woman' without the methodological need to collapse them. While the researchers warn of "an oversimplified and misleading picture of how language conveys personal identity," they nevertheless acknowledge that protocategorical intersectional classifications are also "disarmingly accurate."[123]

Unlike Claritas's profile segments, the measurable types generated from this Twitter research have wholly unimpressive names, ranging from "c1" to "c20." "c14," for example, skews heavily 'female'[124] (89.60 percent) and most often used words such as "hubs, blogged, bloggers, giveaway, @klout, recipe, fabric, recipes, blogging, tweetup" (figure 1.4). As humans, we can infer a bunch of other categories from this list to intersect and refine what kind of 'gender' cluster 14 might be.

At first glance, "c14" seems composed of women who are white, in their twenties and thirties, technologically savvy, heterosexual, and partnered. Of course, we have no idea if any of that is really true, as these emergent 'gendered' categories arise from commonalities in data, not volunteered identities. It's also noteworthy to compare the clusters "c11" and "c20." Cluster 11 skews heavily 'male' (73.80 percent) and uses words like "niggas, wyd, nigga, finna, shyt, lls, ctfu, #oomf, lmaoo, and

	Size	% fem	Dict	Punc	UnPron	Pron	NE	Num	Taboo
Skews...			M	F	F	F	M	M	M
c14	1,345	89.60%	75.58%	16.44%	3.27%	1.93%	1.66%	0.85%	0.14%
c7	884	80.40%	73.99%	13.13%	5.27%	4.27%	1.99%	0.83%	0.37%
c6	661	80.00%	75.79%	16.35%	3.07%	2.15%	1.54%	0.70%	0.32%
c16	200	78.00%	70.98%	14.98%	6.97%	3.45%	2.19%	0.90%	0.10%
c8	318	72.30%	73.08%	9.09%	7.30%	7.06%	1.96%	0.80%	0.56%
c5	539	71.10%	71.55%	14.64%	5.84%	4.29%	1.94%	0.82%	0.77%
c4	1,376	63.00%	77.09%	15.81%	1.84%	1.82%	2.02%	0.78%	0.52%
c9	458	60.00%	70.48%	10.49%	7.49%	7.70%	2.00%	0.89%	0.65%
c19	198	58.10%	70.25%	21.77%	3.72%	2.24%	1.28%	0.31%	0.36%
c17	659	55.80%	72.30%	12.84%	4.78%	5.62%	1.82%	0.65%	1.69%
c1	739	46.00%	75.38%	16.31%	3.15%	1.60%	2.25%	1.02%	0.11%
c15	963	34.70%	74.62%	15.40%	3.29%	2.42%	2.74%	1.05%	0.32%
c20	429	27.50%	75.38%	16.74%	2.09%	1.41%	3.10%	0.91%	0.23%
c11	432	26.20%	68.97%	8.32%	5.95%	11.16%	2.01%	0.88%	2.32%
c18	623	18.90%	77.46%	10.47%	2.75%	4.40%	2.84%	1.07%	0.82%
c10	1,865	14.60%	77.72%	16.17%	1.51%	1.27%	2.03%	0.89%	0.34%
c13	761	10.60%	75.92%	15.12%	1.60%	1.67%	3.78%	1.44%	0.36%

FIGURE 1.4. This table shows each different cluster, its different 'gender' proclivities, and the words most often used by each cluster. Source: David Bamman, Jacob Eisenstein, and Tyler Schnoebelen, "Gender in Twitter: Styles, Stances, and Social Networks," arXiv:1210.4567, 2012, 23.

Hash	Top words
M	
0.13%	hubs blogged bloggers giveaway @klout recipe fabric recipes blogging tweetup
0.16%	kidd hubs xo ~] xoxoxo muah xoxo darren scotty ttyl
0.09%	authors pokemon hubs xd author arc xxx ^_^ bloggers d:
0.43%	xo blessings -) xoxoxo #music #love #socialmedia slash :)) xoxo
0.15%	xxx :') xx tyga youu (: wbu thankyou heyy knoww
0.16%	(: :') xd (; /: <333 d: <33 </3 -___-
0.12%	&& hipster #idol #photo #lessambitiousmovies hipsters #americanidol #oscars totes #goldenglobes
0.30%	wyd #oomf lmbo shyt bruh cuzzo #nowfollowing lls niggas finna
0.07%	nods softly sighs smiles finn laughs // shrugs giggles kisses
0.30%	lmfaoo niggas ctfu lmfaooo wyd lmaoo nigga #oomf lmaooo lmfaoooo
0.18%	qr /cc #socialmedia linkedin #photo seo webinar infographic klout
0.17%	#photo /cc #fb (@ brewing #sxsw @getglue startup brewery @foursquare
0.14%	gop dems senate unions conservative democrats liberal palin republican republicans
0.38%	niggas wyd nigga finna shyt lls ctfu #oomf lmaoo lmaooo
0.19%	@macmiller niggas flyers cena bosh pacers @wale bruh melo @fucktyler
0.06%	/cc api ios ui portal developer e3 apple's plugin developers
0.10%	#nhl #bruins #mlb nhl #knicks qb @darrenrovell inning boozer jimmer

lmaooo." Cluster 20 similarly skews 'male' (72.50 percent) but uses words like "gop, dems, senate, unions, conservative, democrats, liberal, palin, republican, and republicans."[125]

While race, class, political persuasion, age, and education level are not directly stated in this 'gender' formation, their traces are nonetheless present in the resulting clustered measurable types. They are protocategorical intersectionally baked into each cluster. The resulting algorithmic output is, as literary critic N. Katherine Hayles writes in her critique of what she calls the "computational perspective," "understood as the discourse system that mirrors what happens in nature and that generates nature itself."[126] Without the requisite supervision that delimits the world according to categorical identity, the emergence of this new, protocategorical intersectionality is composed by a "knowable and quantifiable phenomenon, freed both from the mysteries of the Logos and the complexities of discursive explanations dense with ambiguities."[127] Certainly we can't free our identities from ambiguity. But this computational perspective reads intersectional patterns without context and thus erases the "complexities" of discourse—and ultimately our lived experience.

Such a nascent intersectional identity does away with the explicit practice of cultural politics that historically describes intersectional theory: elements of race, class, and gender are the lived building blocks of our intersectional identities and, more importantly, the channels through which we encounter relations of power. Instead, protocategorical intersectionality is limited to an incipient politics that engages with race, class, and gender on terms that are unseen but emergent. The possibility for a protocategorical intersectional politics comes into the picture only after the clustered category is created, not before. It is a politics that is useful for whoever is doing the algorithmic processing, not for those who are living the output of that processing.

In this way, this protocategorical categorical intersectionality echoes a larger argument by digital media theorist Wendy Hui Kyong Chun, who writes,

Networks end postmodernism. They counter pastiche with the zoom and the overview; they animate and locate "placeless" architecture; they resolve multiculturalism through neighbor-hood predictors that bypass yet reinforce categories such as race, gender, sexuality; they replace postmodern relativism with data analytics. They do so by moving away from subjects and nar-ratives toward actors and captured actions that they knit into a monstrously connected chimera. They imagine connections that transform the basis of the collective imaginary from "we" to you: from community to an ever-still-resolvable grouping that erodes and sustains the distance between self and other.[128]

And it is here that we encounter the immediate danger in this regres-sive brand of a posteriori politics. It's a politics without a *there there*. It's missing the referent by which one can know, and live, one's identity. Protocategorical intersectionality is instead a moving target. But rather than serving as a more precise intersectional index for life, this algo-rithmic approach produces a data object that flatly rejects that which cannot be datafied.

More specifically, the latent attributes of race that are baked into cat-egories like "c11" and "c20" erase the lived experience of race within the statistical correlations of racialized experience. Without an explicit con-nection to think through and talk about, race becomes an aftereffect, a measurement that can only describe a condition—but fails to critique it. We are forced to read stereotypes of whiteness into "c20" and blackness into "c11" in order to accurately interpret their intersectional characters. Similarly, we have to listen impossibly closely to uncover how black-ness seeps into how Shimon plays like 'John Coltrane.' This postiden-tity function means that algorithmic intersectional identity is not lived through a racialized, gendered, or classed lens. It is instead lived, and compiled, in the wake of acritical, positivist measurement.

Which is to say, neither "c20" or "c11" lets us talk about race as race. Neither lets us think through the power dynamics of white supremacy.

But both produce new terms of racialization, and both let us supplement Judith Butler's theory of performativity as it applies to the intersectionality of gender: "Gender intersects with racial, class, ethnic, sexual, and regional modalities of discursively constituted identities. As a result, it becomes impossible to separate 'gender' from the political and cultural intersections in which it is inevitably produced and maintained."[129]

Butlerian gender performance accepts the knots of entanglement that connect our different identity markers, much like the pantheon of black feminist thought that preceded Butler's analysis. The Combahee River Collective famously stressed the interlocking oppressions of race, gender, sexuality, and class—"the synthesis of these oppressions creates the conditions of our lives"—in 1973.[130] Collective member Audre Lorde singles out the lack of white women's intersectional politics in her *Sister Outsider*, in which she writes, "By and large within the women's movement today, white women focus upon their oppression as women and ignore differences of race, sexual preference, class, and age. The word sisterhood indicates a pretense to homogeneity of experience that does not in fact exist."[131]

Intersectionality for these writers is a critical concept, constituted by political categories, that permits the political act of self-identity in the face of those who are trying to disallow it. But protocategorical intersectionality deprives the potential for critical politics. It ignores that power sees black lesbian women, in the case of the Combahee River Collective, in ways that cannot be fully understood without the a priori intersection of black + lesbian + woman. And it ignores the political possibilities that intersectional analysis, from the work of women of color feminists Cherríe Moraga and Gloria Anzaldúa's *This Bridge Called My Back* to sociologist Patricia Hill Collins's *Black Feminist Thought*, worked to carve out.[132]

The move to define something as multifaceted and multilayered as the connections between gender, race, and class in statistical, quantitative terms originates in what I discussed earlier in the chapter as the clean, procedural logic of engineering. Google's former top visual designer Doug Bowman wrote in a letter following his resignation from the company, "When a company is filled with engineers, it turns to engineering to solve problems. Reduce each decision to a simple logic problem. Remove all subjectivity and just look at the data."[133]

Void of subjective assessment, our 'gender,' 'race,' and 'class' has little resemblance to how we encounter gender, race, and class. This is why the idea of "personalization"—the assumption that you, as a user, are distinctive enough to receive content based on you as a person, with a history and with individual interests—largely does not exist. We are instead communicated to through *profilization*, the intersections of categorical meaning that allow our data, but not necessarily us, to be 'gendered,' 'raced,' and 'classed.'

While Bowman's critique of contemporary engineering logic was a commentary about the future of design, the same logic can be applied to algorithmic culture at large. If gender is framed by the corresponding problematics of engineering, then more data—not different perspectives or voices—determines what 'gender' will look like. The aforementioned research on Twitter is not some insurgent feminist attack on the hierarchies of gender. It's just a more nuanced perspective to construct audiences, using engineering logic, that sanctions a world with more than two 'genders.' This relation to measurable-type identity, nuanced as it may appear to be, dispossesses us of the capacity to determine who we may be. When we perform what "is" for algorithms, we lose control over what that "is" means.

For example, Zach Blas is a queer artist whose work focuses on the intersections of technology and sexuality. In one project, dubbed the "Facial Weaponization Suite," Blas critiques the work by some researchers to assess, through facial features, the sexual orientation of individuals on the basis of digital photographic portraits.[134]

In these studies, a methodological analysis of sexuality ties one's being 'gay' or 'lesbian' to her countenance, authenticating a hypernormative, but scientifically anointed, gaydar. Blas intervened by asking self-identified queer individuals to sit in front of a camera, scanning their features with an Xbox Kinect, and compiling the aggregate bio-metric scans of his participants' faces.[135] After constructing his own measurable type of 'queerness,' Blas toyed with the facial aggregate output, stretching and shaping this new 'queer' 'face' until it was incomprehensible: it became neither 'queer' nor a 'face' but what he calls a "fag face." In other words, he made a face not useful. Afterward, Blas fabricated deformed pink plastic masks with this useless "fag face" model.

These art pieces algorithmically obfuscate any attempt to attach bio-metric value to one's actual face. Blas's work operates on data's terms, the terms of the measurable type. It accepts, analyzes, and critiques according to 'queerness'—not queerness—thus acknowledging the import that datafied sexualities have in our lives. Much like the example of the NSA's 'terrorist,' a measurable type of 'gay' and 'straight' has politically dubious merit. That someone would think, much less care, about an individual's sexuality is not a cute accomplishment of digital technology. It's an unambiguous robbery of the root of our subjectivity, a techno-enthused gall that defines sexual identity through faces, not experience or desire.

Chapter 2 will explore how measurable types do more than just represent ourselves for us, without our knowledge and without our authorship. They also actively control; they modulate themselves to best fit the population they're meant to describe. The fuzziness of the measurable type gives way to the malleability of the measurable type. And this malleability can eventually, and quite directly, sashay into control.

CONCLUSION

Algorithms and data organize our worlds, dually performing a service—Google "make[s] it useful"—as well as prefiguring our lives according to that usage. But data operates on its own terms, not ours. Political scientist James C. Scott, in his own useful book *Seeing like a State*, shows how states manipulate social norms via haphazard rubrics of categorical simplification, an ongoing "project of legibility" that connects populations to power.[136] He writes, "Those who gather and interpret such aggregate data understand that there is a certain fictional and arbitrary quality to their categories and that they hide a wealth of problematic variation. Once set, however, these thin categories operate unavoidably as if all similarly classified cases were in fact homogeneous and uniform."[137]

Measurable types' synoptic data is more than the truth of a population. It is the "departure for reality" as algorithmic processing assumes control.[138] Who we are, in terms of the state consigning us to these rubrics, is owned by the state. We are not just categorized. We are also manipulated and controlled, made homogeneous as entries in lines of a database or records list.

But the measurable types that constitute our algorithmic worlds are unending. Unlike Scott's singular agent of the state, which uses data for its own machinations, there is no single, unique, authoritative category of 'gender,' nor is there a single, permanent idea of 'swingers' that all databases globally share. Measurable types are placeholders for meaning, but those meanings are necessarily local. They are empirical assessments of prejudice and/or patterns that work, according to a particular confidence percentage, at a particular moment and by a particular set of rules. Google might have a relatively booming voice in determining who we are and what who we are means, but there are many, many more agents that call you something different.

Across this data world, we participate in a colossal ecology of data production. We make data, we signify to algorithms what that data means, and what we do differently allows those resulting measurable types to change. A blog post you write might be 20 percent 'sexual' today, but the updated, 2015 version of the LIWC dictionary might change that assessment to 22 percent as new words are included into its catalogues. Like the inclusion of "wardrobe malfunction" into the *Oxford English Dictionary* in 2014, the world hesitantly evolves. Our attempts to corral certain meanings into the backdrop of this evolution is a never-ending process. But measurable types are both incomplete and largely automated. They have no senior editor who publicly declares that yes, "wardrobe malfunction" deserves its own entry into the formal English lexicon.

Think about the use of the word "beta" in software development and how many programs that we all use, including Gmail up until 2013, were labeled as "in beta." These "beta" programs indicate that they are not in their final form and have not been officially released. They are in a developmental limbo, previously known as beta testing, in which users (often a small population) toy with a program in order to find and weed out bugs from its final distribution. Lev Manovich describes our use of digital technology as such, claiming, "a user of Google Earth is likely to experience a different 'earth' every time she uses the application."[139] Both the world itself and the representation that Google presents us of that world are in constant flux.

We should think of algorithmically processed data in this way. Measurable types like 'gender' or Shimon's version of 'you' are not truths but betas. They admit they're not perfect and are invariably changing toward something new. They remain unfinished and thus cannot be expected to be stable. They will never reach 100 percent confidence— but then again, what can? Even death and taxes are potentially avoidable, in light of the millions of dollars being pumped into cryonics and the billions stashed in Caribbean or Swiss tax havens. Computer software that has passed beta and is released into the wild, only to find a bug that remained hidden during its testing phase, is not a stain on modernity's notion of truth and perfection. It's rather the truth of life, a truth without end.

A "beta" next to a program logo or title provides us a Franco Moretti– like distance from finitude. It functionally suggests the portent of error but invites you, through use, to help resolve those errors. With knowledge itself seen to be in beta, we are forever at the whim of the changes made to resolve "bugs" in discourse. As 'woman' sits in beta stage, data that suggests that women are increasingly following soccer allows 'woman' to change in response. Blindly following trends is not just for fashionistas and Brooklyn-based music snobs. It is part of how the measurable types that we inhabit dynamically respond to new inputs drawn from our datafied lives.

So, if we are called 'woman' by a marketer or even 'terrorist' by a government, what does that really come to mean? The reference to legal scholar Frank Pasquale's *Black Box Society* made in the introduction needs to be reframed: while we don't know what we're being called, we are also unaware that what we're being called is changing all the time. Multiple voices hail us according to different, dynamic measurable types.

With the Althusserian ideological work implied, if a cop yells, "Hey, John!" I know who he is talking about. But a computer that says, "Hey, 'John!'" is hailing me on different terms. It's talking *about* me, not to me. It's not trying to communicate with me as a person or individual subject. It instead interpellates me according to a category-based profile.

But that profile is remapped every day, cybernetically sustaining 'John' not as a unified subject but as a mathematically equilibrated, multitiered aggregate of knowledge. 'John' is a "just-in-time" identity, an arbitrarily closed subject that gets articulated across a range of different interpretations and registers of knowledge. As of 6:24 p.m. on July 30, 2016, 'I' am what Google + NSA + Shimon think of me, ad infinitum. And, after a full minute of web surfing at 6:25 p.m. on July 30, 2016, 'I' am someone different.

The field of cybernetics helps us understand how we, as users, are perceived as stable, controllable entities by computers. In what will be discussed in chapter 2, to cybernetically maintain equilibrium is to accept fluidity in a system's inputs while calibrating its revised outputs in accordance. How our algorithmic identities wield power over us is less about inputs (causes) and more about outputs (effects). What makes the outputs—the algorithm itself—is the steward of our futures.

What we and knowledge become is not a function of truth. It's a function of the algorithm's output that we are told is 'truth.' What Google says 'I' am, I am. If I significantly modify my web-surfing habits,

Google won't abandon me as a user. Instead, it will reconceptualize its interpretation of me according to how my data fits within its algorithmic life-world.

As we will investigate in chapter 2, this reconceptualization suggests that the origin and meaning of life is unimportant, so long as how that life is lived can be measured, made useful, and eventually controlled under the guise of systems of power: Google, advertising companies like Quantcast, and even the NSA.

2

CONTROL

Algorithm Is Gonna Get You

To be governed is to be watched, in-
spected, spied upon, directed, law-driven,
numbered, regulated, enrolled, indoctri-
nated, preached at, controlled, checked,
estimated, valued, censured, commanded,
by creatures who have neither the right
nor the wisdom nor the virtue to do so.

—Pierre-Joseph Proudhon[1]

"Today's fitness test uses a Nunchuck. Are you able to use the Nun-chuck?" You select "Yes." The first event is "Target Practice: Volley the ball off the wall and hit the targets. Controlling your swing speed and strength is essential in aiming your shots." The word "start" flashes, and you see your small, overly lit avatar crouched over, racket in hand. A large target is affixed to the brick wall in front of you. You use your baton to serve the ball, hitting the target directly in the center. The "Targets left" count goes from ten to nine. Based on movements from your own newly cyborg arm, your avatar follows the ball as it ricochets off the bricks. After hitting the target ten times, the word "finished" appears, and the screen fades to black.

The second event is "Batting Practice: The pitcher will keep throwing those balls, so focus on making fast, compact swings!" Transported to a baseball diamond, your avatar stands eerily still, wearing pinstripe pants and gripping a baseball bat with a single spherical hand. "Start" flashes again, and the pitcher hurls a ball in your direction. Gripping the baton, you swing and hear the sound of cracking wood. The tally in the upper-left-hand corner now says, "Hits: 1, Left: 29." There are twenty-nine more pitches, and each time you concentrate and swing, your avatar swings with you. "Finished."

The third event is "Dodging: Your trainer throws ball after ball at you. Move left and right to avoid getting hit." "Start" flashes a final time, and a goateed man reaches out his right hand. A red-and-yellow tennis ball is launched toward you. You move your baton and Nunchuck to the right and successfully avoid the projectile. The score increases to

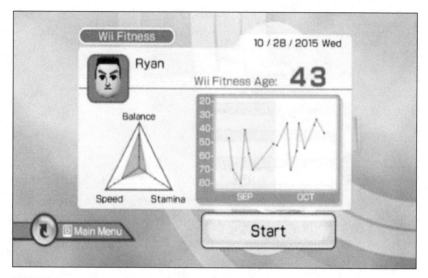

FIGURE 2.1. A screenshot from Nintendo's *Wii Sports*.

plus one. For sixty seconds, this character flings balls in your direction, sometimes with one hand, other times with both. After the frantic assault, "finished" appears one more time, finally, and you put your real hands on your real knees, trying to catch your real breath.

You wait for your results. After three random activities, your avatar's athletic ability is evaluated: your "Wii Fitness Age" of '43' pops up in red. A triangle on the left side of the screen has three axes: "Balance," "Speed," and "Stamina." A teal-colored triangle fits inside the larger lines, filling the "Balance" trisector by three-quarters but only covering about half of "Speed" and one-quarter of "Stamina" (figure 2.1).

This evaluation comes from the 2007 Nintendo Wii game *Wii Sports*. For those who have played it, one quickly realizes that this Wii 'age' is not about age at all. It's about accuracy, dexterity, and endurance. The measurable type of 'age' is an abstraction, indexical of nothing other than the data Nintendo says makes you '43.' Every day you play the game—unlike those 364 days that aren't your birthday—your 'age' will change. That numerical change then appears on a graph that tracks your standing over time. You can go from '43' today to '80' tomorrow and then, with enough luck and practice, to the coveted '20,' the lowest 'age' possible.

Millions of people have played this game, and millions of people have felt themselves somewhat deflated by their resulting 'age' after a particularly unlucky string of performances (boxing is the most disheartening). Your 'age' serves as the empirical stand-in for your apparent physical capacity, a gauge of your in-game success as well as a reminder that you haven't been to the gym in a while. The number then haunts you for the rest of the afternoon. In fact, so hallowed is this particular measurable type that if *Wii Sports* assigns you a particularly high 'age' and you want a mulligan, you aren't allowed to retest yourself until the following day.

On the one hand, our 'age' connects to power in clear-cut ways. Like 'age,' measurable types produce meaning about who we are, and in the case of *Wii Sports*, that meaning might make us feel good or bad about ourselves. This is the disciplinary mode of power, most famously theorized by philosopher Michel Foucault and made diagrammatic by the panopticon prison: if there's surveillance/interpretation by the other, we do the work of power by disciplining ourselves in accordance with perceived social norms.[2]

Measurable types are also biopolitical. They compile different data into an intelligible whole, which then is used to manage the "stock" of a population. Through a simple, three-event evaluation via *Wii Sports*' algorithmic logics, a single 'age' folds the complexities of our individual histories into a unitary, abstracted categorical scale. You are not you, with all the intricacies that make you you. You are a temporal member of one in sixty-one different categories ('20 years old' to '80 years old'). We might be sick, disabled, or a novice at gaming in general, but unless *Wii Sports* transcodes that information into data that its algorithms can understand, it will have no bearing on our score.

This newly minted index of health, well-being, and general state of living, unintentionally or not, steers the life of the population.[3] While *Wii Sports*' 'age' articulates the Foucauldian slogan of biopolitics, the "power over life," in a lighthearted, aesthetically childish manner, the game might encourage us to behave differently or choose healthier habits.[4] And since biopolitics relies on data about a population, our lives are controlled based on how we, as members of that population, are made intelligible by data. So with only a three-button, gyroscopic *Wii* controller in our hand to describe the ins and outs of our life's affairs, we are intelligible to the game in technologically range-bound ways.

On the other hand, our 'age' also connects us to power "at a distance," to borrow Nikolas Rose's understanding of Foucauldian governmental-ity.[5] From afar, this governmentality, quoting Foucault, "undertakes to conduct individuals throughout their lives by placing them under the authority of a guide responsible for what they do and for what happens to them."[6] More specifically, measurable types like 'age' do more than enable channels for disciplinarity. They also produce the knowledges that "conduct" who we are seen to be, who we see ourselves to be, and how we are assigned resources.

In this case, being '80' may not mean you've successfully rotated around the sun eighty times, but it does lodge you within an un-known relation to discourse. While a medical test might alert an ac-tual old person to high cholesterol, there is no scientific evidence that indicates one is more or less likely to suffer a heart attack at '80.' In-stead, *Wii Sports'* measurable type of 'age' floats around, ontologically and epistemologically separated from age. But 'age' still "conducts" through discursive definition. It still allocates attention to our health. It establishes what it means to be 'young' versus 'old.' It reifies youth as good and seniority as bad. In short, measurable types determine what different discourses come to mean in their datafied form: from what is 'age' to who has 'health' and even to what is 'good.' But what if these categories are unknown? What if, unlike the panopticon, there is no identifiable entity that we perceive to be watching/evaluating/disciplining us?

More specifically, what if we don't know we're '80 years old,' but we're still treated that way, much like Google's 'gender' described in chapter

1? If '80' and its accompanying conception of health attaches to your profile without your consent, how might your world be different? What would that world look like if the category of '80'—indexical to nothing more than an algorithmic assessment of baseball, tennis, and dodging data—changes? What if '80' is now based on how well you score in golf, boxing, and bowling? And what if Nintendo updates its algorithms, modifying how it values golf given users' higher-than-average scores on golf versus other sports? '80' still means something, but what it means transmutes without announcement.

This chapter aims to answer these questions through the lens of control. Digital theorist Seb Franklin describes control as "a set of technical principles having to do with self-regulation, distribution, and statistical forecasting . . . [that] also describes the episteme grounding late capitalism, a worldview that persists beyond any specific device or set of practices."[7] This episteme, then, serves as "a wholesale reconceptualization of the human and of social interaction under the assumption . . . that information storage, processing, and transmission (as well as associated concepts such as 'steering' and 'programming') not only constitute the fundamental processes of biological and social life but can be instrumentalized to both model and direct the functional entirety of such forms of life."[8]

These terms of control regulate, as well as epistemologically establish, the standards by which we, reconceptualized as measurable types, are positioned as subjects through data. In this chapter, I explore how control becomes manifest in what some theorists have called "algorithmic regulation." To better understand the role of this algorithmic regulation, I employ the concept of "modulation" as described by Gilles Deleuze. And lastly, I explore how control can be marshaled without traditional control (control that is difficult to perceive or control that is distanced and rarely felt).

Up till now, many of my examples have revolved around online marketing and advertising. These types of identification are easiest to point out because of their ubiquity and seeming innocuousness. But as

I elaborate in this chapter, our algorithmic identities also regulate us in many different, and much less visible, ways.

To describe this control without control, I look to several examples of algorithmic regulation, particularly those with biopolitical dimensions. Google Flu, the famed big-data project for predicting flu epidemics six weeks before the U.S.'s Centers for Disease Control does, will play a starring role. I look at how researchers algorithmically curated the idea of 'Santa Claus' and how a simple mobile application can tell us if we're 'depressed,' 'anxious,' or 'suffering from PTSD.' Using these examples, I explore the concept soft biopolitics, or how algorithmic agents create measurable-type categories according to biopolitical mechanisms. And I tread through the field of cybernetics to understand how exactly concepts like 'gender' can enforce norms *and* create space for dissident behaviors or new trends.

ALGORITHMIC REGULATION AND CONTROL

While philosopher Gilles Deleuze's oft-cited essay "Postscript on the Societies of Control" is only five pages long, its publication in 1990 has been anointed as an important turning point for theorizations of digital culture. Terse and atypically clear in prose, the essay may have surprised die-hard Deleuzeians if not for the fact that the "Postscript's" conceptual heart beats across several decades of Deleuze's work. Seb Franklin traces this trajectory from designs emerging in *A Thousand Plateaus* to *Cinema 2* to Deleuze's mid-1980s book on Michel Foucault to a published lecture in 1987 and to a transcribed discussion with Italian autonomist Antonio Negri in 1990.[9]

Ultimately, the "Postscript's" philosophical kernel details an epochal shift from disciplinary power to control, a transformation that has since been debated and critiqued, resulting in provocative scholarship and interpretations for, in particular to this book, work on surveillance, identity, and politics.[10] But for the purposes of this chapter, I want to emphasize two general themes to cull from Deleuze's lineage. One, power can operate through the permissive distancing of "an open environment" while simultaneously attending to a relational intimacy in which "perpetual training tends to replace the school, and continuous control to replace the examination."[11] This theme is best described by the concept of modulation. And two, "we no longer find ourselves dealing with the mass/individual pair. Individuals have become 'dividuals,' and masses [have become] samples, data, markets, or 'banks.'"[12]

First, detached from Deleuzeian specificity, modulation has many different meanings that all share one central idea: dynamism and variance according to stability.[13] In music, it's the shift from one key to another; the melody continues, even while the tonic scale changes. In electronics, it's varying the properties of a wave form; the analogue wave continues, even while its frequency and/or amplitude changes. And in some forms of philosophy, it's the idea of variability in order to better manage metastasis.

Deleuze defines modulation accordingly, usefully contrasting it with the rigid molds of disciplinary enclosures (like the prison): "a self-deforming cast that will continuously change from one moment to the other, or like a sieve whose mesh will transmute from point to point."[14] While the molds of disciplinary societies are strict and static, the self-deforming cast of control's modulation is flexible and dynamic. In this case, modulation is similar to Silly Putty. When you play with it, the silicon substance maintains some degree of its integrity, despite being pulled, squished, blotted with newspaper ink, and eventually put back into its red plastic container.

This Silly Putty of modulation defines the regulatory frame for control's self-reflexive episteme. It also serves as an accessible metaphor for the contemporary, computational processes of algorithmic identification. Unlike disciplinary institutions of the police, school system, and factory supervisor that make subjects patently aware when they step outside the rigid molds of norms and power relations, the modular character of the societies of control ideally allows for an economy of tolerable aberration.

For example, if we took a non–Silly Putty egg and started to play with it, we would eventually be covered in odorous whites and yolk. While the intolerant molds of the enclosure might be good at keeping the insides of an egg within its shell (or a prisoner in her cell), they aren't as effective when it comes to managing the dynamism and playfulness of noncarceral life. Singular, static ideals of man, good, and illegal will all, sooner or later, outlive their purpose and eventually become obsolete.

A modulating silicone egg tolerates dynamism, change, and eventually reconfiguration. As an element of control, it cares less about being an egg. Its focus is trained to the changing, "point to point" nature of the world: from egg to flat surface to mashed-up clump and maybe even back to egg. Modulation rejects the essentialism implicit in an egg's fixed material integrity across time, preferring instead to identify what an egg is according to its state and substance at any given moment.

And second, while disciplinarity speaks to a unique, nameable individual, Deleuze suggests we look instead to "the code of a 'dividual' material to be controlled," the various point-to-point representations of our subindividual selves.[15] We see control's dual distance/intimacy in how I, as John the individual, might appear unaffected while the elements that regulate me online—my dividual data, my measurable-type identity, and ultimately the affordances algorithmically allocated to me according to that data—get modulated and manipulated.

This kind of dividual modulation is more prevalent than we might recognize. For example, Blizzard Entertainment's multiplayer online role-playing game *World of Warcraft* (*WoW*) is renowned for its persistent updates to the game's code in order to maintain a balanced game environment for players. A single update can instantly increase or decrease players' stats—for example, strengthening a spell (buff) while weakening a sword attack (nerf). More specifically, if you choose to play as a certain class, like the spell-casting mage, you will have to cope with these changes as they affect both your character and others you play with.

In 2012, a mage who habitually used the spell "Combustion" in *WoW* found herself having to adapt after the game's version 5.1 patch reduced the spell's periodic damage over time. A year later, this same mage had to adjust yet again to the version 5.4 patch that nerfed "Combustion" even further. Every character's playing ability changes based on how Blizzard developers perceive imbalances within the game. Overpowered classes and skills reduce fun, subscription rates, and ultimately sales. So Blizzard employs periodic updates to even out game play, modifying spell-casting, item, and resource variables in order to produce a notion, albeit temporary, of fairness.

The idea of what a mage *is* depends on these coded, modulating game mechanics. The modification of one spell-casting ability, alongside the hundreds of other nerfs and buffs that accompany each update, carves out an undulating digital landscape that users navigate on a day-to-day basis. These changes affect entire "communities of play," citing games scholar Celia Pearce, forcing users to adapt, sometimes explicitly (debates arise over each update, with players diligently consulting patch notes) but most often through unconscious adjustment.[16]

Steady updates to the game also fuel class-based stereotypes, in which playing a mage may be seen as easy (having to be repeatedly nerfed suggests an overpowered status), while the recently buffed class of priest may be seen as more difficult. The knowledge of what makes a mage, and the subsequent challenges and benefits of being a mage, vary across the life of the game and eventually spill into off-game forums. Both the identity of mage and the surrounding culture of the game morph according to each Blizzard univocal redesign.

For most players, updates have an indescribable effect on their game play. Whether they know it or not, the programmed changes in each new version mean that players play within a moving, magic-circled terrain.[17] Every altered, ludic element empirically readjusts what makes up a mage not by disciplining individuals but by reconfiguring the constitutive identity of their in-game characters. For the millions who log onto *WoW* every month, the possibilities for game play are conditioned in ways they may not know nor understand.

This moving terrain is a practical, preliminary consequence of what Tim O'Reilly, Internet entrepreneur, first formalized in the concept of "algorithmic regulation." For O'Reilly, this algorithmic regulation "should be regarded in much the same way that programmers regard their code and algorithms, that is, as a constantly updated toolset to achieve the outcomes specified in the laws."[18] Pursuant to this formulation, while the law formally exists as a stable edict of right, the mechanics by which that same law is understood, maintained, and implemented modulate according to these metaphorical "updated toolsets."

The capacity for control offered by algorithmic regulation goes beyond the future of jurisprudence or a transcoding of the 7,591 words that make up the U.S. Constitution. Updates in *World of Warcraft* do more than enforce the legalistic elements of the game's terms of service. They structure what life is and can be according to the rule set expressed in the game's code, structuring what legal theorist Lawrence Lessig describes in *Code 2.0* as "architectures of control."[19] *WoW* users play, and are controlled by, the logics written into the game's software. A wall in a dungeon prohibits you from walking through it. The spell "Combustion" is only as powerful as the programmed value that establishes its damage over time.

Legal scholar Julie E. Cohen revises Lessig's theory to think outside the confines of the liberal self—the unitary individual who theoretically participates in a one-to-one dialogue with her surroundings. For Cohen, code operates in a dividual, networked form. Users encounter multiple codes in different contexts that overlap, overdetermine, and thus confound Lessig's singular "code is law" framework.[20] Continuing with Cohen, code is a "modality of governance not reducible either to law or markets. . . . It should acknowledge and allow examination of the ways that artifacts and architectures configure their users."[21] The "updated toolsets" are precisely those that "configure" us, regulating not just our legal system but also our day-to-day lives.

Let's consider a futurist example dating from back in the 1980s, when famed French psychotherapist (and Deleuze's collaborator and friend) Félix Guattari imagined a world where algorithmic authentications granted residents conditional access to certain areas of a city.[22] Here, possibilities to navigate Guattari's world are conditionally regulated by the dividual identity of one's electronic card. This card ostensibly communicates with a central server, which then authorizes entrance into buildings or exit from houses according to a programmed rule set. While this type of access is routine today, reflect on the apparatus's portent for control.

Today, university networks grant conditional access to most academic buildings: professors often enjoy 24/7 entry, while students might be limited to a window of eight a.m. to six p.m. These rules are accepted and institutionalized—and remain unapparent until you find yourself locked out and no one is around to let you in. Here we encounter an algorithmics of space, as geographers Nigel Thrift and Shaun French write, that "animates," and thus produces, our lived, physical experience.[23] The societies of control are effective because we rarely see this animation at work. We often accept regulatory logic with scarcely a question, precisely because it interfaces not with our individualities but with our electronic cards as dividual proxies.

Yet this kind of control also occurs without physically locking you out. It can discursively lock you out (as well as lock you in), "animating," in this case, knowledge about the world that then has direct effect on who we are, who we can be, and what can be uttered and understood about both. Certainly, power resides in the strong-armed batons of police violence and military bombs. But power also governs us—through the now-common Foucauldian concept of power/knowledge—by informing what the state is called, what society looks like, what the body politic can do, and how a population is defined.[24] In this framework, the goal of control is not the production of individual, docile bodies. Rather, the goal is a stabilizing definition of society's discursive topography, the parameters of knowledge that structure our lives.

More to the point, power produces and constrains discourse for its own needs. To define discursive topography governs what can or cannot be said and what is interpretable or not. This is what philosopher Judith Butler describes as the "limits of acceptable speech."[25] But knowledge is much more than speech and its subsequent intelligibility. It is also the matter that regulates, in the case of this book, categorical membership and meaning. This defining of discursive topography intersects with Butler's earlier work on the production of sex, in which the "discursive limits" of sex set "the limits to what will qualify as a body by regulating the terms by which bodies are and are not sustained."[26] For Butler, individual bodies—and not just speech—must fit within these defined limits in order to be legible.

Returning to our university building example, one's dividual ID card determines legibility within the system. But professors are not individual people with names. 'Professor' is instead a category, made explicit in a database (where a user ID card is attached to an identity like "professor," "staff," or "student"), that is eventually populated by a dividual listing of certain ID card numbers and access permissions. The lives of all those who hold a 'professor' ID card are governed by the rule set programmed by a database engineer. And this engineer can also, either arbitrarily or during a security threat, disallow access on the basis of these categorical identities. What it means to be a 'professor,' previously known as the free rein to jaunt around campus unencumbered, evolves accordingly. I, John, am not personally regulated by this access restriction. But those who currently hold 'professor' ID cards are.

These conditions of possibilities regulate not just where 'professors' can go but who 'professors' can be. The subsequent modulation governs what some scholars have described as the "conduct of conducts": the norms and practices of life that determine both who we are and what who we are means.[27] O'Reilly's "updated toolkits," then, are not just one-off calibrations of law or conduct. They are constant, abiding revisions—or, to think alongside Butler, new limits—of those conducts that enforce discursive stability on a modulating, "point to point" moving structure.

In the preceding examples, it is a human engineer who facilitates these abiding revisions through a continual rewriting of a system's algorithmic rule set, or architecture of code. Yet, as we'll discover later in this chapter, algorithms can also rewrite these algorithmic rule sets, programming not just each system's governing regulations but the process itself by which those regulations change. Here, our database engineer charged with administering categorical access, that is, what buildings 'professors' can enter, might be replaced by an algorithm that performs a similar task. But rather than privileging a human interpretation of what constitutes a viable security threat, an algorithm can automatically determine what abiding revisions are necessary on the basis of available data—for example, constantly mining online news reports, CCTV footage, or even the local Twitter stream for reference to any incipient 'threats.'

More generally, in this type of algorithmic regulation, we see how the current, almost obsessive push toward datafying everything and anything (like our fitness routines, ovulation cycles, sleep patterns, even the quality of our posture) becomes much more than a simple transcoding of life into machine-readable information. This process of datafication is also the process of materially connecting these data "points" with power. By checking up on us each and every time we make a datafied step, rather than only when we stand before a judge or a police officer detains us, power becomes exceptionally intimate and efficient. It knows us. It learns from us. It becomes an author of our lives' knowledges, and all we have to do is provide it the words. This intimacy is what Deleuze's societies of control rely on. As subjects, we tortuously facilitate mobile but constant contact with a regulatory regime that effectively recalibrates the nuances of our own making at the moment of each and every encounter.

COFFEE AND DATAVEILLANCE

"Our data set is so extensive, it's equivalent to having coffee with every U.S. online user every hour," brags Quantcast, the San Francisco, California, web-analytics company mentioned earlier in this book.[28] As of 2014, Quantcast is a firm that processes "up to 30 petabytes" of data a day, a quantity that contains "40 billion media consumption events."[29] Indeed, Deleuze's theoretical "point to point" intimacy finds practical correspondence in the vast world of Internet tracking. Which websites we visit, which products we purchase, which queries we search for, and even which words we type are all vacuumed up via the technological surveillant assemblage for the near entirety of the Internet marketing and profiling industries. Without tracking, these multibillion-dollar analytics systems would fall apart. Without a mechanism to connect our data, we are forgotten.

But with tracking, we are remembered, almost forever.[30] This is what makes companies like Quantcast (or Google or Facebook) so profitable. For example, you may go to Wordpress.com. Upon access, a "measurement tag" cookie (a small text file saved onto your computer that holds a unique, random number) "phones home" to the Quantcast server, telling Quantcast that the unique number assigned to your computer went there. You may then go to Live.com, only to have your Quantcast cookie read and "phone home" again, now from Live.com. As you go from site to site, this hypervigilant tattletale / coffee date accumulates an immense list of cross-server activity: Quantcast "sees each U.S. online user on average 600 times a month."[31]

Who Quantcast thinks we are is based on the iterative logging of each available datafied move. With this dividual cookie data and nothing more, a marketing company can compare your web-browsing habits with the measurable types of different 'genders,' 'ethnicities,' 'classes,' 'education levels,' 'number of children,' 'age,' 'political affiliation,' and 'political engagement.' It's possible that you never tell Quantcast, 'I am a forty-six-year-old white man,' but like Google in chapter 1, it infers your

	FACTORS					
	VISITED SITE X	VISITED SITE Y	USED APP Z	VISITED CATEGORY K	DEVICE TYPE M	KNOWN MALE
MALE ATTRIBUTES	●		●	●	●	X
VISITOR 1		●		●		
VISITOR 2	●		●	●	●	X

	VISITED SITE X	VISITED SITE Y	USED APP Z	VISITED CATEGORY K	DEVICE TYPE M	KNOWN COLLEGE GRAD
COLLEGE GRAD ATTRIBUTES	●	●		●		X
VISITOR 1			●	●		
VISITOR 2	●	●		●		X

[REPEAT PROCESS FOR EACH ATTRIBUTE]

Note: example for illustration only; actual models include hundreds of factors

FIGURE 2.2. This Quantcast matrix demonstrates how its inference model uses site visits, phone apps, website categories, and types of device to determine a user's 'gender' and 'education level.' Source: Quantcast, "Understanding Digital Audience Measurement," 2014, www.quantcast.com.

identity based on your online behavior. It makes 'you' using everything it can measure, a point best put by Quantcast itself: "actual models includes hundreds of factors" (figure 2.2).[32]

The Quantcasts of the world understand 'you' as an evolving digital species. The sum of who you are is based on a matrix of datafied "factors" and the measurable types that those factors best fit into. And with more data comes more pieces of datafied meaning, which then can yield a higher statistical significance that *userX* belongs in *measurabletypeY* (see figure 2.3). Marketing companies often boast about the efficacy of their inference models, with one claiming that it can confidently know your 'gender' after visits to only eight different websites.[33] Yet we rarely visit just eight sites when we're online. We visit hundreds, if not thousands, in a single month. And for a tracking company like Quantcast, the more the better: "Machine-learning inference

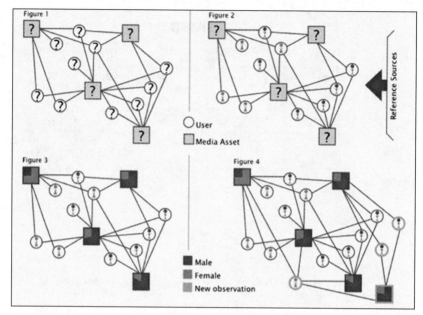

FIGURE 2.3. A composite Quantcast image from a 2008 methodology white paper explains how its 'gender' inference model works across websites. Source: Quantcast, "Quantcast Methodology Overview," 2008, www.quantcast. com [no longer available].

model just gets smarter over time. As additional media assets and re-lated exposures are continually added to the model, a ripple effect oc-curs. Real-time updates to the estimates are made not just to the added observations, but also to all relevant exposures and web assets along adjacent parts of the visit graph."[34]

The manner by which this model "gets smarter" is best explained by the statistical method of Bayesian probability. Thomas Bayes was an amateur mathematician whose 1763 posthumously published "Essay to-wards Solving a Problem in the Doctrine of Chances" asserted, among other things, a simple fact: we update a phenomenon's meaning when new data about that phenomenon arrives.[35] Media scholar Finn Brun-ton offers us an excellent exposition:

Imagine someone new to this world seeing the first sunset of her life. Her question: will the sun rise again tomorrow? In ignorance, she defaults to a fifty-fifty chance and puts a black marble and a white marble into a bag. When the sun rises, she puts another white marble in. The probability of randomly picking white from the bag—that is, the probability of the sun rising based on her present evidence—has gone from 1 in 2 to 2 in 3. The next day, when the rises, she adds another marble, moving it to 3 in 4, and so on. Over time, she will approach (but never reach) certainty that the sun will rise. If, one terrible morning, the sun does not rise, she will put in a black marble and the probability will decline in proportion to the history of her observations.[36]

Bayesian probability is a statistical rendering of how we revise our opinions and interpretations of the world. We don't reformat our brains every day, nor do we expect the world to remain stagnant. Bayes tried to mathematically pinpoint this dynamic worldview through a process of inverse probability. Quantcast's model "gets smarter over time" not because it studies really hard but because it uses already-defined information to reduce the possibility of unknown information.

Much like our alien woman's incrementally progressive knowledge about the sun, any marketing company that tracks users over time will benefit from the improved probability afforded by inferential statistics. And much like a sunrise can never be a foregone conclusion, our membership within our measurable types will never find certainty, either. We are always in the in-between.

If this alien woman went online, she might be understood as 99 percent 'woman.' But due to the impossibility of 100 percent statistical confidence, she could also be 4 percent 'man.' Even a day later, that same alien might be understood as 97 percent 'woman,' as the sites that previously identified her as 99 percent 'woman' had statistically become more 'manly' due to the ripple effect from new data acquired the previous night.

Modulation of this kind produces a sense of conceptual equilibrium. The reflexive measurable-type identification of 'woman' responds to the general practices of the population, learning (and thus changing) while also controlling the conduct of conducts of those who make contact with Quantcast's surveillance network. This change has no linearity, as transmutation—the word Deleuze chooses to use—urges us to think of modulation as evolutionary, without telos or explicit purpose. But this change is algorithmic in the way that philosophers Paolo Totaro and Domenico Ninno describe algorithms' recursive function of "an operation that operates on itself," echoing the progressive continuity of Deleuze's "point to point" relation in both materiality and process.[37]

Yet despite a lack of linearity or absent the perceived push toward a singular norm, algorithmic regulation still sets the "discursive limits" of identity. Through modulatory identification, power orders and controls us in ways that are implicit. While our data is collected under incredibly intimate conditions, the enactment of this control comes at us from a distance. Scores of scholars have remarked on power's increasing distance from the subject, such as philosophers Michael Hardt and Antonio Negri, who succinctly write in *Empire* that "communication and control can be exercised efficiently at a distance."[38] Or we can return to Nigel Thrift, who explains how software "consists of rules of conduct able to be applied to determinate situations. But these rules of conduct operate at a distance."[39]

An important caveat to these discussions is that this distanced control does not make one immune to actual violence. Anthropologist Aihwa Ong reminds us in her own distant, modulatory term "latitudinal citizenship" that while "latitudinal activity is continually monitored, not least by the fluctuating bottom line and unknowable market risks, it is also parasitic on older disciplinary forms."[40] And digital scholar Tung-Hui Hu describes how our network society facilitates the "variable ways that sovereign power interfaces with data-centric tools," or what he calls "sovereignty of data."[41] Seemingly anachronistic modes of power surely remain in the most high-tech of our experiences. People are jailed, injured, killed, or intimidated often because of, not despite, their access to digital technology.

Yet algorithmic regulation signals something theoretically new for our digital, datafied selves. There's something distinct about the dual distance/intimacy afforded by the technologies that compose the Internet—something that a third-rate advertising executive would probably want to call the "digital difference" but that we will think about in terms of Seb Franklin's episteme of control. If we, and the measurable types that compose us, are reconfigured and instrumentalized according to methods like Bayesian confidence measures, we will always be both 'man' and 'woman' at the same time. By processing our data but never revealing what that data means to us, the discursive topographies that shape our lives are black boxed into a state of procedural, algorithmically inferential unfolding.

To repeat a point made earlier in the book, the control implicit in algorithmic regulation is distinct from critiques of algorithmic "personalization" that assail a fragmentation of the liberal public sphere. In these arguments, news sites and search engines target data-based profiles with specialized content, profiles that in turn build self-affirming echo chambers that rupture the possibility for ideal democratic discourse.[42] As an example, a user might see articles from the conservative FoxNews.com on the basis of his profiled measurable-type identities. While we could focus on the resulting polarization of opinion and dearth of accurate information, I want to instead emphasize the process by which knowledge about what it means to be 'Republican,' 'male,' and 'white' conditions the possibilities for our present and futures.

The measurable types of 'Republican,' 'male,' and 'white' are more than just conduits that allocate content or FoxNews.com stories. If you as a user fit in 'Republican,' 'white,' and 'male' measurable types, the sites that users visit will have been visited by a 'white,' 'Republican' 'man.' This information extends past one's own immediate experience, as that same data can be used in more foundational editorial decisions.

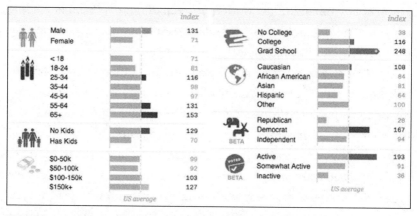

FIGURE 2.4. The demographic breakdown of TheNation.com in 2014, according to Quantcast's inference analytics. Source: Quantcast, "TheNation.com's Audience Profile on Quantcast," 2014, www.quantcast.com.

For instance, if a progressive news site like TheNation.com glances at its Quantcast demographic profile, it would find that the majority of its users are 'male,' went to 'college' or 'grad school,' and are 'Caucasian' (figure 2.4). An editor with this data might make one of two decisions. One, she could expand her audience by producing content that might appeal to non-'Caucasian' 'ethnic' groups, put more emphasis on women's issues, and even talk about gaps in access to education. Two, she could double down, identifying the several dominant measurable types that compose the *Nation*'s audience and focus even more to provide even better content for those loyal readers. How news sites use measurable-type data has discursive effect on content, audience assessments, and even staff-hiring decisions.

But while the *Nation* might hire a writer to produce Hispanic content, it might discover that those 'Hispanics' visiting TheNation.com were not Hispanic/Latino at all. The demographic makeup of these sites is fluid, and there is a lived separation between an identity like 'Hispanic' 'woman' and actual issues that Hispanic women might care about.

And unlike a writer who targets a Hispanic or Latino audience, a writer on the 'Hispanic' beat has no real clue what her job should be. Is it about Spanish-language content? Is it about immigration and Latin America? Is it about something else entirely, unavailable for identification because even if this writer identifies as Hispanic/Latina herself, she might not be categorized as 'Hispanic' by Quantcast's inference algorithms? This discursive incommensurability is a consequence of transcoding identity into data, in which each redrawn category is often unrecognizable to the lived experience of those who compose it.

And as 'Hispanic' users move on to visit different sites, the measurable type of 'Hispanic' changes in accord. In this case, we can also see how a progressive reconfiguration of categorical meaning establishes a permanent transience of identity. Using 'Hispanic' as an index for knowledge becomes analytically problematic if it is applied as anything more than just a passing referent. In the current moment, 'Hispanic' might mean something. But when the moment passes, 'Hispanic' means something else. No latent politics remain. There is no grounded, political identity—no connection of 'Hispanic' to what it means to be Hispanic/Latina. 'Hispanic' orders life solely according to temporal correlations of measurable, datafied behavior.

This "algorithmic governmentality," as philosopher Antoinette Rouvroy writes, "simply ignores the embodied individuals it affects and has as its sole 'subject' a 'statistical body,' that is, a constantly evolving 'data body' or network of localisations in actuarial tables."[43] With the knowledge component of Foucault's power/knowledge constantly evolving, we can better witness Deleuze's "perpetual training" in how it generates new discursive pathways on the basis of a clustering of the steps we have already taken. A 'man' is what users who are 'men' do most. As those 'men' form new habits, try new things, and grow as human beings, 'man' keeps up "point to point," organizing the world for us directly, through profilization or prefigured life, and indirectly, through reforming what it means to be a 'man.'

In this direct form, we see the import of scholars like theorist Tiziana Terranova and digital media theorist Wendy Hui Kyong Chun, who argue that "soft control," as Terranova labels it, or "soft government" /

"programmable visions" as Chun writes, predictively shapes our future within network culture. For Terranova,

> Emergent output needs to be carefully collected and valorized at the end of the process with a very fine-toothed comb; it must be modulated with a minimum amount of force. . . . This is a control of a specific type, it is a soft control. It is not soft because it is less harsh (often it has nothing gentle about it) but because it is an experiment in the control of systems that respond violently and often suicidally to rigid control.[44]

And for Chun, "[The] future . . . is linked intimately to the past, to computers as capable of being the future because, based on past data, they shape and predict it. . . . This future depends on programmable visions that extrapolate the future—or more precisely, a future—based on the past."[45] This programmable, soft control is all around us. When we shop in an online store, we're never followed by a security guard because we look suspicious. But we *do* see a very limited view of that store. We're recognized and evaluated as an aggregation of different measurable types.

Yet beyond these predictive futures, algorithmic regulation indirectly modulates the present tense of our measurable-type classifications. The consequences of this regulation are more than a particular perspective enforced through a litany of algorithmic fine-tuning. Namely, algorithmic regulation articulates the knowledges that compose us, the productions of "limits of acceptable speech," in ways that give us no recourse. Who we are as data becomes an enunciation of another's algorithmic interpretation. And those interpretations abandon prior meaning—quite unlike the politics surrounding our identities—as soon as that meaning becomes statistically ineffective.

THE BIOPOLITICS OF THE MEASURABLE TYPE

Biopolitics is, as Michel Foucault writes, the "power over life."[46] It is a power that first speaks to its subjects as part of a population, in which individual lives get lumped together into a composite "stock" like cattle, flattening out the amorphous mess of love, loss, and joy that traditionally defines the human condition. I am not John, the individual biopolitical subject with particular wants and needs. I am John, an astonishingly unimportant member of a much-larger populace.

From this razed ground of the population, biopolitics builds us anew. From the stock emerges new forms of categorical demarcation. A population might be composed of men and women who are single or married, young or old, with kids or without. These constructed caesuras of natural life form the avenues of distribution for resources and governmental power that define biopolitical action.[47] A domestic health campaign, for example, rarely targets the broad, unintelligible idea of Americans but rather narrows its focus to Americans who are teenagers, and the message is often different for girls and boys.

First Lady Michelle Obama's 2010 Let's Move! program, aimed at reducing obesity in children, is but one example. With Let's Move!, the U.S. stock is narrowed to "kids and teens" (six to seventeen years old) and "adults" (eighteen and older), and different exercise goals are assigned to each group "so that children born today will reach adulthood at a healthy weight."[48] Government policy and public education take their cues from these programs, using propaganda and physical-education classes to emphasize stated public-health goals. In this case, a healthy exercise regimen is not a personalized routine attendant to each individual's needs and circumstances but a categorical quantity anointed by government bureaucrats.

On the surface, these health campaigns are not bad, but they are necessarily controlling—and quintessentially biopolitical. In this example, the U.S. government uses its position of power to produce a change in our habits, something that proponents might call "nudging" while naysayers might claim manipulation.[49] Yet implicit in how we conceive biopolitics is a baseline dependence on data, the abstraction of a population into dividual, datafied forms in order to assign those forms quantifiable goals: "Kids and teens" should either be active for sixty minutes a day, at least five days a week, for six out of eight weeks, or take twelve thousand steps a day.[50] For the latter, with even the most rudimentary pedometer, or step counter, an individual can monitor the aggregate steps she takes during the day. More contemporary pedometers can count how many steps your child takes and upload that information into an existing cloud-based data set, recording a string of historical data about your and/or your child's walking patterns over time.

These datafied trails we tread as users of digital technologies have profound biopolitical applications. Health and medical data that was once painstakingly collected by governments, scientists, and doctors is now automatically monitored and uploaded by our own personal devices. While the "power over life" might be impressively imperial as a catchphrase, the technologies facilitating that power are as ordinary as our cell phones. And with these technologies both decreasing in price and increasing in availability, large numbers of individuals around the world, most notably those organizing around the Quantified Self community, or QS, use this mode of self-tracking to sleep better, eat healthier, and exercise more efficiently.

QS is the practice of datafying bodies and environments (the types of food consumed, calories burned, moods, blood oxygen levels, insulin levels, and even sleep quality) in order to know more about one's self. This is what QS people call "self-knowledge."[51] QS community members use self-datafication both to track their progress toward whatever goal they have and to create relationships between two or more previously unrelated phenomena. For example, "every time I eat more than three thousand calories a day and don't go to the gym, I tend to sleep worse."

For many QS users, technologically mediated self-tracking often allows for healthier, more productive, and more fulfilling lives. If individuals can monitor their daily caloric intake, they might avoid obesity and the health problems surrounding it. If they understand what negatively affects their sleep patterns, they can rest and work more effectively.

But through these new regimes of self-tracking, we also develop divergent relationships to what is and is not 'healthy.' In what anthropologists Dawn Nafus and Jamie Sherman term "soft resistance," there exists a constant tussle between QS users (who often "critically question what constitutes relevant information, whether individual data points or entire categories of knowledge") and dominant forms of "healthiness" defined by QS app makers and the mobile health industry (who try to "cajole people into conforming to standards").[52] But in the case of Let's Move!, you, as an individual adult, may be a picture of health despite a disappointing daily step count below twelve thousand. You will not be algorithmically considered as 'healthy' until your data corroborates the self-tracking device's own assessment.

The same evaluative logic that authoritatively establishes the twelve-thousand-step measurable type for 'healthy' also applies to a variety of different 'moods' like 'depressed,' 'general well-being,' 'head injury,' 'anxiety,' 'stress,' or even 'PTSD.' Take the Pentagon-funded mobile application *T2 Mood Tracker*, which alerts you to how 'anxious' you may be on the basis of nine sliding continuums with opposing dispositional polarities such as "Worried/Untroubled," "Distracted/Focused," and "Anxious/Peaceful" (figure 2.5).[53] As you plot your current mental state according to each of these nine scales, the application calculates your 'anxiety' with an assigned quantitative value that, when tracked over time, might clue you into a previously unavailable diagnosis.

In this case, 'anxiety' becomes an actionable stand-in for use in subsequent biopolitical activities, striating the once smooth, unruly complexity of our mental states into a cardinal array between 'anxious' and 'not anxious.' With *T2 Mood Tracker*, you can track your 'anxiety' over time, and that datafied 'mood' can then be calculated, connected to, and analyzed alongside other pieces of self-quantified data. High levels of *T2 Mood Tracker* 'anxiety' matched with weeks of consistently low Let's Move! step counts might signal a correlation. And that correlation might

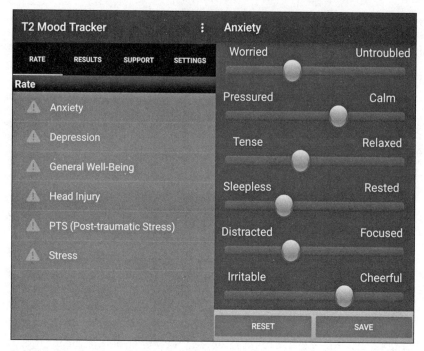

FIGURE 2.5. Two screenshots from the *T2 Mood Tracker* mobile application. Source: T2, "About T2 | t2health," 2014, http://t2health.dcoe.mil.

encourage a range of amateur diagnoses and "soft resistance" practices. Nevertheless, these different datafying technologies move biopolitics' "power over life" to a more personal level—and in doing so modify the definition of biopolitics in the process. In the case of QS, biopolitics is not just the politics of life itself but the politics of data itself, which has also become a new index for life itself.

Put more concisely, what data materially represents is now tied to biopolitics. So let's ask ourselves, if an iPhone application, not a mental health professional, can assess and diagnose your 'anxiety' and 'depression,' what other effects would this shift to the measurable type have for our biopolitical futures?

Let's continue with physical diseases. Historically, countries like the U.S. used their version of a Centers for Disease Control (CDC) to study public health, record medical trends, and eventually alert the populace and medical practitioners to outbreaks of infectious diseases such as the flu. If state officials in Des Moines, Iowa, saw an abnormal number of patients coming to the hospital with flu-like symptoms, that patient data would be gathered, analyzed, and eventually used as evidence to declare a flu epidemic in central Iowa. Authorities could shut down schools, issue public-service announcements about hand washing, and even quarantine people they suspect are sick.

However, this method has a hidden flaw: it operates on a delay. Individuals with the flu will not be classified as sick until they are diagnosed by a doctor—which can take weeks from the onset of symptoms. Burdened by this inherent latency, any biopolitical agent must wait to make decisions until that data arrives. But what if you had access to people before they went to the doctor or even before they suspected they had the flu? What if you could diagnose the 'flu' in a similar way that *T2 Mood Tracker* assesses 'anxiety,' Quantcast assesses 'gender,' and even the NSA assesses 'terrorist'?

This is what Google had in mind when it launched Google Flu Trends in 2009. Using its stream of millions of hourly search queries, Google had access to the world's 'health' data without really knowing it. Searches about different illnesses, types of medicine, and alternative treatment methods all might be "good indicators of flu activity," which led Google Flu Trends to "[use] aggregated Google search data to estimate flu activity."[54] With near-real-time, mass dataveillance of search queries, Google discovered it was able to report flu epidemics a whole six weeks prior to CDC estimates.[55] The CDC model, which relies on human volition and visits to medical facilities, suddenly seemed old-fashioned, conservative, and in need of an upgrade.

Google Flu Trends, the CDC's data-based heir apparent, relied instead on a "bag of words" to connect search terms with historical flu data. This bag of words was sewn from the remains of hundreds of billions of queries from 2003 to 2008, resulting in the fifty million most common search terms. These fifty million terms were then regressed over 1,152 different flu date data points, arriving at n = approximately 160. To phrase it differently, the terms that Google users most frequently searched for during periods of flu epidemics became the new indicator for 'flu' symptoms. Google's datafied model of the 'flu' comprised the ~160 most appropriate terms that statistically fit those flu date data points best.

If Iowa experienced flu outbreaks in October 2005, February 2006, February 2007, and March 2008, Google could query its giant search repository and discover which terms were most common across all four years. Through this process, the 'flu's' bag of words might include "my daughter has a runny nose," "omg my son is vomiting help me now," and "I can't sleep because I am sweating way too much." In fact, due to Google's informational secrecy, it is actually impossible to know the ~160 terms used in this analysis. While Google's engineers did curate its data model (removing, for example, "high school basketball," which strongly correlated with U.S. influenza rates), statistical regression played the biggest role on the diagnostic front. Data ruled, on its own terms and according to Google's own algorithmic logics.

But when these ~160 different queries became the new index for what makes a flu epidemic, Google drastically altered what the flu meant. The flu was no longer about actually having a runny nose, throwing up, or enduring a fitful sleep. It was about searching for "vomit" over and over again when it happened to be flu season. The flu became the 'flu,' indicating a unique shift in its biopolitical future.

Google Flu Trends assigned the 'flu' to web behavior in certain cities, states, and countries—not to people with symptoms. We know that federal officials, including Lyn Finelli, chief of surveillance for the CDC's Influenza Surveillance and Outbreak Response Team, used Google Flu Trends' data and other governmental and nongovernmental sources "all the time."[56] For Finelli, Google Flu Trends "could conceivably provide as early a warning of an outbreak as any system. . . . The earlier the warning, the earlier prevention and control measures can be put in place, and this could prevent cases of influenza."[57] Accordingly, the U.S. government's response to a flu epidemic was directly linked to how Google defined 'flu' and how its algorithms recognized 'flu's' activity.

In the world of commerce, companies like Vicks hired marketers that used Google Flu Trends data to target advertisements for its Behind Ear Thermometer. In this case, Chicago-based Blue Chip Marketing World-wide located states that had high 'flu' activity. It then targeted users in those states on the basis of their 'gender,' 'age,' and 'marital status' and if they were a 'parent.' Finally, Blue Chip would wait until those profiled users' GPS locations were within three miles of a retail store that sold the Behind Ear Thermometer and then trigger a targeted advertisement on those users' phones.[58] Google's measurable type of 'flu' was not just an experimental analytic but an actionable category that required—from a state and capital perspective—precision. In this sense, Google's measurable type was both powerful and profitable. If only it were accurate.

In 2012, Google's predictions turned out to be a bit overblown. Only about half of Google's forecasted 'flu' epidemics actually happened. The race toward datafying the 'flu' through big data skipped over many of the complexities that small data, like doctor visits and the number of actual flu cases, accounted for.[59] To repurpose an idiom used in chapter 1, Google hadn't missed the forest for the trees. It missed the sick tree for all the other trees who'd been frantically Googling ways to help the sick tree.

Many people rushed to critique Google after "Flugate," with some going so far as to deem it—and big data in general—a failure, emblematic of the almost doctrinaire way that patterns in data were regarded as the digital skeleton key for life's mysteries.[60] But lacking in these critiques was an explicit account of what was really happening in Google Flu Trends' algorithmic models. Google wasn't measuring the flu; it was measuring the 'flu.' The measurable type of 'flu' is conceptually separate from the flu. You might be talking to someone with the 'flu.' You might even kiss her on the mouth. But she won't be able to give you the flu. The 'flu' is not transmittable across the quotation-mark gap—unless, of course, the person with the 'flu' also has the flu.

Had Google Flu Trends failed, as some commentators declared? In one way, the answer is yes, since Google's prediction missed the mark of actual CDC figures in 100 out of 108 weeks.[61] But in another way, it hadn't. If we take the idea of a "beta" introduced in chapter 1 and operationalize 'flu' not as a static list of ~160 keywords but as a dynamic, reflexive measurable type, then, at least theoretically, the 'flu' shows potential for improvement. It hadn't failed; it just did poorly on its first exam.

Back during biopolitics' birth in the early eighteenth century, nation-states used data to intervene in the lives of citizens on behalf of the people in power—just like Google Flu Trends did. Unlike more immediate, disciplinary forms of power, biopolitics wasn't exclusively about the quelling of dissent or imperial expansion of territory. It was about a politics that fostered a temporary homeostasis of life. If people were healthy and free of blight and disease, they could work harder for the king's honorable realm.

Biopolitical action then served, quoting Foucault, as "a technology which brings together the mass effects characteristic of a population, which tries to control the series of random events that can occur in a living mass, a technology which tries to predict the probability of those events (by modifying it, if necessary) or at least compensate for their effects."[62] As a site of prediction, aggregation of mass effects, and ultimate control of resources, this is the exact technology of Google Flu Trends foretold only decades prior.

The technological failure of Google's 'flu' wasn't an error of biopolitical action. Its problem was the rigidity of the category of 'flu' itself. Methodologically speaking, Google decontextualized ~160 search terms away from their individual contexts and collapsed them into a single measurable type, functionally ignoring the variability that might differentiate one data element ("I am sick [physically]") from another ("I am sick [mentally]"). If only Google could make the 'flu' in the same way it predicted the flu, taking the swaths of available data in order to dynamically update its interpretation of 'flu.' With an updated 'flu,' the immediate failure of the category could potentially be resolved.

And this is precisely what a group of U.S. researchers did from 2012 to 2013.[63] Rather than monitoring the constant $n = {\sim}160$ of Google's bag of words, these researchers wrote an algorithm that tracked not the flu but the 'flu,' examining how certain 'flu'-like queries' values changed over time. It was discovered, for example, that the phrase "rapid flu" had little to no correlation with overall flu incidents in 2009. In the years that followed, however, it became highly correlative. And in 2013, it was deemed a wholly "positive influence." More interesting still, the query for narcotic cold medicine Robitussin was a slightly "positive influence" on 'flu' cases in 2009, became "no influence" in 2010, fell to a slightly "negative influence" in 2011, returned to "no influence" in 2012, and then resiliently crept up again in 2013 as a "positive influence" (figure 2.6). The emergent 'flu' measurable type adapted to this modulatory weighing of search-query accuracy.

Week by week, when official CDC sources published new, small flu data, the researchers' adaptive flu algorithm assessed how accurate their 'flu' was and recalibrated its definition accordingly. The persistently updating algorithm yielded markedly better results using data from 2009 to 2013, with the alternative 'flu' outperforming Google's on almost every metric.[64] This new measurable type of 'flu,' mechanically recorrective rather than reliant on Google's human intervention, exemplifies the practice of discursive algorithmic regulation. But as a process, it's also not at all new.

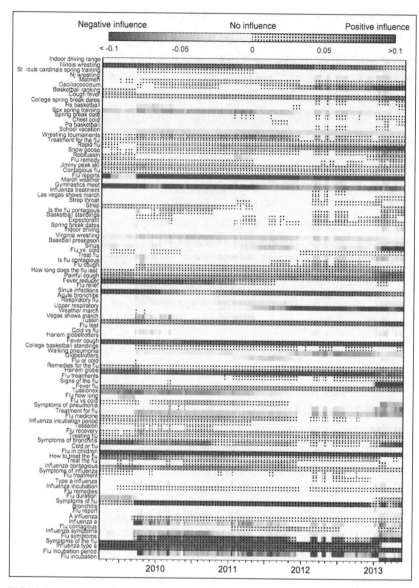

FIGURE 2.6. A breakdown of each search term's efficacy as it correlates to the 'flu.' Source: Mauricio Santillana, D. Wendong Zhang, Benjamin Althouse, and John Ayers, "What Can Digital Disease Detection Learn from (an External Revision to) Google Flu Trends?," *American Journal of Preventive Medicine* 47, no. 3 (2014): 345.

CYBERNETICS AS ALGORITHMIC REGULATION

While an automatic, persistently recalibrating 'flu' might seem impressively futuristic, the theory that grounds it is quite familiar. This self-updating 'flu' closely resembles the mid-twentieth-century systems and computer-science writings that founded the field of cybernetics.[65] Cybernetics is the study of regulation as a technological problem. An ideal cybernetic machine performs an automatized balancing act to both prevent failure and ensure functionability, like the most basic of cybernetic examples, a thermostat. While research on cybernetics by notable figures like Norbert Weiner largely framed control in terms of social homeostasis, we can see a similar homeostasis emerging in the form of measurable-type modulation.

Drawing further, the 'flu' is this cybernetic machine in epistemic form, a discursive vessel whose defining composition changes over time on the basis of new inputs. While the dictates of cultural gatekeepers invested in the status quo establish and reaffirm traditional categorical definitions, cybernetic systems are devoid of these kinds of conservative politics. It's the machine itself that is valued, just like 'flu,' 'woman,' and 'sixty years old' are heralded as truth. The machine's inner workings, of what is the 'flu' and what isn't, are theoretically happenstance processes that ensure its vitality.

Thinking through the cultural history of cybernetics as outlined by literary critic N. Katherine Hayles, when cybernetic systems chug along to maintain stability, they also have the ability to produce new emergent meanings.[66] In the case of Google Flu Trends, this emergence arrives in the epistemological work that the 'flu' does upon algorithmic output. Emergence in cybernetics begins with deviations from the once-standard norm—we might choose to call them differences. These differences, write philosophers Luciana Parisi and Tiziana Terranova, "are generated, therefore putting in motions the turbulent machine of life . . . [as] life does not tend towards entropy but towards deviation, mutation and variation leading to increased levels of complexity."[67]

The epistemological difference of 'flu' means that new inputs, like a query for "college spring-break dates," might have no correlative consequence on 'flu' until 2012. Then, from 2012 to 2013, we see a slight but prevalent increase of the query's "positive influence." 'Flu' isn't just composed of existing terms that modulate accordingly. It also accepts new terms unrelated to the flu but increasingly 'flu'-like, such as when exactly college students enjoy a week off from their classes.

The emergence in this cybernetic system is greedy, and in its greediness, it ingests as many inputs as possible in order to assure the system modulates itself toward operable stability. This is a deviation that is not a bug but a feature. A medical doctor might scoff at a patient who tells her about his spring break in a conversation about the flu. A traditional biopolitical system would consider the patient's vacation plans irrelevant. But a tolerant system, one that cares little for the flu as a historical idea, finds this off-the-wall deviance and entropy statistically intriguing.

It is precisely because one system cannot foresee every possible variant that enters into it—think about how the flu itself is as much an evolving biological phenomenon as the measurable type that describes it—that entropy in that system is a productive, if not premier, attribute. This routine of free-flowing self-organization according to a set of (dynamic) rules embodies what philosopher Eugene Thacker describes, in his work on swarms, as a control without control: "a totally distributed, self-organizing, flexible and robust model of group organization, that can be directed towards certain ends, that is able to mobilize in a particular way, and that is able to express purpose or intention on a global scale."[68]

This flexible, self-organizing proceduralism means there is no doctor dismissing a patient's spring-break query, but there is an algorithm calculating its "positive" or "negative influence" week in and week out. A robust, emergent tolerance allows almost anything to be part of the prognosis for 'flu.' It is only up to the correlative patterns made through calculations of data to decide what is an emergent property, what is an outdated or submerging property, and what has no relevance to 'flu' whatsoever.

By statistically determining the ins and outs of the 'flu,' Google and its academic revisionists refined the 'flu's' discursive limits. And this new meaning can have direct effect on our lives. The U.S. government, Vicks, and anyone else who used Google Flu Trends in their health analysis required that the 'flu' be useful. Accordingly, its cybernetic system privileged 'flu' above anything else. Ironically, Google Flu Trends' primary goal was not about health at all. It was about the production and subsequent maintenance of 'flu' as a valid and accurate measurable type, which only later might lead to real-world health benefits.

No matter the 'flu's' real-world efficacy, the 'flu' was perceived as meaningful. Advertising money was spent. News and state officials referred to the 'flu' as real. The 'flu' became part of our world whether we wanted it to or not. Consider a hypothetical. You and your neighbors may wonder when spring break begins, so each of you goes to Google and searches for "spring break." A spike in these "'flu'-like" queries from the same zip code might lead to the local elementary school shutting down.

Or more hypothetically, due to your "spring break" queries, maybe your profile is 'flu'-ed. And because your profile has the 'flu,' you might fail to see that your favorite band is in town due to state health officials requesting that ticket vendors hide the event from those who are potentially contagious. You might not have the flu, but your data says you do. And ultimately you can't understand what the 'flu' is because it's both impossible to know and changing by the week.

Or even more hypothetically, imagine you're a world superpower, and you want to overthrow a sitting, unfriendly government. Because of your superpower status, you have access to a large repository of that foreign country's Internet traffic, meaning you can pattern analyze all data traveling across the country's Internet tubes. And with that available data, you might go about creating several different measurable types: 'pro-revolution,' 'anti-revolution,' and 'apolitical.' With this data, you could better understand who supported the government, who despised it, and who couldn't care less. Quite saliently, this is what political campaigns call "microtargeting," in which data-driven profiles tailor political messages to potential voters on the basis of demographics, interests, and hobbies.[69]

And quite unsurprisingly, this is also exactly what the U.S. Agency for International Development (USAID) did from 2010 to 2012 in a haphazard attempt to destabilize Cuba with a "Cuban Twitter" named ZunZuneo. Reaching forty thousand Cuban users at its height, the U.S.-government-funded microblogging service connected Cuban users to initially apolitical content through a network of text messages. Yet beneath its "social networking" front overseen by Cayman Island and Spanish holding companies, U.S. state-employed contractors also developed the aforementioned three political measurable types with goals of fomenting what was optimistically called a "Cuban Spring."[70] While the project was canceled when funding ran out only two years into operation, these static measurable types constructed by ZunZuneo let us better appreciate the cybernetic power of the modulatory measurable type.

That is, if researchers at USAID/ZunZuneo expanded their work to identify not just who was 'pro-revolution' but what 'pro-revolution' people wanted, the U.S. government could use this pattern-analyzed data to demonstrate how daily life was no longer satisfied by the regime. 'Anti-revolution' users might be considered defenders of the regime, but the data that fabricated 'anti-revolution' could also suggest the best ways to suppress their loyalist support. Even those who were 'apolitical' might be mobilized if data could algorithmically identify what might drive them to insurgency.

By using the company's founts of data to not just order but predict collective identity before that identity had the chance to collectively understand itself, ZunZuneo would govern a considerable portion of political discourse. Geographer Louise Amoore describes this potentiality as a changing calculus of risk: in addition to managing known risk, corporate and government actors now enjoy the capacity to act on what is not yet known or what could potentially happen.[71] If Zun-Zuneo tracked these categories over time, adapting 'anti-revolution,' 'pro-revolution,' and 'apolitical' to variations in the political climate, the notion of 'pro-revolution' could be theoretically understood, and potentially prefigured, by the U.S. government.

Of course, while many of these variations would include error (think "spring break" and 'flu'), the prospect that 'pro-revolution' can clue USAID into an unknown political project, nascent event, or yet-defined consensus shows the epistemological danger of life understood through ubiquitous surveillance and measurable-type analysis. And unlike a 'flu' that keeps you from a concert, this hypothetical goes beyond regulating mere user behavior to defining categorical identity itself. Effectively prefiguring 'gender' leaves little room for political struggle over 'gender.' And effectively prefiguring 'anti-revolution' gives a state considerable power over the political future of another body politic.

This future is entirely speculative, crass even, but it gets at the underlying danger of a digital life ordered and reordered beyond our pale and without our knowledge. In this algorithmic forging, who we are in terms of data is constructed as an analytic, all while that analytic is treated as an identity. This collapsing of analysis and identity might signal a reason for the downfall of Google Flu Trends, which in August 2015 shuttered its operations, passing its 'flu' data to its partner health organizations that compile their own predictive models.[72] While the rationale for Google Flu Trends' closure remains unstated, we nonetheless encounter a key dynamic for the future of our algorithmic identities. Without making our identities and thoughts social, and without a general understanding of how resources and rights are asymmetrically distributed, that distribution is unavailable for critique.

SOFT BIOPOLITICS

The control in Google Flu Trends was quite unlike the "walk, not drive" *Wii Sports* example discussed at this chapter's beginning. While our 'age' might discipline us toward certain normativities (like the nubile, ideal 'twenty-year-old' who is really good at baseball), the control implicit in a cybernetic measurable type is a control of allocation. In the case of Google Flu Trends, it's the allocation of health resources. In the case of Vicks's use of Google Flu Trends, it's the allocation of advertising dollars, attention, and potential health remedies. But in all three, it's also about something much more lasting and profound: the allocation of knowledge, including what sociologist David Lyon labels "social sorting" and what geographer Stephen Graham describes as "software sorting."[73]

What it means to have the 'flu' and to be a certain 'age' is not really up to us. We are 'flu'-ed and 'age'-ed by an algorithm. And when an algorithm determines discursive construction, we will always be one step behind it. 'Flu' and 'age' are made and deployed on data's terms, not ours.

So when 'flu' has the capacity to change its meaning week by week, not only are we a step behind, but we're also using an outdated map. Imagine you are a marketer for Vicks and want to target an advertisement to only 'women' who live in a state that has the 'flu.' The measurable type of 'flu' is potentially mobile, modulating according to the new patterns found in time-sensitive data pieces weighed each week.

But 'woman' is similarly itinerant: what a 'woman' is changes just like the 'flu' can, dynamically adapting to the emergent ideas that define 'woman' according to how its cybernetic model processes new data. Now, if a significant portion of 'women' started to show interest in Argentine soccer-related sites and products, those Argentine soccer elements would slowly become part and parcel of what it means to be a 'woman.'

To return to an earlier example, Quantcast's analytic algorithms look at users' web-browsing data in order to make various measurable-type inferential identifications such as what a user's 'gender' is and whether that user is 'with children.' When a new website like WeAreDataBook.com launches and connects to the Quantcast dataveillance network, its audience is initially unknown. No one has visited it, and it remains untouched by prior demographic valuations.

But as profiled users arrive in droves, the site's 'gender' and 'children' makeup subsequently changes in correspondence to the relative frequency of visitors who are 'male,' 'female,' 'with children,' and 'without children.' As a new data element in the Quantcast universe, WeAreDataBook.com is quickly canonized with weighted membership as 65 percent 'female' and 35 percent 'male.' These percentages empirically denote the arbitrarily closed, momentary, but empowered 'gender' of WeAreDataBook.com.

Yet as visitors to WeAreDataBook.com visit different sites or as those sites themselves 'demographically' change according to the flows of new visitors, the 'gender' breakdown of WeAreDataBook.com necessarily realigns. Its 'gender' value is now 66 percent 'female' and 34 percent 'male.' As a category deployed across the web in targeted advertising, a company like Vicks must accept that 'women' is whoever is categorized as a 'female' at the very moment an ad launches.

Thinking for the moment outside the complexities of percentages and machine-learning inference algorithms, this type of dynamism is common sense. A machine-learned model of 'woman' from 2008 is archaic, most definitely out of fashion, and most likely passé. 'She' has no idea what Snapchat or Tinder is. 'She' might not know there was a global financial collapse around the corner. 'She' has never heard of the Arab Spring and wouldn't know what an Uber or Lyft "ride-sharing" car was, even if it drove back in time and hit 'her' on the street. The measurable-type models that Quantcast developed in 2008 need to account for the dynamism of life itself. New sites, new words, new interactions, and new types of performance, when datafied, maintain these recursively updated versions of 'gender' (as well as 'ethnicity,' 'class,' 'age,' and even 'education').

We can better understand these updating algorithmic versions of demographic identity using Quantcast's own, dual-sourced inference methodology. First, "Quantcast directly measures more than 100 million web destinations, incorporates over 1 trillion new data records every month," collecting and aggregating small pieces of cookie information (*userX* went to *websiteY*), which in turn lets it process an estimated thirty petabytes of data a day.[74]

Second, Quantcast also employs supplementary "multiple reference point data" that combines data sources from "market research companies, ISPs (broadband and dial-up) and toolbar vendors and cover in excess of 2 million individuals (1.5 million in the U.S.). . . . Quantcast is continually adding new reference data sources to validate, establish and improve the inference capabilities of its models."[75] Quantcast's 'male' and 'female' are recompiled ad infinitum on the basis of new data sets, improvements in Quantcast's inference models, and the daily rhythm of life and death in cyberspace.

This procedure of automatic categorical recompiling is what I have previously called soft biopolitics.[76] Like wearing a so-last-season sweater to Paris Fashion Week, any marketing campaign using 2008 measurable types today would fail spectacularly and be subject to unpleasant scorn. To communicate using 'Women 2008' would mean you are neither able to speak to the current state of identity nor able to understand anything that has happened since 2008. And because measurable types enjoy no timeless essence—no shared, stable identity outside of what is currently available to be empirically measured—their modulation is a requisite feature.

A company like Vicks sends out targeted ads to 'women' without really knowing if they're women, so long as 'women' continually recalibrate to ensure effective legibility as an accurate measurable type. Soft biopolitics attends to the definition of categorical identity itself, allowing that identity to cybernetically take shape according to the most current, and correlative, patterns of data.

This softer brand of biopolitics uses the same methods of traditional biopolitics (statistics and population-level analysis) to generate the exclusive discursive limits that then represent a certain population. And this new mode of representation abandons the singular truth of identity often anointed to state-based census rolls and even volunteered identification. Instead, those census rolls and "I am a: Man" drop-down-menu options become mere shards of data that accompany other shards to produce a synergistic, composite algorithmic category of 'man.' In hard biopolitics, the state separates kids and teens from adults in order to assign different exercise objectives. In soft biopolitics, the state—or most likely a company contracted by the state—sends out emails, targeted content, or coupons for cough syrup to users who have the 'flu.'

The dominion of soft biopolitics is much more than an inventory of individual policies that govern the life of a population. It's also the manner by which these policies are communicated through what sociologist Nikolas Rose calls "circuits of inclusion" to that population.[77] Those who are empowered to construct the categories that define life have authorship over the future of biopolitical life. And those who have the most adept measurable types are most likely to be the conduits used for biopolitical intervention.

More explicitly, hard biopolitics engages life on a social level, assessing populations in compliance with the rigid, ready-made constructions of gender, race, class, age, and so on. Soft biopolitics makes 'gender,' 'race,' 'class,' 'age,' and so on using biopolitical means, via statistical clustering models and vast databases filled with pieces of our datafied lives. Accordingly, soft biopolitics engages life on a techno-social level, employing measurable types as mere temporal casings for what 'gender,' 'race,' 'class,' 'age,' and so on need to be. The resulting measurable types become an epistemic average for what Foucault describes as the "fundamental codes of a culture—those governing its language, its schemas of perception, its exchanges, its techniques, its values"—that "establish for every man . . . the empirical orders with which he will be dealing and within which he will be at home."[78]

By constructing categories from the ground up, Google Flu Trends, Quantcast, and Vicks don't just engage us through biopolitical policies. They also modulate the medium that policy arrives in. The "empirical orders" of our behavior arrive from afar. And while these orders might not be published or immediately perceptible to us, their quiet regulatory fortitude defines what is true, what isn't, and how we're biopolitically seen in the world.

Soft biopolitics is one way to think about how power operates in the seemingly unobstructed superhighway paved by digital technology. On this road, we often conceive of control as a stale red light or an aggrieved police officer walking toward your car—or, in Internet terms, of an HTTP 404 Not Found error message that alerts you to the fact that a certain site is unavailable due to a government take-down request, Internet outage, or poorly written code.

But, as Alexander Galloway argues, the protocols of the Internet also regulate traffic: they standardize communications, distribute packets according to the logic and rule set of TCP/IP, and assign domain addresses in line with the contested politics that surround DNS name servers.[79] Put this way, other cars on the highway, road construction and repair, and Google Maps' algorithmic routing instructions also serve as elements of control. While these examples might not be overt and intentional, their presence nonetheless prohibits certain life choices and political activities.

We might then return to the discursive topographies of changing knowledges, à la Judith Butler, and concentrate more fully on what theorists like Stephen Collier have called a "topological" approach to power, one in which a wide array of different and recombined techniques work in concert to create a unified state of power relations.[80] In this framework, there may not be a single, deep-rooted institution (like a government) that makes decisions that directly affect your life. Rather there is something else, latent and distant, that preserves stability through heterogeneous methods. Soft biopolitics is one attempt to demonstrate how this stability becomes manifest.

FINDING THE CENTER OF A MEASURABLE TYPE

As we shift our analysis toward a more topological understanding of power, we might be tempted to disregard the very real social norms that enforce hegemonic meaning. With no single institution that pompously declares "*this* is what it means to be a man," the norm of masculinity becomes unsettled. But in the nonalgorithmic world, there still remain grand arbiters of party-line gendered meaning: religious institutions, families, doctors, government bureaucrats, and even media representations like the predatorily oversexed Pepe Le Pew.

Nevertheless, the norms that sustain masculinity's definition necessarily move. They realign through explicit struggle and the implicit churn of social change. But in the algorithmic world, this movement of norms most often operates in the distance. Norms come at us unevenly, gradually, and quietly. We do not know what they are, nor do we know if, or if not, we're a good 'man.' So what happens when we don't know we are being positioned? And even if we are lucky enough to know that we are being positioned, what happens when we don't know what that positioning means?

This line of questioning leads us to an even more productive question: what is a "norm" in the algorithmic world? In most instances, it's simply the mathematical average of key elements, like Google's 'man' or Quantcast's 'Hispanic.' Or, for researchers at UC Berkeley, it's the algorithmic average of one of the most popular social constructions of recent history, 'Santa Claus.'

Created by an algorithm called AverageExplorer, 'Santa Claus' is the visual average, or distilled, apparent key elements, of a series of Santaclaus.jpg digital images that obviously contain a Santa Claus.[81] These key elements are the sections of those photos that change rarely, if at all: a white beard, a red hat atop a white face, a large body dressed in red, and a child on Santa's lap.

This average is the essential kernel of a stable cybernetic system. When new Santaclaus.jpgs are input into the algorithm, its cybernetic output is the redefined, averaged 'Santa.' In AverageExplorer's case, 'Santa' is white and man-like, a bit fat, with children on his lap, a red-and-white hat, and a white beard (figure 2.7). If an individual, let's call him Reza, used this averaged 'Santa' image as the template for assigning Santa Claus jobs at malls during Christmas, the type of person who could be hired as 'Santa' is quite limited.

But what if we used other types of Santas as additional inputs, including black Santas, thin Santas, Santas who are women, and Santas with trouble growing facial hair? Reza would have a new average to use and thus a new pool of potential employees. With variance in skin, body size, gender, and facial hair, the resulting average would be slightly different while still appearing as Santa: there could still be a red coat, a red-and-white hat, and a child on a lap.

This 'Santa' cybernetic model calibrated a new visual mean that adjusted to the myriad datafied differences of each succeeding photo. The key elements that arrive from this output, necessarily different from before, become the updated statistical identity of 'Santa.' More practically for Reza, they are the norms that decide who is, and who is not, a good 'Santa.' A bad 'Santa' might dress in blue and not get hired. The model of 'Santa' rejects the historical lineage of Santa and instead depends only on the Santaclaus.jpgs used as algorithmic inputs.[82] The key elements that make up the output are all that matter.

Key elements are the calculated norms that control how these algorithmic clusters are made, used, and reconfigured. Similarly, 'gender,' 'race,' and 'class' have key elements, but unlike the handpicked photos that become the inputs for Reza's 'Santa,' it is our mundane, datafied lives that feed our algorithmic futures. For a company like Quantcast, the inputs it uses in its cybernetic modeling can include everything from "viewing a web page, downloading an MP3, responding to an ad,

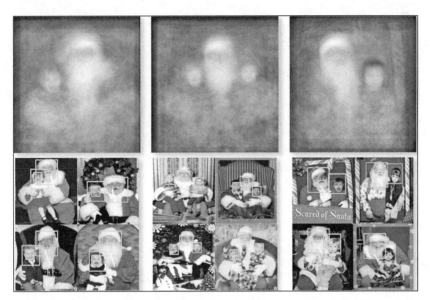

FIGURE 2.7. Three different visually averaged photos from AverageExplorer's 'Santa Claus.' Source: Jun-Yan Zhu, Yong Jae Lee, and Alexei A. Efros, "AverageExplorer: Interactive Exploration and Alignment of Visual Data Collections," *ACM Transactions on Graphics (TOG)* 33, no. 4 (2014): 160.

launching a widget, watching a video, purchasing a product, chatting on IM" to "playing an online game."[83] All of these activities, when datafied, become descriptors of some larger categorical membership—just like photos of 'Santa.' When processed, the average of these activities forms the statistical core of our algorithmic identities.

While Reza is charged with the crucial job of deciding who gets hired as Santa Claus and who has to settle for the title Elf 1, the algorithms that evaluate 'gender,' 'race,' and 'class' have no comparable personal duty. Instead, the key elements of these measurable types are abstract, disinterested models. Whatever data temporarily fits those models is conferred provisional membership. You might not get a job as 'Santa' because you refuse to wear red, but your datafied whiteness may mean that you'll instead get advertisements and content aimed to 'Caucasians.' An online health campaign for 'women' 'with children' will bio-

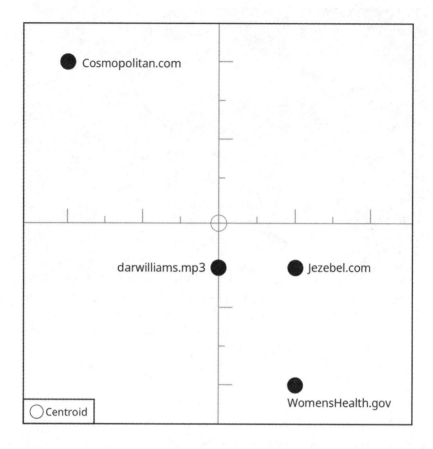

FIGURE 2.8. The centroid of (0, 0) suggests a diagrammatic stability that defines 'woman.'

politically target you on account of your preceding data trail. And now, a subsequent visit to LetsMove.gov to find out more suggests to the U.S. government that its campaign is effective in communicating to 'mothers.'

In the unrelenting ebb and flow of these data streams, the primary cybernetic instruction, then, is to constantly find a center—a clustered density of datafied meaning that supplies a cybernetic machine its temporal definition. For Reza, 'Santa' wears red and has a red-and-white hat.

For Quantcast, 'woman' might hypothetically contain four elements: WomensHealth.gov, Jezebel.com, Cosmopolitan.com, and MP3s of singer-songwriter Dar Williams.

In data-mining speak, this average that defines 'woman' is a centroid. For purposes of this example, this centroid is the point on a 2-D graph that establishes the statistical mean of each measurable type.[84] In the first instance, the idea of 'woman' may unsurprisingly find its normative center in the exact middle of a graph ($x = 0$, $y = 0$; figure 2.8). Like a Mercator Projection map, this empowered perspective has perfect staticity—cybernetically continuing, if all things remain equal, without need for alteration. Its stability will sustain forever: if you go to WomensHealth.gov, Jezebel.com, and Cosmopolitan.com and download Dar Williams MP3s, you are a 'woman.' If you don't, you aren't.

On the basis of these 'womanly' inputs, the average 'woman' would look very, very white. But let's say a bunch of 'women' started visiting different sites such as queer of color blog BlackGirlDangerous.com, went to Chinese search portal Baidu.com, searched for terms like "Nairobi, Kenya weather," and downloaded Persian singer Delkash's music (figure 2.9). The new average for 'woman' would look a bit different. The resulting centroid defining 'woman' moves to the whims of 'women,' serving as a temporary, statistical anchor leveraged to analyze consumer behavior.

In this case, the identity of 'woman' hasn't changed because white women gave up some of their hegemonic dominance in their 'gender' formation. It's merely that 'women' started visiting different sites in statistically significant numbers. And with the accumulation of more queries and sites, the statistical identity of 'woman' will slowly float away from (0, 0) and reattach to each new, ensuing centroid.

In this type of algorithmic regulation, there is no explicit struggle over the discursive soul of 'woman.' Exclusion is barely felt, if at all, and the racial and class distinctions that historically separate people within a gender identity can exist only insofar as the resulting 'gender' model includes statistically significant data to prove it. Inclusion therefore

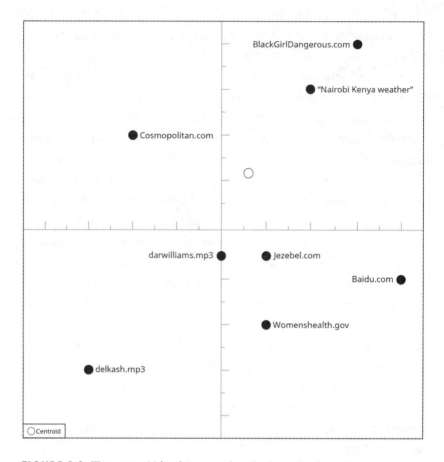

FIGURE 2.9. The centroid (2, 1) moves after the introduction of new inputs.

becomes the elementary axiom, since a company like Quantcast cares very little if the key elements of its model of 'woman' are consistent with what cultural gatekeepers may define as authentically woman.

If we're always one step behind algorithmic classification, then the idea of who 'women' are is akin to a simple trend meter. But unlike one of the central theorists for this chapter, Judith Butler, who looks to parody and drag to destabilize hegemonic truth of identity and thus to establish a radical tactic for liberatory politics, variance in 'women,' if performed en masse by 'women,' quickly becomes 'woman.'[85] In other words, any collective action performed according to identity is territorialized by Quantcast's cybernetic feedback loop before constituents of that identity even have the chance to realize those performances' consequences.

Instead of abiding by a hard-coded fixity, the category of 'woman' quietly changes, strategically locating new key elements for its 'gender' while abandoning those that are ineffective. These relentlessly recalibrating containers are how we are measured, talked about, and represented on the fly. Over time, then, we do not typically hold onto an algorithmic identity, cultivating it through practice and conflict in sociological terms best laid out by Manuel Castells.[86] Rather, it is algorithmic knowledge that temporarily incorporates us within its models, making our datafied life useful for the various neoliberal inclinations of marketers and governments.

'Gender' is first and foremost a cybernetic system, not a gendered politics. The emergence of novel key elements in 'gender' reifies the idea of 'gender' while simultaneously repurposing the category for something new. Any ensuing cultural politics that may attempt a 'gendered' critique are unable to grasp at a firm identity of 'woman' because it doesn't exist. It is a fleeting historical artifact with neither longitudinal scope nor agents empowered in its stability. As new inputs come in, 'gender' recalibrates its centroid, finding better key elements that better classify new data, which provides a better fit to newly redefine 'woman.'

However, much like the NSA's 'terrorist' becomes terrorist, from chapter 1, 'gender' eventually becomes gender. What 'woman' is leaks its discursive meaning across the quotation-marked gap into the idea of woman itself—similar also to how the 'flu' influences how the state and companies think of the flu. And a surge in 'women' visiting Cosmopolitan.com will suggest to *Cosmopolitan*'s editors that their new, women-focused content is successfully reaching its intended audience. But most importantly, 'women' will serve as the temporary notion of womanhood for anyone who wishes to target women online. No matter how wrong a measurable type may be, there exists a baseline, statistical confidence rating that eagerly facilitates the tirelessly optimistic belief that 'women' are women.

Measurable types are useful because they are tolerant. Those who employ them trust that meaning will arise from flows of data, not in spite of those flows. And since there is an assumed dynamism within these flows, we can interpret the data-driven, discursive flexibility of the measurable type as metaphorical coil springs in a vehicle suspension. While structurally malleable and thus practically able to withstand difference, a truck's shocks leave the vehicle intact and relatively undisturbed (figure 2.10). Or, in the terms of soft biopolitics, the policy maintains even while the categories that deliver it change.

These measurable-type cybernetic systems constantly move the goalposts of what membership in a category means, a control without control that articulates a new relationship to biopower. They define from a distance but assess us with an incredible intimacy. As Quantcast's extensive data coffers, for example, may order us from afar, the data that Quantcast surveils is a point-to-point, hourly coffee date that connects us, and our innermost selves, to an apparatus of control. While this type of algorithmic processing of our data might not know us as us and on our terms, these systems more pertinently, and perilously, learn who we are and might become on theirs.

This kind of programmed, constraining vision structures what sociologist Gabriel Tarde described in the late nineteenth century as an "elastic milieu." More specifically, as philosopher Mauricio Lazzarato cites Tarde, "in the public, invention and imitation are disseminated in a manner which is 'almost instantaneous, like the propagation of a wave in a perfectly elastic milieu,' thanks to technologies that make possible the action at a distance of one mind on another."[87] These thanked technologies bring our datafied interactions into increasingly close proximity to one another, connected together by surveillant assemblages and the insatiable appetites of big-data research and analytics.

Lazzarato's "invention," and subsequent "imitation," of social life transforms into the creation, and subsequent modulation, of social

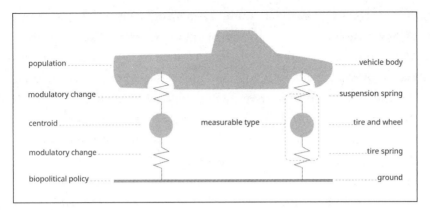

FIGURE 2.10. A diagram connecting the conceptual diagram of soft biopolitics with the mechanical structure of a truck's vehicle suspension.

facts. Thinking through the concept of the measurable type, this social life modulates according to the soft-biopolitical dynamism of 'gender,' 'flu,' or even 'Santa Claus.' When we are connected to others in ways neither voluntary, known, nor able to be managed by ourselves, this constantly adjusting social world becomes a production that can never truly square with our own, individual perspectives. Like a scorned lover, it is both intimate and distant at the same time.

The inability to square the modulatory flexibility of our algorithmic identities with our own nonalgorithmic identities recalls philosopher Walter Benjamin's concept of the aura. For Benjamin, an aura can be viewed as "the unique phenomenon of a distance, however close it may be."[88] "Those mountains," *over there*, oblige a sense of distance that avoids a precise, tangible quality. They are too far away to permanently connect to a certain history, to a certain point. They emanate meaning rather than define it. And any attempt to reproduce that mountain will necessarily lose its essence.

Similarly, any imitation of invention, or modulation of social life, embeds a comparable deletion of distance. Benjamin presciently described what politically happens when objects lose their aura in reproduction, a move he conveniently, for us, finds evident in the "increasing importance of statistics," in which "the adjustment of reality to the masses and of the masses to reality is a process of unlimited scope."[89] And in a world of constant readjustment, this mass control finds theoretical resemblance in what sociologist Zeynep Tufekci describes as "engineering the public." Blessed with a bounty of individual-level data and a capacity to see that data on an immense, big-data-level scale, we encounter what Tufekci then defines as "computational politics" that engineers the range of possibilities available to our political world according to distanced, big-data interpretations of our intimate, datafied lives.[90]

And just like with the distant reading of literary scholar Franco Moretti, from chapter 1, the space between us and a text produces an original, emergent epistemological perspective. Our experience with measurable types parallels this detached-but-intimate thinking—but never intersects it. The distance of measurable-type analysis isn't based in far-off physicality or hazy imprecision. Rather, measurable types are a unique phenomenon in cultural analysis because they can be defined at a particular moment. While distant in their conceptual proximity, they rebuff their auras with an immediate empiricism. 'Rich, white women' actually means something that is locatable and identifiable, if only for a fleeting, between-CPU-cycles millisecond.

But with the emblematic distance implicit in opacity and temporality, our individual ability to react to these algorithmic knowledges—to locate ourselves as a subject and make an enunciated claim based on that subject position ("I am a white man, and I say x")—is rendered functionally useless ("I am a 'white' 'man' at this very specific moment, and I say x, even though what 'white' and 'man' may mean tomorrow is different from what it meant today"). This separation between life and algorithmic life is not a redefinition of the metaphysical division between the real and not real. Algorithmic interpretations are just as real as our identities are, and our identities are just as constructed as their algorithmic counterparts are. Instead, it's an acceptance of the fact that cybernetic algorithmic identifications locate us in novel subject positions that we can never be too sure of.

CONCLUSION

In 2008, former *Wired* editor Chris Anderson wrote an article announc-
ing the "end of theory." In this ode to big data, Anderson proposed that
with an *n* = *all* world, theory as we know it would be obsolete. If you
have access to "all," he explained, there's no need to hypothesize what
"all" means. While the argument was lambasted for its unrepentant
techno-utopianism, Anderson did manage to introduce readers to an
insightful quotation from British statistician George E. P. Box: "all models are wrong, but some are useful."[91]

Once we accept all models' functional imperfection, we start to see
how the second half of Box's comment is actually the most significant.
What is useful in a model is what's empowered. Or what Google or
Quantcast decides is useful is what becomes true. Which algorithmic
model is implemented, regardless of its faults, determines what big data
"says" and how populations are then defined. The totality of Anderson's
end of theory is distilled into an actual algorithmic output.

It is this universality of wrongness—coupled with this particularity
of usefulness—that makes algorithmic models so powerful. Like gen-
eralizations themselves, the knowledges that come from algorithmic
work are viewed, even with explicit error percentages, as more or less
true. It's here that a comment like "men are *so* boring, except you, Gene!"
meets the claim that *userX* is 92 percent confidently 'man.' In both cases,
we hold onto an essence, a sense of categorical authenticity that ema-
nates outward because, without it, membership in that group would
appear to mean nothing.

But unlike masculinity, the measurable type of 'man' truly holds
onto nothingness, tying its informational value to the aimless fluidity
of our datafied behavior. An algorithmic agent captures data, assigns
it 'man' meaning, and calibrates its generalization accordingly. It then
looks to capture, assign, and recalibrate even more. In a way, making
knowledge and identity like this is liberating. It temporarily removes
the shackles placed on conventional discourse. But it also reframes

knowledge in ways that we're not fully cognizant of or, I wager, comfortable with.

By reframing knowledge creation as an algorithmic phenomenon, one in which "models are wrong" but still employed, we see the swindle of big data's theoryless objectivity. What is useful is what is decided to be useful. Use isn't contingent on anything outside the model's authors' intentions or haphazard creations. The "end of theory" means that if Quantcast wants to make a profit, who cares about who a 'woman' really is so long as that person buys like a 'woman'? The programmers who made *Wii Sports* know that your age doesn't change day by day, but the game's own version of 'age' bends time to fulfill its entertainment function.

Google Flu Trends, despite its failings, might embody Anderson's repurposed mantra best, in that use comes full circle. The 'flu' wasn't the flu at all, and in the majority of instances, Google Flu Trends was dead wrong. Did that immediately stop Google? Not at all, because the logic of big data is on the side of neither truth nor empirical, real-world accuracy. Rather, $n = all$, and the use of measurable types to produce meaning, is constantly "in beta" and valued according to this empowered use. With enough data, correlation, and modulation, Google's 'flu' might still be wrong but increasingly useful at the same time. It's this finger-crossed hope that grounds algorithmic knowledge on an engineering-based telos toward 'truth.'

The control in this chapter is not a control that guides you against some presumed, autonomous will. Instead, it's a control that frames your world. It conditions the possibilities available for you to live your life as a user—as well as a member of a category. With measurable types, knowledge and categories lose their politics and their history. They lose their *there there* because without a stable sense of identity, the modulatory, temporal conduits of meaning that we inhabit, and that describe us, become facile and immune to critique. Who we algorithmically are is not an intelligible list of adjectives but a mishmash of patterns that, at the moment, is good enough for Google, Quantcast, and the U.S. government. They're useful for them but ultimately meaningless for us.

Accordingly, 'swinging,' from chapter 1, is simply a categorical place-holder sold to companies that want to communicate with 'swingers.' Citing sociologist Kai Eriksson, for the 'swinger,' there is no "major confrontation between privileged institutions or principles, but rather . . . an endless struggle and a transformation within [what Foucault calls] 'the multiplicity of force relations . . . which constitute their own organization.'"[92] These relations are "incessantly reorganizing"; they make connections and build things without us fully realizing they're there. Quite vanillaly, 'swinging' isn't about switching sexual partners. It's just about, *ugh*, being discursively ordered.

And with this incessantly reorganizing discourse, there is no stability in who we are. 'You' is a collection of different measurable-typed pots of meaning, and when these pots change, 'you' transforms in kind. Neither 'you' nor these pots hold permanency, as each pot is recast every time new data gets poured in. Any claim that a pot is 'yours' is upended by the fact that the pot is no longer what it was. It has changed.

SUBJECTIVITY

Who Do They Think You Are?

Stupid sound and screaming
with one voice we leave out everything

—Black Eyes, "Letter to Raoul Peck"

The RSVP link for Julian Assange's 2014 book-launch party in New York City was posted on the Facebook page of Manhattan art gallery Baby-castles. Although it was met with skeptical comments such as "Is this supposed to be white irony Or this Actually happening?" and "Is this real?," the guest list filled up weeks before the event.[1] Assange, famed for founding WikiLeaks and defamed by sexual assault charges in Sweden, was in de facto detention in the Ecuadorian embassy in London. But, thanks to broadband video chat, his face was temporarily freed and beamed onto the gallery's walls for a conversation with those guests who believed enough in the event to RSVP.[2]

During the party, a discussion sparked by Assange's book, *When Google Met WikiLeaks*, highlighted the striking similarity between the mission statements of Google and the U.S.'s National Security Agency. Google takes the world's information and makes it "useful."[3] The NSA vacuums up the world's data so as to "gain a decision advantage for the Nation and our allies under all circumstances."[4] The former uses data for knowledge, order, and advertising. The latter uses data for knowledge, order, and state power.

Regardless of the state/capital distinction, the endless production of data about our lives means that there will always be some piece of us to be pooled, stored, sorted, indexed, and exploited. The knowledge-producing challenge found in these two bodies' missions is to take the seemingly indiscriminate world of search queries, social network connections, and GPS locations and make it meaningful. The results, when cast into categories, are the measurable types of the world. And our resulting algorithmic identities—of us as 'terrorist' or 'swinger' and whether we like 'sports' or not—form what philosopher Judith Butler calls the "field of enabling constraints" that constitute users as actors and subsequently regulate who we are and who we can be online.[5]

These constraints on our algorithmic identities position us within a unique kind of subject relation, one that both Google and the NSA exemplify when they make our data useful according to each institution's profiling needs. This subject relation begins with what artist Mary Flanagan describes as a "combined subject position," in which virtual systems allow for a "multiple positioning of the user" that pairs a user's corporeal body with her avatar's digital body.[6] As our algorithmic identities incorporate an almost endless combination of these different positionalities—via Google, the NSA, and many more agents—I want to single out a relational logic within this combined position: one that discursively locates and relocates us according to patterned, associative interpretations of our data.

In these associative terms, we are not made subject but, referencing philosopher Rosi Braidotti, made "as if" subject.[7] To tease an example to come, a user is not a citizen of the U.S., but a user is "as if" a U.S. 'citizen' on the basis of the NSA's algorithmic interpretation of her data. In this "as if" relation, we are defined according to digital theorist Seb Franklin's understanding of "control as episteme" from chapter 2, a "wholesale reconceptualization of the human and of social interaction . . . to both model and direct the functional entirety of such forms of life."[8] For the NSA, these reconceptualized constraints were largely fashioned in secret, hidden behind an opaque suite of classified documents, practices, and technologies.

That was until May 2013. In the beginning of that summer, Edward Snowden told his supervisors in Hawaii that he had epilepsy and would need to take medical leave. With four laptops in tow, the NSA contractor quietly landed in Hong Kong. In the weeks that followed, Snowden leaked to journalists hundreds of thousands of classified documents regarding the U.S. government's global surveillance and data-mining programs.

These materials revealed the top-secret specifics of the NSA's "collect it all" approach, aimed to "gain a decision advantage for the Nation and our allies under all circumstances." An intergovernmental surveillant assemblage recorded and processed billions of people's data and personal details.[9] Metadata from our cell-phone conversations, lists of our Bing search queries, our Facebook account information, our instant messages on GChat, even screenshots of our video conferences on Yahoo!—nearly all of it was blindly recorded and algorithmically catalogued within U.S. government databases. The NSA's surveillance program collected the "whole haystack" so that, citing then–NSA director General Keith Alexander, "whatever it is you want, you [can] go searching for it."[10] The ensuing debate over surveillance, privacy, and the dynamics therein took hold of global public discourse for years.

As we learned from these Snowden-leaked NSA classified documents, the most ordinary of datafied events can determine how we are situated within the NSA's rubrics of identification. In an interview in Russia with NBC's Brian Williams, Edward Snowden described how an NSA analyst might use supposedly inconsequential data pieces to construct an idea of who you are as a user, thus adding yet another condition to your combined subject position:

WILLIAMS: Did anyone [at the NSA] know or care that I Googled the final score of the Rangers-Canadiens game last night because I was traveling here?

SNOWDEN: You might say, does anybody really care that I'm looking up the score for the Rangers game? Well, a government or a hacker or some other nefarious individual would say yes, they're very interested in that, because that tells a lot about you. First off, it tells you probably speak English. It says you're probably an American, you're interested in this sport. And they might know what your habits are. Where were you in the world when you checked the score? Did you check it when you travel, or did you check it when you're just at home?

They'd be able to tell something called your pattern of life: when are you doing these kind of activities? When do you wake up? When do you go to sleep? What other phones are around you when you wake up and go to sleep? Are you with someone who's not your wife? Are you doing something? Are you someplace you shouldn't be? According to the government—which is arbitrary, you know. Are you engaged in any kind of activities that we disapprove of, even if they aren't technically illegal? And all these things can raise your level of scrutiny, even if it seems entirely innocent to you, even if you have nothing to hide, even if you are doing nothing wrong. These activities can be misconstrued, misinterpreted, and used to harm you as an individual even without the government having any intent to do you wrong. The problem is that the capabilities themselves are unregulated, uncontrolled, and dangerous.

WILLIAMS: All because I Googled "Rangers-Canadiens final score"?

SNOWDEN: Exactly.[11]

A Googled sports score might serve as the datafied preamble that goes on to tell the story of your 'nationality' or even 'marital status.' The NSA makes 'you,' and infers much about 'you,' according to these tiny, apparently useless fragments of data.[12] A sports game here and your phone's GPS location there likely mean nothing at all. But examined together, and with an algorithmic eye for patterns, this data might come to mean everything.

The Snowden leaks alerted the world to the vast scope of the NSA's ubiquitous state surveillance. And in doing so, they cast into doubt the legality of its spying. To "collect it all" necessarily meant NSA surveillance would collect U.S. citizens' data, and the NSA's inescapable approach to surveillance fundamentally questioned the tried-and-true notions of how the nation-state historically allocated citizenship. Pre-

viously, one was formally viewed as a citizen according to jus sanguinis or jus soli.[13] According to jus sanguinis, to be a legitimate part of a
national body politic meant one's parents were citizens. According to
jus soli, to be a legitimate part of a national body politic meant one was
born within the borders of that nation-state.

These Latin-named poles of formal state belonging identify the
highly politicized conferral of what political theorist Hannah Arendt
calls "the right to have rights."[14] But absent on the Internet was an identifiable individual with blood or birth certificate, added to the fact that
the NSA wasn't really spying on discrete individuals—it was spying on
everything and anything it could. So how could the NSA know exactly
who was and was not a U.S. citizen? Or more specifically, what is the
subject relation between U.S. citizens and the state online? Certainly,
it's near impossible to reproduce jus sanguinis or jus soli on the Internet. We don't surf the web with a passport or identity card. Our IP
addresses can change every time we log on. And what would happen if
both a U.S. citizen and a foreigner were to simultaneously use the same
computer?

In response, the NSA legally maneuvered around this political-
technological impasse by etching out a new algorithmic identification
that serves as the introductory example of this chapter. Instead of limiting the scope of state surveillance, the U.S. intelligence community created an entirely new conception of citizen and thus actively reframed
how we can think of ourselves, as users, as subject to state power online.
So just as Google made individual names into 'celebrities' or Quantcast made profiles into 'women,' the NSA made users into 'citizens' by
implementing a data-based assessment that assigned 'foreignness' (and,
in turn, 'citizenship') to targeted Internet traffic, authorizing "legal" surveillance if a targeted data subject was deemed to be at least "51 percent
foreigner."[15]

This mode of citizenship is what I have previously called *jus algoritmi*.[16] Jus algoritmi is a formal citizenship that, unlike its soli and
sanguinis counterparts, is not theorized as ordained and stable.[17] It's a

temporal, informationalized citizenship that is constantly reevaluated according to users' datafied behavior.

Accordingly, jus algoritmi serves as a useful model to understand the nascent potentialities found in what I later define as a datafied subject relation. One day a user might be a 'citizen' of the United States. Another day that user might be a 'foreigner.' Jus algoritmi 'citizenship' is a legally enshrined categorical assessment based on an algorithmic interpretation of one's data and nothing else—not one's lineage, not one's birth certificate, and not one's passport. To the NSA, 'citizenship' is something that can't be proved once and for all. It can only be continuously performed for these algorithmic arbiters of 'citizenship.'

The job of this chapter is to outline the problems, possibilities, and theoretical issues that arise when we are made subject (or made 'citizen') according to relations of data and only data. Importantly, this chapter does not attempt to think about subject relations outside of data. The datafied subject relations of our algorithmic identities are meant to be understood as an "add-on," in web-browser speak, to the already-theorized subject interfaces we have with the world. Or the relation in jus algoritmi acts as a layer atop our jus sanguinis and jus soli state belonging. It serves as just another stratum within Flanagan's "combined subject position."

The purpose of this add-on is twofold. First, I do not wish to theorize *the* datafied subject but rather a datafied subject relation in order to identify a larger logic, returning to what anthropologist Tom Boellstorff calls "platform-agnostic theory," "that make[s] claims about patterns and dynamics beyond the case study and the individual field site" of algorithmic classification.[18] The datafied subject relations that arise from our algorithmic identities construct a general frame through which we can analyze how algorithmic processing constrains or facilitates datafied life.

Second, I want to identify how our algorithmic identities may not perfectly align with the lived experiences we have in a data world, an unspoken misalignment that I loosely term the else. As we'll read below, contemporary theories of subjectification often focus on a direct, power-person relationship that engages a human reflexivity requiring self-recognition. But in the case of the NSA's 'citizenship,' these datafied subject relations are distinct in how they position us from afar—and how we respond to them—and thus require a distinct analytical mode to understand their operation.

In the following pages, we'll explore how language is algorithmically transcoded, in the example of Google Translate, which produces a 'language' that doesn't perfectly mirror our own. We'll look at how who we 'match' with on the dating site OkCupid is not necessarily a faithful interpretation of who we really might romantically click with. But we'll begin with how the U.S.'s jus algoritmi 'citizenship' and 'foreignness' unevenly sit atop our offline citizenships and foreignness, producing a subject relation unique to its nondatafied form. More succinctly, we'll see how a user can be a 'citizen' and a foreigner, or a 'foreigner' and a citizen—at the same time.

ALGORITHMIC 'CITIZENSHIP'

The NSA's 'citizenship' is an algorithmic reconceptualization of Hannah Arendt's "the right to have rights" in the online world. And that original "right" is parceled out if, and only if, a user's data speaks jus algoritmi citizenese. That is, even if a user is a U.S. citizen—and even if she buys a new computer, installs a new router, diligently washes her hands before she logs on, and tapes her passport to her monitor and birth certificates to her keyboard—that same user must still prove her citizenship to the NSA's algorithms and/or analysts.[19] We are all 'foreigner' until proven 'citizen,' or in the words of Attorney General Eric Holder in the 2009 memo "NSA FAA Minimization Procedures A,"

In the absence of specific information regarding whether a target is a U.S. person, a person reasonably believed to be located outside the U.S. or *whose location is not known* will be presumed to be a non-U.S. person unless such person can be positively identified as a U.S. person, or the nature of circumstances of the person's communications give rise to a reasonable belief that such person is a U.S. person.[20]

Unlike the legalistic cliché of innocent until proven guilty, the rights guaranteed by the U.S. Constitution—the formal advantages to being a citizen-subject—are activated online only if a user behaves according to the NSA's established template of datafied associations. Jus algoritmi relies on a provisional 'citizenship,' a modulatory and unstable assignment of state belonging, in which an NSA target is 'foreign' if there is at least "51% confidence" in her "foreignness."[21] And the NSA calculates "foreignness" according to various unconventional declarations of national belonging (figure 3.1): communications with an "account/address/identifier reasonably believed by the U.S. Intelligence Community to be used by an individual associated with a foreign power or foreign territory"; presence on the "'buddy list' or address book" of someone "reasonably believed" to be "associated with a foreign power or foreign territory"; metadata records "acquired by lawful means" that reveal an individual to be "associated with a foreign power or foreign territory"; and "Internet Protocol ranges and/or specific electronic identifiers or signatures (e.g., specific types of cryptology or steganography)" that are associated with foreign people.[22]

Even more incredibly, other documents leaked to Brazilian paper *Jornal O Globo* showed that the language used in emails and phone conversations (read: everything but English) also serves as a variable that produces "foreignness."[23] Indeed, being "buddies" with a tech-savvy, Portuguese-speaking Brazilian with whom you communicate over encrypted instant messaging will likely make you a 'foreigner.'

Online, our data is what articulates our relationship to the state, precisely because it is the most procurable and thus easiest way for the NSA to represent its surveilled population. This distinction founds the origin difference of what I refer to as the datafied subject relations of our algo-

b. With respect to Internet communications:

- Information indicates that the electronic communications account/address/identifier has been used to communicate directly with an electronic communications account/address/identifier reasonably believed by the U.S. Intelligence Community to be used by an individual associated with a foreign power or foreign territory;

- Information indicates that a user of the electronic communications account/address/identifier has communicated directly with an individual reasonably believed to be associated with a foreign power or foreign territory;

- Information indicates that the electronic communications account/address/identifier is included in the "buddy list" or address book of an electronic communications account/address/identifier reasonably believed by the U.S. Intelligence Community to be used by an individual associated with a foreign power or foreign territory;

- Information indicates that the electronic communications account/address/identifier has been transmitted during a telephone call or other communication with an individual reasonably believed by the U.S. Intelligence Community to be associated with a foreign power or foreign territory;

- Public Internet postings match the electronic communications account/address/identifier to an individual reasonably believed by the U.S. Intelligence Community to be associated with a foreign power or foreign territory;

- Information contained in various NSA-maintained knowledge databases of foreign intelligence information acquired by any lawful means, such as electronic surveillance, physical search, the use of a pen register or trap and trace device, or other information, reveals that electronic communications account/address/identifier has been previously used by an individual associated with a foreign power or foreign territory;

- Information made available to NSA analysts as a result of processing metadata records acquired by any lawful means, such as electronic surveillance, physical search, or the use of a pen register or trap and trace device, or other information, reveals that the electronic communications account/address/identifier is used by an individual associated with a foreign power or foreign territory; or

- Information indicates that Internet Protocol ranges and/or specific electronic identifiers or signatures (e.g., specific types of cryptology or steganography) are used almost exclusively by individuals associated with a foreign power or foreign territory, or are extensively used by individuals associated with a foreign power or foreign territory.

FIGURE 3.1. An image from the leaked 2009 "NSA FAA Minimization Procedures A" document shows eight different ways that an Internet user's communications might be seen as 'foreign.' Source: Eric Holder, "Exhibit A: Procedures Used by the National Security Agency for Targeting Non–United States Persons Reasonably Believed to Be Located Outside the United States to Acquire Foreign Intelligence Information Pursuant to Section 702 of the Foreign Intelligence Surveillance Act of 1978, as Amended," 2009, 5–6, www.aclu.org.

rithmic identities, wherein the lack of a stable, citizenship-identifying core (like a body or a name) means the NSA constructs a user's "right to have rights" through an interpretation of that user's arrayed data trail. Each user's designation of state belonging is exclusive to the information produced through her datafied behavior.

Of course, our worlds have always been made through registers beyond primary thought or self-identity, a point well made by philosopher Gilles Deleuze and his revisionist reading of David Hume's empiricism.[24] Interpreting Hume as a philosopher of associations, Deleuze understands subjectivity and experience itself as conjunctive: both are theorized within a co-occurrence between subject and object, self and other. This permeating subjectivity finds consonance within a larger antihumanist shift in contemporary feminist theory around what some scholars have termed "new materialisms."[25]

And in the practice of jus algoritmi, we see state power explicitly interfacing with elements outside the liberal confines of an individual, organic self, an extracurricular subject relation made familiar for us by the work of feminist theorist Donna Haraway. Haraway's technologically augmented self, the cyborg, rejects traditional ontological distinctions between the natural and artificial and thus invites us to consider a subjectivity that extends into the nonhuman world.[26] Writing against the naturalized essentialism built into categories like woman, Haraway posits a humanity that is altered, but not disfigured, when that naturality is perturbed—like when a cell phone allows social interaction beyond one's natural capacity. Ultimately, we are ourselves plus the technology we make and use, a refounding of our status of self (Haraway writes that the cyborg is "resolutely committed to partiality, irony, intimacy and perversity") as well as a revaluation of our actions as routed through technology (she continues, "our machines are disturbingly lively, and we ourselves frighteningly inert").[27]

Literary critic N. Katherine Hayles's analysis of the posthuman further distances subjectivity from an idealized, contained naturality. For Hayles, posthumanism augments these techno-infused subject relations beyond the material body and its accompanying machines to also include information, a coproduction among who we are, our capacity to think, what machines do, and their capacity to process.[28] This body/technology/informational "amalgam," in her words, is a "collection of heterogeneous components, a material-informational entity whose boundaries undergo continuous construction and reconstruction."[29]

We encounter Hayles's amalgam in the perpetual assessment of our data for jus algoritmi interpretations of 'citizenship.' And we similarly encounter this informational assessment in sociologist Alondra Nelson's work on state interpretations of DNA, anthropologist Kim Tallbear's research on tribal interpretations of blood quantum, and sociologist Clara Rodriguez's writing on the U.S. Census and hegemonic interpretations of ethnicity.[30] As cyborg/posthuman selves, both of which refuse an overly simplistic, individual-state relationship to power, who we are in relation to the state is clearly much more than an individual body gripping a passport.

And quite plainly, the idea of citizenship itself must always return back to how states read their own subjects in uneven ways. Many individuals are formally guaranteed citizenship by certified state documents but fail to enjoy inclusive practice of those rights. For instance, historian Mae Ngai argues that Asian immigrants to the U.S. are "impossible subjects," who even after naturalization as citizens are not treated as full citizens due to their migratory and racial identity.[31] Or we can look to scholar Edlie Wong, who highlights the "fictions of citizenship" that reasserted whiteness as the default racial norm of citizenship in the post-Reconstruction U.S.[32]

Eventually, we arrive at the work of philosopher Rosi Braidotti, whose concept of the "nomad" might serve as the most apropos way to theoretically merge the amalgamed unnaturality of the posthuman/cyborg with the modulating algorithmic identifications exemplified in jus algoritmi. As a theorized subject, the nomad spurns life in the center, living instead in the joinders of the pastiche and interstitial. This nomad is fully relational, intersecting our social and objective associations with our body/

technology/data. Braidotti's work, by refusing to center a concept of subjectivity on one's body, unique name, and even individuality, recruits Deleuze and psychotherapist Félix Guattari's own theory of nomadism as that which lives outside the state and institutional organization.[33]

In line with Braidotti's nomadic thought, the apparent essentialism of jus sanguinis and jus soli is supplanted by the relational, associative terms of jus algoritmi. For the NSA, a user is never just a 'citizen' but a 'citizen' according to that user's datafied social relationships. Who a user talks to or has on a "buddy list" has productive, associative qualities that determine each Internet user's datafied relation to the U.S. state. Recalling the "as if" production of social reality from chapter 1, Braidotti's nomad follows an "as if" philosophy of association, too: a nomad experiences x "as if" it was y. With an "as if," there is no home, no stability in identity, and thus no ability to inhabit some permanent sanctity of ideal citizenship. Rather, the nomad lives "*as if* some experiences were reminiscent or evocative of others . . . [with an] ability to flow from one set of experiences to another."[34]

It's useful to contextualize Braidotti's nomad as a response to modernist structures of power that employ an essentializing fixity of identity, like woman = x. The "as if" allows subjects to understand each other in a relationship of solidarity void of any dependency on a static, x idea of woman. But without the epistemic stability of x, an "as if" subject relation that requires an "affirmation of fluid boundaries, a practice of the intervals, of the interfaces, and the interstices" is also wholly indicative of the regulatory restraints found in algorithmic processing.[35]

And this is why Braidotti's associative, assemblaged subject relation is both problematic and freeing. A nomad can respond to a fixed frontier (woman = x) with a liberatory move against that frontier ("I declare y!"). But the NSA's interpretation of her as a 'citizen' is similarly itinerant. It changes day to day, dispassionate about who a woman *is* so long as that subject behaves "as if" she was a 'citizen.' Correspondingly, Braidotti's "as if" antiessentialism is liberatory insofar as it liberates itself from rigid structures of essentialism.

Deprived of a localized, stable index endowed with citizenship, jus algoritmi's associative "as if" 'citizenship' is ecologically overdetermined. It connects to the many different things that graze us as we shuffle through datafied life: friends, geographies, modes of communication, and even what language we use. As a formal legal apparatus, jus algoritmi's concern is not the production of "good citizens." Rather, it is a citizenship whose exclusive requirement is to satisfy U.S. constitutional legal precedence while simultaneously maintaining the NSA's "collect it all" approach.

This is how, based on NSA procedures, a search query in Spanish for plane tickets to Milan, Italy, from an IP address in Canada made four years ago on a computer running Linux can potentially affect your 'citizenship' and right to privacy today. Even the person sitting next to you on that flight is bound to you in both a datafied and nondatafied "emphatic proximity" and "intensive interrelationality."[36] Braidotti introduces these two phrases to describe the associative nature of her nomadic subject, but we can also use them to describe the subjective emergence implicit in our "as if" datafied subject relations. You are forever connected to your seatmate, both by the life-changing conversation about soccer and politics you had on the flight and by the database record saying you were in seat 14A and she was in seat 14B.

I need to reiterate the dual potential/problems of this association-based subject relation. While Braidotti writes that her interpretation of the nomadic subject "entails a total dissolution of the notion of a center and consequently of originary sites or authentic identities of *any* kind," the NSA allocates its algorithmic 'citizenship' according to this very same process.[37] While Braidotti's "as if" might facilitate a subjective transition across gendered experiences, for example, the distinct but similar experience of two individuals' lives under patriarchy, the U.S. government might comparably claim you're a 'foreigner' because you have 'foreign' friends. Again, unlike the hypothetical stability of jus sanguinis or jus soli, there's no center to being a 'foreigner,' just a roaming sense of "as if." The formal ability to knowingly relate to a state as a verified, authentic citizen is thrown into disarray.

But with a concept like "emphatic proximity," we can see how shared social relations become inextricable in the process of subject making and, by corollary, the possibility for political action. Associations matter not just in who we are but in how those associations set the terms for what subjectivity is and can be. With both sides of this modeled subject arrangement tangoing with each other "as if" they were something else, our algorithmic lives lack the epistemic solidity of an unmoving self-identity: "I am a woman" or Sojourner Truth's more defiant "Ain't I a woman?"

On both sides, the "as if" rejects these singular statements in favor of an endless daisy chain of associations: I am like a, b, and c, while Google thinks I'm like x, the NSA thinks I'm like y, and data analytics company comScore thinks I'm like z. Yet both a, b, and c and x, y, and z are only meaningful according to others like us. We rely on our friends and accomplices to figure out what a, b, and c mean. And marketing and NSA algorithms rely on networks of dataveilled users to determine what x, y, and z are, too.

I propose that we see our position within this assemblaged algorithmic identity as unsuited for fixity and thus akin to gossip. Scholar San Jeong Cho writes in her work on women's subjectivity in nineteenth-century English literature that "gossip is a vehicle of making what is considered the 'trifling and silly' personal matters in the discourse of official histories meaningful and significant, because gossip secularizes the universalized notion of life by representing the specific ordeal of life and immediate human frailty."[38] Following philosopher Lorraine Code, gossip provides a space for what she calls a "successor epistemology," a "located, situated discourse, subtly informative, yet never stable or fixed."[39]

Devoid of discursive officialism, the "secularization" of social life elevates the "specifics" of who we are into fuller view. In nondatafied worlds, these specifics traditionally get lost in the chaos of mundanity. It's quite difficult to remember what you did every night during the past year and even more difficult to recall with whom you were. But in a world of ubiquitous dataveillance, these experiential specifics are recorded with ease.

To elevate our specifics brings us to a key documentary condition of the Internet, something privacy theorist Daniel Solove details in his theorization of reputation in a dataveilled world: "In the past, people could even escape printed words because most publications would get buried away in the dusty corners of libraries. . . . The Internet, however, makes gossip a permanent reputational stain, one that never fades. It is available around the world, and with Google it can be readily found in less than a second."[40] A similar point is made in the 2010 film *The Social Network*, when Mark Zuckerberg's ex-girlfriend berates him after a late-night round of boorish, sexist blogging: "The Internet's not written in pencil, Mark; it's written in ink."

While the practical permanency of the digital archive has long been called into question by digital scholars like Megan Sapnar Ankerson, this use of ink as metaphor bleeds beyond instances of mere blogging to also include the logging of our datafied associations into a database.[41] Indeed, to return to gossip, people don't just say they saw someone walking down the street. They also make sure to include the detail of with whom they were walking. *What* they were talking about is frequently a moot point, as the topic of conversation may be either unknown or too convoluted to make sense of. Often with *whom* they were talking matters most, as it's the only piece of information available to a mere observer.

It is this appending of character to content that former deputy CIA director Michael Morell valorized in testimony to the Senate Judiciary Committee: "there is quite a bit of content in" this associative network, otherwise known as metadata.[42] For example, my own Gmail email address produces metadata that tells a nuanced story of who I am, the patterns of my social relationships, and the daily schedule I keep—all without considering any of the actual words I type. While my inbox might just look like a motley collection of spam and last-minute student requests/excuses, the data detailing with whom I communicate assembles a descriptive social network that can be algorithmically used to speak volumes about me and my social world.[43]

Indeed, so valuable is this data that, as noted earlier, it is one of the defining features of our jus algoritmi "foreignness" and who deserves a higher "level of scrutiny," to use Snowden's terms. As media theorist Matteo Pasquinelli argues, the current mode of Deleuze's "societies of control" might be termed the "societies of metadata," wherein metadata serves as the "measure of value of social relations" and thus the arbiter of what our algorithmic associations come to mean.[44] This value comes in the form of the NSA's facile assumptions of homophily, in which citizens speak to citizens, foreigners speak to foreigners, and bad seeds speak to bad seeds. We can be "intensely interrelated," but that interrelation is neither patently good nor comforting.

For example, I remember receiving an email immediately after the Snowden revelations in the summer of 2013. It was from a friend of my brother who wanted tips for traveling through southern Europe. He also happened to work as a developer for Tor, the powerful anonymizing proxy service that technologically masks the origin and destination of users' web traffic. And thanks to the Snowden leaks only weeks prior, this friend was made aware that his work with Tor would flag any recipient of his emails as a Kevin Bacon–esque degree away from the "scrutinized."

The email my brother's friend sent to me was a run-of-the-mill introduction and inquiry about good pizza in Rome. But, even though he avoided any serious technological or political discussion in his email, he still knew the influence of this single, associative metadata connection. With an acknowledged "emphatic proximity," there was a candid levity in his default signature: "welcome to the watch list :)."[45]

While the Snowden leaks made the world aware of this aspect of the NSA's extensive data dragnet, the datafied subject relation of jus algoritmi may confuse more traditionalist interpretations of subjectivity.

What happens to subjectivity when we don't necessarily know if we're a 'citizen' or a 'foreigner'? Or what happens when we are algorithmically identified but we don't know exactly how? In the next section, I explore what a subject relation might look like without direct, human reflexivity. And later, I explore how this disjunction might function in terms of what I call the else.

ON ALGORITHMIC INTERPOLATION

The political act of making subject is famously, and rather overreliantly, described in philosopher Louis Althusser's allegory of ideological interpellation. A cop yells, "Hey, you!" and "hails" an individual. Like a frog to a prince, that individual turns into a subject, even before she hears "you," via the ideological apparatuses of the dominant class.[46] But requisite in this communicative diagram is the act of self-recognition—a becoming subject in response to the act of the other. While we may theoretically acknowledge our algorithmic identities, jus algoritmi's black-boxed opacity means we won't immediately encounter the hail of 'citizenship.'

Yet algorithmic identifications like jus algoritmi rarely hail users directly. They instead structure users' conditions of possibilities, be it their access to privacy rights, social relations, or knowledge itself. In this way, the process of making subject is indirect. It is a relation of power more akin to the psychoanalytical framework of theorist Jacques Lacan—which, as it happens, fundamentally influenced Althusser's theory—than to the metaphorical potency of some overly salutational police officer.

In initial theorizations of Lacan's "mirror stage," he proposed that infants become unified individuals upon recognition of themselves as an object in a mirror and thus begin to identify themselves with their own image.[47] Or, as author Curtis White summarizes, "'I' looks into the mirror and says, 'I am that.'"[48] But Lacan soon expanded this stage into a more general interpretation of subjectivity: subject formation also occurs through our encounters with what he calls an "introjection" of language, or the internalization of symbolic identification.[49]

More relevant to this chapter, information scholar Ronald Day broadens introjection's definition to "the mental coding of the subject by cultural forms and social norms, forming unconscious systems of semantic forms and of rules and roles for expression."[50] The process of subjectification may not route through a direct heeding to power. It rather structures and mediates life (from language to culture and to social norms) by constantly retouching our own subjective positioning (of how language, culture, and social norms necessarily change).

For example, we can look to Day's own work on what he calls the "documentary subject." This emergent subject relation positions individuals within a field of documents "about something or someone, some object or some person." "Wanting to know about, in a documentary sense," Day continues, "is wanting to understand something or someone within a context of a system of knowledge."[51] This focus on "aboutness" is helpful on many counts, not least of which is how Day wordplays a connection between Althusser's "interpellation" and the statistical method of "interpolation."[52]

In an interpolative method, new data points are generated using patterns of existing data points (like predicting future behaviors on the basis of an existing data set). An interpolated subject, then, is not identified according to a preexisting, one-to-one relationship of one's self. Rather, that subject is understood in the context of statistical estimation that fills in the holes of existing data with new algorithmic approximation. Like Day's documentary subject, an interpolated subject is only talked *about*, not *to*. Ultimately, this subject can be expressed as a type of composite algorithmic identity: the particularity of one's individual identity is replaced by an aboutness of one's identifications. A documentary or interpolated subject may not necessarily feel the "Hey, you!" hail of a police officer but will sense the accompanying introjection through the flows of language, culture, and social ordering.

The aboutness of Day's documentary subjectivity nicely sashays into an aboutness of Rosi Braidotti's "as if." A suite of documents may situate individuals in terms that define who they are, just as a user's "as if" intensive interrelationalities position her within a suite of antiessential associative networks. The NSA, for example, assesses assemblages of social connections on the Internet, labeling users 'citizens' according to its own, classified system of interpolative knowledge. Here, individuals' actual citizenships need not apply, just as a foreign user might pass unnoticed through an NSA dragnet due to a datafied interrelationality with other 'citizens' that quantitatively fill in the holes to identify her as 'citizen.'

This imprecision of "as if" identification dirties, while also making more empirically loyal, the theoretical polymorphing of Althusser's "clean cut" (the phrase philosopher Mladen Dolar uses to critique the disconnecting move from individual into subject with a simple "Hey, you!") of interpellation.[53] And from within this identificatory messiness, it becomes easier to see why Félix Guattari describes subjectivity as an "ensemble of conditions which render possible the emergence of individual and/or collective instances as self-referential existential Territories, adjacent, or in a delimiting relation, to an alterity that is itself subjective."[54] More pointedly, this imprecision provides a depth of perspective to answer Guattari's own framing question regarding subjectivity: "How can I maintain a relative sense of unicity, despite the diversity of components of subjectivation that pass through me?"[55]

One way to conceive of this ensemble is media theorist Mark Poster's superpanopticon from back in 1990—a year after the World Wide Web was invented and four years before the first online tracking technology (cookies) was devised.[56] Poster argued that digital technology extends the diagrammatic boundaries of philosopher Michel Foucault's panoptic prison, where the networked circuits of our subjectivity escape the conceptual prison walls of traditional discipline and make a break for cyberspace. This superpanoptic subject is a posthuman subject, one "that threatens the stability of our sense of the boundary of the human body in the world. What may be happening is that human beings create computers and then computers create a new species of humans."[57]

While this "new species of human" may have a body, its relations exceed our immediate corporeal interactions and leak into the contemporary postmodern arrangements of deinstitutionalization, decentering, and deindividualization. In this deconstructed milieu, institutions are disassembled, meaning become multiple, and individuals lose their idealized autonomy and authorship of life. Media theorist Mark B. N. Hansen frames a similar subjective setting: "In our interactions with twenty-first-century atmospheric media, we can no longer conceive of ourselves as separate and quasi-autonomous subjects, facing off against distinct media objects; rather, we are ourselves composed as subjects through the operation of a host of multi-scalar processes."[58]

But the messiness of this claim, that we do not "face off against distinct media objects," identifies the conceptual limit of the superpanopticon. It also signals the importance, for me, to align the datafied subject relations of our algorithmic identities with Guattari's "diversity of components of subjectivation." In the early 1990s, Poster was unable to consider how these database discourses might serve as more than just a dispersed dossier of our individual selves. Today, it's quite obvious that a record in a government database has extraordinary effect on an individual's ability to board a plane, pay a tax, get a tax refund, not go to jail, or enter or leave a country.[59] What's less obvious, though, is how the superpanopticon lets us appreciate data's role in subject making as more than a prosthetic accouterment that eventually returns to an individual existing body, name, or U.S. Social Security number.

To theorize beyond the superpanopticon is to transcode our posthuman individuality into data. Or it is to follow the conceptual move from the individual to the "dividual." "We no longer find ourselves dealing with the mass/individual pair. Individuals have become 'dividuals,' and masses, samples, data, markets, or 'banks,'" writes Deleuze in his "Postscript on the Societies of Control."[60] And online, where our individualities are recoded into units of data, our dividualities are the only things available to be counted. As digital theorist Seb Franklin argues, "the dividual is the subject digitized," not only positing an ontology of subject relations functionally distinct from our nondigital lives but founding a productive framework to think of how the specific, lived complexity of one's individuality is divided from within.[61] It is decontextualized, dehistoricized, and thus modular in operation and application.

This form of divided individuality reconceptualizes much of identity into an aggregation of membership in different modulating measurable types. The individual is dislodged from its apogee of identity and thus the index for subjectivity. Without an embodied, always complete and unique identifier to call John, 'John' is an unstable inventory of potential meaning. 'I' get assembled at the whim of my assemblers, an algorithmic calculation of my different, nonspecific dividual selves that eventually come to determine my 'citizenship,' 'celebrity,' and 'gender.' The attending epistemological distance between I and 'I' parallels the subjective distance requisite in Day's aboutness and Braidotti's "as if."

This subjective distance, of one being a 'citizen' while not a citizen, serves as an important distinction that complicates many existing theorizations of algorithmic regulation. For example, in what philosopher Antoinette Rouvroy calls "algorithmic governmentality," algorithmic processing is theorized to produce a preempted, contextually and behaviorally managed world. She writes, "Algorithmic governmentality does not allow for subjectivation processes, and thus for recalcitrance, but rather bypasses and avoids any encounter with human reflexive subjects. Algorithmic governmentality is without subject: it operates with infra-individual data and supra-individual patterns without, at any moment, calling the subject to account for himself."[62]

In this insentient, perfectly attuned algorithmic system, we are preempted by distance. Algorithmic power "does not confront 'subjects' as moral agents (avoiding to question them about their preferences and intentions, about the reasons and motivations of their actions) but attunes their future informational and physical environment according

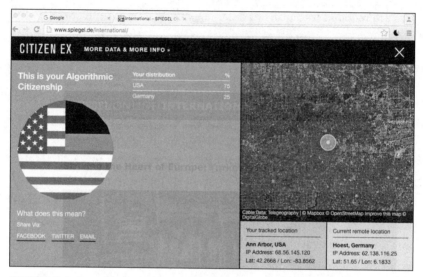

FIGURE 3.2. A screenshot from James Bridle's *Citizen-Ex.*

to the predictions contained in the statistical body."[63] While the empiricism of this irresistible control still remains hypothetical, as in the Zun-Zuneo example of chapter 2, I want to emphasize the yet-completeness of such a theorization. Online we recognize ourselves not necessarily as unique subjects or "moral agents" but as entities who can be reflexive in ways that might not come in the form of direct, bare-knuckled recalcitrance.

In the case of jus algoritmi, we encounter reflexivity in the fact that we know it exists. The datafied subject relation that assigns 'foreigner' and 'citizen' might seem hidden from us as a secret interpretation of our metadata. But the 2013 Snowden leaks alert us to the possibility, and underlying logic, of how this kind of algorithmic 'citizenship' works. Accordingly, we recognize that any interpretation, from state power to metaphysical claims to identity, orders our lives in inconsistent ways. In this formative disconnection, we can feel the space between one's citizenship and one's 'citizenship.'

For instance, upon learning that the NSA valued Internet metadata to ascertain users' 'foreignness,' UK artist James Bridle and others developed a browser add-on called *Citizen-Ex* that, following my earlier work on jus algoritmi's logic, made users aware of NSA surveillance through a "just-in-time," artistic interpretation of their quantitative 'citizenship' (figure 3.2).[64] The fact that one's *Citizen-Ex* 'citizenship' is more than likely distinct from one's formal citizenship alerts us to our reflexivity and thus conditions how we experience the multiplicities of our algorithmic identities. In this case, users do not directly face off with the NSA's subject-making power. But a program like *Citizen-Ex* emphasizes the possibility for subjective response, nevertheless.

"CONTIGO, MANOS E PAIS"

To be reflexive to our jus algoritmi identification requires a knowingness of how the NSA can make our data meaningful. While one might not feel the sway of being identified as 'foreign,' *Citizen-Ex* alerts users to the kinds of valuations the NSA makes about our Internet metadata. But in other algorithmic instances, we feel not a sway but a perturbing inappropriateness—a strangeness that we take as creepy, suspect, or even derogatory in its manifestation.

For example, take a 2014 conversation, recounted by historian Marissa Moorman, between two friends. One spoke only Portuguese, the other only English. Both used Google Translate as their automatic linguistic mediator: "Olá caríssimo amigo, espero que esteja tudo bem contigo, manos e pais. Eu e minha irmã estamos bem. Gostaria de manter contacto com vocês. Abraço forte."[65] What began as a mundane greeting made our English-speaking recipient turn her head after she read Google Translate's rendition: "Hello friend caríssimo, I hope all is well with you niggas and parents. My sister and I are fine. I would like to keep in touch with you. Big hug."[66]

For those who read Portuguese, you might identify two idiosyncratic vagaries. One, "caríssimo," wasn't translated in the English version. The word, which means "very dear" or "dearest" in a friendly context or even "unreasonably expensive" in others, is quite common in Portuguese. Its nontranslation seems slightly off. The more jolting change, Moorman notes, comes in the translation of the word "manos," which means either "brother" or "friend" but also can be a slang word for "gang member" and even, in some cases of rap music, "nigga."

The semantic output of a Google Translate translation is always a bit off. Although in this case, it's downright racist (or, in the parlance of this book, 'racist'). As anyone who has used the service to complete her foreign-language homework knows, one learns not to take Google Translate 100 percent literally. For one, Google Translate Portuguese seems to prefer the formal second-person pronoun of "you." "Do you want an apple?" will be translated into Portuguese as "você quer uma maçã?"[67] The formal "você" takes the place of the more informal "tu."[68] At the outset, Google Translate's tone appears overly ceremonial—a tad too professional. Its underlying politics might seem to be classist and impersonal.

This is principally due to Google Translate's methodology, which relies on already-translated documents for its datafied inputs. As it turns out, states and international organizations are some of the biggest employers of translators who subsequently produce an endless flow of publicly available, multilanguage documents. The United Nations, for example, provides Google a handy translation bounty when it publishes versions of every organizational text in Arabic, Chinese, English, French, Russian, and Spanish. Perhaps even more useful is the cache of the European Union, which translates all documents dating from 1957 into two dozen languages.[69]

It's unsurprising, then, that Google's translations adopt the decorous vocabulary of the state. The tone, word choice, and lack of slang in these documents turn "you" into "você" and lend Portuguese a stringent and courtly quality. A Google Translate that relies almost exclusively on official state or academic documents will sound like a punctilious diplomat, and millions of high school students have turned in technocratic-sounding foreign-language homework assignments because of it.

These are the linguistic politics of Google's algorithm in action. A user of Google Translate participates in a datafied subject relation similar to our algorithmic identities. And after using Google Translate in a conversation like the preceding one, one notices something is strange. Regional dialects and vocabulary are often ignored or normalized. Words like "manos" become racial epithets.

This strangeness happens on the quantitative level. First, we have to think about how computers actually make sense of words. Google prides itself on abandoning the old form of grammatical translation, one in which the translator would tirelessly contemplate a certain word or phrase, agonizing over whether the Portuguese "cinza" means "gray" or "ash" or whether "não faz mal" means "don't worry about it" or "it won't hurt."[70] Google's method for translation, which dates back to the 1940s, is mathematically comparative. It assembles measurable types for each language according to statistical connections between words and phrases, not poetic expertise and the affective renderings of semantic distinction. Google Translate doesn't know English, but it knows 'English.'[71]

Second, Google tellingly translates most everything to 'English.'[72] This imperial "all roads lead to 'English'" methodology skips the language-to-language parallel ('Portuguese' to 'Russian') and instead employs 'English' as its linguistic liaison ('Portuguese' to 'English' to 'Russian'). Google uses the lingua franca of 'English' under our radar. But a sentence translated between 'Portuguese' and 'Russian' doesn't focus on specific English words and their individual, historical meanings. Rather, it follows an unremarkable list of associations between billions of different linguistic examples.

That is, if Google's computers see the word "olá" in a bunch of Portuguese European Union documents in the same place that they see the word "hello" in a bunch of similar English documents, the algorithm learns, with strong confidence, that "olá" means "hello." The same process also works between English's "hello" and Russian's "привет" (privet). Google Translate then converts this linkage into a transitive equation: "olá"[Portuguese] = "hello"[English] = "привет"[Russian]. These statistical associations, calculated at immense speed, close the once-vast foreign-language gap.

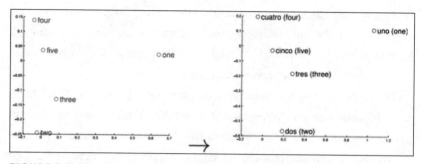

FIGURE 3.3. This graph shows how Google Translate connects different words, in this case the numbers one through five in English and Spanish. Source: Tomas Mikolov, Quoc Le, and Ilya Sutskever, "Exploiting Similarities among Languages for Machine Translation," technical report, arXiv:1309.4168, 2.

But the mathematical relationship between "manos" and "nigga" didn't come from UN or EU documents. There is no pre-2014 Googleable document that publicly connects these two words together. If linguistic translation becomes, like visual designer Doug Bowman's critique of Google from chapter 1, exclusive to the logic of engineering—in which every word or phrase is turned into a contextless logic "problem"—then the circumstances for the translation of "contigo, manos e pais" into "you, niggas and parents" is treated the same as the translation of "two" into "dos" (figure 3.3). The former's output is not the work of a racist programmer.[73] Rather, the phrase simply found statistical commonality in those semantic connections as it compared 'Portuguese' to 'English' using pre-existing data sets and rules.

Quite revealingly, if you Google Translate only "manos e pais" to 'English,' the output is "brothers and parents." It is the prompt of the preceding word, "contigo," that serves as the statistically significant contextual cue for the racial epithet. Somewhere, in some document unavailable to us mere Googlers, there exists a mathematical connection between "contigo manos e pais" and "nigga." As it happens, "contigo manos" (without "e pais") changes to "you niggaz."[74] Even the spelling of the racial epithet is based on frequency and variance within the available data set.

Despite all this racialized and technocratic baggage, Google Translate has become the predominant linguistic window to our foreign-language worlds. For users of Google's Chrome browser, its algorithm offers to translate any web page outside your customized preferred languages. The United Kingdom's National Health Service enlists Google Translate "as an effective alternative way of communicating with non-English speakers."[75] Even the *Hartford Courant* newspaper, in 2012, relied entirely on Google Translate to launch its "Courant en español" Spanish-language portal.[76]

It is Google Translate's dependency on preexisting semantic data that cavalierly calls someone the n-word, a 'racism' based on statistical significance, not malign prejudice. And a similar dependence will also deny a certain word, such as "irregardless," legibility across this language gap if it isn't found in Google's already-translated data sets. This introjection of subject making bluntly demonstrates how Google's algorithmic arbitration of language restates our relations to subjectivity in general. The gap between English and 'English' isn't just epistemological but also subjective.

This language gap runs analogous to the multiple gaps that define the junction between datafied and nondatafied life: the ontological split from bytes to atoms; the epistemological split between 'true' and true; the control split between soft-coded modulation and hard-coded disciplinarity; and the field of study split between mathematics/engineering and sociology/linguistics.[77] But there will always be wiggle room within the partitions. This wiggle room is what I broadly define as the else. This else refers to a general conditional statement in computer programming that follows an "if-then(-else)" logic: if x, then do y, else do z. If user='citizen' then user=citizen. Else is the subjective surplus that maintains the gap between.

The else is the lever that our subjectivity uses to address and account for these inescapable slippages of algorithmic life. It is the way we subjectively react to—and are thus made aware of—the functional differences between a sentence in English and its 'English' translation. This else, or the fact that something "else" is up that we sense or indirectly know about, reifies the contemporary impossibility to perfectly transcode life/control into a digital form. The else is getting an advertisement for baby formula when you're past menopause. The else is an HP computer camera being unable to recognize a black face. And the else is a resolute suspicion of algorithmic systems in general. Overall, the else serves as the procedural moment when human reflexivity enters into this new datafied subject relation.

This else relies on geographer Nigel Thrift's observation that software is an "imperfect medium," ripe for the possibility of Deleuzeian "bad mimesis" and thus with ability to appreciate the creative distinction that exists between English and 'English.'[78] Correspondingly, cultural historian Hillel Schwartz reminds us that "copying is ultimately imperfect, our errors eventually our heirs. The more widespread the act of copying, the greater the likelihood of significant mistranscription."[79] With this establishing distinction between algorithmic and non-, we experience the world on two fronts that cannot be collapsed into one.

'WE' ARE DATA

Google's transcoding of English into 'English' connects Portuguese speakers and English speakers to Google Translate's particular, pattern-based logic of algorithmic processing. Accordingly, we shouldn't overlook the fact that this 'language' arbitrates our social world, expanding past algorithmic identifications of 'you' and 'me' and into algorithmic mediations between 'us' and 'we.'

For example, log into your Facebook account (if you have one, of course) and behold the ragtag cast of characters that populates your News Feed. This ensemble of irate status updates and heavily filtered digital photographs is not a random occurrence, nor is it chosen by you. It's algorithmically curated—a datafied ordering of your friends according to a quantitative matrix of over one hundred thousand variables.[80] In fact, Facebook ranks every last one of your Facebook friends with a numerical appraisal based on things like how often you talk, how recently you became friends, and how many times you visit their profile and comment on their posts.

Who is visible on your Facebook is who is active and datafied as 'close' to you; who is not is someone who is inactive, non-data-producing, and thus 'far.' This "algorithmic visibility," as media researcher Tania Bucher writes, is based on "the assumption that users are not equally connected to their friends. Some friends thus 'count more' than others. The friends that count more are those with whom a user interacts on a frequent basis or on a more 'intimate' level; say by communicating with a friend via 'Chat' rather than on the 'Wall.'"[81] Our friendships become 'friendships,' so while your 'friends' might not help you move, they sure do post a lot of stuff on Facebook.

The associations made from this data frame the temporal and spatial dimensions by which we interact with others. They align our subjective experiences to the rapid cadence of what sociologist Adrian Mackenzie describes as "machine time," which "ruptures habits of communication, perception, and representation" and thus "can enlarge the frame of the now itself."[82] Here, one's 'friendships' cycle from 'far' to 'close' and to 'far' again in a dynamism attuned to the rapidity of algorithmic processing and data collection, not human evaluation of our mutual attachments.

These associations also intersect with what geographers Rob Kitchin and Martin Dodge call "code/space," which "occurs when software and the spatiality of everyday life become mutually constituted, that is, produced through one another."[83] How Facebook configures our 'closest' 'friends' can situate the potentialities for bodies within certain spatial relationships, like when the site alerts you that a 'friend' "is attending an event near you later today." The algorithmically arbitrated associations of your Facebook social network allocate the attention, discourse, and definition of 'friendship' online. Upon connecting you to me using the data that makes 'us,' the enabling constraints of algorithmic assessment must also include self, algorithm, and others.

This datafied 'us' is the empirical bridge between two algorithmically mediated subject positions. In this case, 'friendship' can be easily datafied. But so can your 'enemies.' And so can your 'lovers.' As it happens, these three measurable types also defined how users on the dating website OkCupid quantitatively connected to each other.[84] The "Google of online dating," OkCupid is a tech-friendly, Generation Y dating site that prides itself on using fine-tuned data to algorithmically prune out your relative undesirables and thus emphasize your relative desirables.[85]

OkCupid calculates an algorithmic 'you' alongside your algorithmic 'others' in order to supply a customized window into the pool of online dating. Inputs come from survey questions ("How messy are you?"), answers ("very messy," "average," "very organized"), what your ideal match would answer (using the same answer choices), and how important that is for you ("Irrelevant," "A little important," "Somewhat important," "Very important," and "Mandatory") (figure 3.4). The site's "compatibility calculation" algorithm does the rest.

By processing users' answers to thousands of different survey questions, OkCupid provided users three metrics for each potential mate: 'match,' 'friend,' and 'enemy.' A user you fancy might be 89 percent 'match,' 50 percent 'friend,' and 1 percent 'enemy.' If you answer a few more questions, these temporary percentage indices might change to 87 percent 'match,' 45 percent 'friend,' and 15 percent 'enemy.' *Whoops.* OkCupid's measurable types will always be less than 100 percent because they are probabilistically incomplete. Only the most hopeless romantics among us would ever expect a 100 percent match in real life, and it's rightly mathematically impossible as well.[86]

OkCupid frames its digital meat market through an algorithmic array of potential versions of 'us.' Each 'match' percentage gives rise to a quantitatively specific scheme by which users understand each other in a universalist, data-driven way. By defining the likelihood for love through algorithm, the resulting jointly produced measurable types mean that we can put actual filters on our flirting (it's possible to decline any message from users with whom you are less than an 80 per-

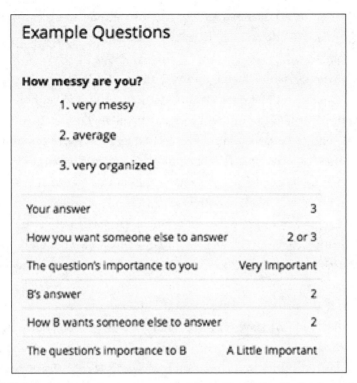

FIGURE 3.4. An example survey question from the OkCupid site shows how the question, answer, and importance of those questions/answers produce quantitative value for subsequent algorithmic processing. Source: OkCupid, "Match Percentages—A Detailed Explanation," https://okcupid.desk.com.

cent 'match') or troll those who are not our algorithmic type ("you are my 95 percent 'enemy'; prepare to die!").[87]

Furthermore, your datafied behavior adds value onto OkCupid's initial survey-based structure. What you do on the site—whose profiles you click on, whom you rate and how you rate them, and more consequentially, how often people value, click, like, message, rate, or ask you out—also plays a significant role in who sees your profile and whose profile you see. Get a high user-like rating, and you'll be much more prominent on the site. Ask out everyone and receive no responses, and you'll fall into dating obscurity. This data-based courtship cares little if your last name is Casanova or your face can launch an excessive number of ships. Your desirability must be translatable into clickable, ratable, 'matchable' data.

Importantly, while 'matchability' defines users' social value on Ok-Cupid, data is not just data. Offline stereotypes that we either negotiate and/or witness (or ignore) every day inevitably translate into what digital scholar Lisa Nakamura has coined as cybertypes that enforce hierarchies of attraction, race, disability, and sexuality online.[88] OkCupid's own internal site analytics have shown that heterosexual black women find lower levels of both messages received and average scores (a median of 2 out of 5, when all other racial groups are close to 3).[89] And surprise, surprise, "whatever it is, white males just get more replies from almost every group," even when controlling for user-rated 'physical attractiveness.'[90]

Theorist Geoffrey Bowker's general claim around our online interactions, that "what we leave traces of is not the way we were, but a tacit negotiation between ourselves and our imagined auditors," easily expands to this larger bounty that constitutes the 'we.'[91] Facebook's News Feed determines how we are made socially available to others on the basis of our datafied proximity, a reading of our traces not as we individually decide them but as we are interpreted to be. Our sexual availability on OkCupid is a function of how our survey and behavioral traces are relationally valued. Membership in measurable types writ large actively produces the enabling constraints on our lives that regulate both us and the idea of 'friendship,' 'sex,' or 'enmity' itself.

But key to this 'we'-based subject relation is our everyday use that undercuts the assumed fidelity and permanence of these variables. We might laugh at 'matching' with someone we would never, ever click with in real life. We might delight in discovering that an offline friend has an unusually high 'enemy' score with us. And we might ignore the fact that a 'match' ranks at 7 percent—a score that OkCupid would sassily tell us means "y'all got issues"—because we find that specific user beautiful, interesting, wicked smart, or compelling beyond algorithmic evaluation. This more empirical manifestation of the else becomes an *"are you serious?"* eye roll that defines many of our datafied subject relations. It reaffirms a sense of collective disbelief in algorithms' certitude.

This kind of 'we'-based subject relation necessarily extends to how we understand resistance, too. Returning to Lisa Nakamura, surveillance is "a signifying system that produces a social body, rather than straightforwardly reflects it."[92] While Nakamura was writing explicitly about the physical, human body, I want us to think through this quotation alongside the Foucauldian biopolitics of chapter 2. Surveillance also produces the *social body* and, by doing so, produces a distinct form of surveillance-based, algorithmic sociability. Users of OkCupid and Facebook are not just profiles but mediated social actors whose relations are made, according to traces of data, in a "just-in-time," on-the-fly algorithmic interpretation.[93]

"Just-in-time" means there's another space and yet another politically productive gap in the progression of subject making. To make a claim about something or to have any position from which to act (or not) requires a pause, like cultural theorist Stuart Hall's arbitrary closure, from chapter 1, or the Turing Machine's staccatoed, sequential processing. For Hall, this closure constructs a theoretical stasis that is present at every imagined moment, a hypothetical suspension to life and discourse that lets us, briefly, make a temporal claim about who we are.

In algorithmic processing, there's an empirical stasis that accompanies this suspension. If we hold our breath, pause, and release, we mimic a digital computer's calculation of a one (inhale), then a zero (exhale), and then a one (inhale). We can envision a temporary halt of discourse's dynamism that enables us to figure out where and who we are. This envisioning offers us the space for reflexivity that might not be apparent in most algorithmic productions.

If we were in constant motion without this pause, we would be impossibly disadvantaged, assailed by a flurry of meaningless indeterminacy: 'citizenforeignermanwomanmanhotnot.' In the pause, we encounter the material temporality of what digital scholar Tung-Hui

Hu describes as the "dead time" "between action and response in everyday life."[94] Yet datafied subject relations are overloaded with various measurable-type meanings. We can't think of "dead time" as a distinct, unified instance. OkCupid's analysis of our dating prospects and Facebook's News Feed output provide us their own, temporal pauses. And each pause operates on its own, temporal logic, a "dead time" of "machine time." Or it's what media theorist Mark B. N. Hansen has referred to as a "host of multi-scalar processes" that become the patchwork terrain from which we identify the space "between action and response in everyday [datafied] life."

THE IMPORTANCE OF BEING SOCIAL

To appreciate the else in these multiscalar processes—to acknowledge the epistemological gaps between an algorithmic identification and one's lived experience with that identification—is to appreciate the multiple ways our datafied subject relations connect to us as users. Google's 'English' might let us recognize its subjective influence in an errant epithet, OkCupid's 'match' gives us reflexive possibility in its quantitative overconfidence, and leaked NSA documents alert us to the legal incompatibility of jus algoritmi with jus sanguinis or jus soli.

But online we are much more than an 'English'-speaking 'citizen' who is a 'match.' We are subject to the more general practice of algorithms making data useful, in which a discordant chorus speaks for our data with different voices, calling us their own versions of our different names. In this way, Google might think you're a 'celebrity,' while Microsoft might infer that you're 'painfully quotidian.'

Who we are online is made from an infinitely material posthuman assemblage. We can be connected, and thus made subject, according to many things and many people. Consequently, a user cannot simply think of herself in terms of the NSA, because that same user could be in datafied contact with the UK's Government Communications Headquarters as well as Pakistan's Inter-Services Intelligence. Added onto this, that user's subject position is produced according to where her phone is, whose phones are nearby, what was the last search term she searched for, who was the last person she texted, who was the next person that person texted, and so on.

Or a user might want to anonymously book a bargain hotel room on Orbitz.com, yet her dividualities have given her away: she is using a new MacBook Air computer with OSX 10.10.5 installed. While this information might seem piecemeal and a bit flashy, it can suggest to Orbitz that she's more 'affluent'[95] and willing to pay higher prices than someone with a PC and an older operating system would.[96] Like someone whispering her class status to Orbitz's CEO when she walks into the room, presto: the prices on her query, without Orbitz knowing her actual net worth, appear a bit higher than they would be for someone else.[97]

Orbitz clearly doesn't know this person as a unique, historied individual, but it knows enough about her dividualities to make an "as if" pricing decision. Existing on data's dividual terms means that the space between what is and what is measured will always remain unbridgeable. Accordingly, that same user could use her friend's OSX computer and—knowing that discriminatory pricing happens on the basis of hardware specs—refrain from purchasing a higher-than-usual plane ticket to Islamabad. But Orbitz could subsequently perceive her restraint (and others') after seeing a mass of OSX users leave its site without purchasing anything and decrease the variable weight of OSX in its pricing equation.

In this case, the else is the productive feeling that something is askew and affected. It's living your life with a skeptical and perceptive side eye. This else is like walking into a room and knowing, without necessarily hearing, that someone was talking about you. It's how gossip forces us to engage with a world that is outside ourselves, one that locates us in subject arrangements we might not immediately perceive.

Rephrasing San Jeong Cho's comments on gossip earlier, data is made technologically useful by locating the same personal matters within discourses of official, and unofficial, databases. It is, as scholar

Victor Mendoza interprets cultural historian Lisa Lowe, "distinctly de-territorialist" in its "negation of the state's official discourse," which also "dramatizes the ways in which the dominant discourse incorporates [gossip] into its arsenal, the ways in which official discourse itself cites and 'seizes'" gossip.[98] In other words, just because something is said in a hushed, nonofficialist manner doesn't meant it can't be reterritorialized within a governing apparatus.

To understand gossip as deterritorializing as well as reterritorializing lets us see how ordinary, seemingly unimportant events—with whom we talk on our phones, via email, and even while in the same room—possess constitutive bearing on whether we're a 'citizen,' a 'foreigner,' someone deserving of 'scrutiny,' or a 'terrorist' who merits death. Take the example of the NSA's 'terrorist' from chapter 1. A single cell-phone conversation produces several different dividual pieces of data. Not only are there records of one's phone number, the phone number called, and the day and time the call was placed, but there's also data about the caller's and receiver's geographical locations.

If you track this dividual data across several weeks, you might discover a pattern that $phoneX$ calls $phoneY$, $phoneY$ calls $phoneZ$, and $phoneZ$ then calls $phoneA$. Then, two weeks later, X, Y, Z, and A's phones (or, more technically, their SIM cards) are seen in the same place for ninety minutes on a Tuesday afternoon. This could mean nothing at all, as data is trivial without inference.

But imagine that X and A are believed to be 'terrorists' by the U.S. government. And imagine that X, Y, Z, and A have "patterns of life" that have produced suspicion among NSA analysts for the past several years. Rather than accepting these as mere coincidences of data, you might come to believe that there was actually a 'terrorist' meeting happening that Tuesday. And imagine that X, Y, Z, and A call each other a second time, and two weeks later, they are found to be together again, though now in a different location, for ninety minutes.

There isn't a direct connection that says X is, for sure, a terrorist or A is a terrorist or Y and Z are 'terrorists' or terrorists. But according to this data association, and with indifferent confirmation from both the NSA general counsel and the NSA director themselves, this could very well lead, and has led, to assassination by way of signature drone strike: "we kill people based on metadata."[99] The terminology of a "signature" is more than mere semantics but a datafied pattern that becomes the signed stand-in "as if" a phone belonged to a 'terrorist.'

Online we engage with an ecology of datafied subject relations, and many individuals have been killed because of it. Our datafied subject relations do not free us from our bodies or control us completely. Rather, they produce a subjective index for encounter. This is similar to what philosopher Grégoire Chamayou has described as a coconstruction of a "patterned individuality that is woven out of statistical dividualities and cut out onto a thread of reticular activities, against which it progressively silhouettes in time as a distinctive perceptible unit in the eyes of the machine."[100] And it is aligned with how Ronald Day describes "the codes for the subject's social positioning and expressions by others and by itself" for algorithmic discussion—a datafied reference point that lets us communicate with power, and vice versa.[101] This positioning is best described by a former Joint Special Operations Command (JSOC) drone operator: "People get hung up that there's a targeted list of people. . . . It's really like we're targeting a cell phone. We're not going after people—we're going after their phones, in the hopes that the person on the other end of that missile is the bad guy."[102]

JSOC's hope-based identification is a tragic reminder of the intersections between the "real world" and the "virtual." But this identification also allows one to ask how these kinds of horrific decisions based on metadata can be wrong, unjust, and moreover, messed with. Soon after aerial strikes started terrorizing communities across Pakistan, Afghanistan, Iraq, Yemen, Syria, and Somalia, 'terrorists' became aware of the execution orders authorized by their information signatures. They knew their behaviors were being recorded. And they knew that their datafied "patterns of life" correlated to the kiss of death carried out by unseen aerial drone strike.

In response, many individuals redistributed their SIM cards—by meeting in person and switching, through random assignment, one individual's SIM card for another, thus confusing the stories seemingly written by metadata's associative ink.[103] *X, Y, Z,* and *A* might have been the 'terrorists' the United States was looking for a week prior. But now *X, Y, Z,* and *A* are all somebody else, and horrific would be the day that they decided to call each other to meet for tea one Tuesday afternoon.

This is another example of the else at work. Many individuals—knowing their data trails were used as telltale signifiers for NSA surveillance and without direct, explicit encounter—subsequently challenged the NSA's datafied subject relation by asserting their own freedom on data's terms. It is precisely due to the associative quality of these terms that the decenteredness of datafied subject relations comes to the fore. We are who we are *because* of our connections to people, places, and things—not despite them. And without a stable, centered identity, both algorithms and our responses to their identifications must attend to the intensive interrelationality of our associative connections.

Like the "just-in-time" temporalities of our algorithmic identities, our associative networks also change by the second. Who calls us on the phone, who sits next to us at a cafe with a computer, and who sends us an email all produce datafied relations. These relations are temporarily enacting but quickly eradicated. Their untethering erases the periods at the end of the sentences "I am me" and "you are you," rejecting the "either/or" of relative difference while favoring the endless "and" of Deleuze and Guattari's conceptual basis for rhizomatic becoming.[104] As with the idea that our algorithmic identities add yet another layer to ourselves, "and . . . and . . . and . . ." rejects any semblance of static being as we indefinitely barrel through time, producing more data that algorithms then use to modulate that data's meaning en masse.

The use of "and" and its conceptual coupling with impermanence sets the tempo of each datafied subject relation. The modulation of algorithmic belonging, in which one's jus algoritmi 'foreign' identification might be 51 percent today but 49 percent tomorrow, means that any concrete assessment of who we are will be perpetually outdated. Yet this dynamic subjectivity is theoretically fruitful. So long as our data keeps us alive, our "and"-based identities fit better with the lived realities of our political world than some fantasy ideal of an egalitarian citizenry does. And so long as our data connects us to others, our "and"-based identities emphasize the intensive interrelationality that we always have lived.

OR ELSE

What I have written regarding the else is an attempt to think through the particularities of how algorithmic agents interpret our data traces, and the knowledges that compose us, in "as if" ways. Donna Haraway writes that "no objects, spaces, or bodies are sacred in themselves; any component can be interfaced with any other," a proposal of identity antiessentialism that rejects any notion of naturalist purity while simultaneously accepting the political limits that haunt a hybrid subjectivity.[105] One of these limits is a decentering alienation of who we are when we become cyborg or posthuman. Queer theorist J. Halberstam and media studies scholar Ira Livingston ask us if posthumanity "props itself up against a human body or does it cannibalise the human?"[106] This fitting inquiry of the term carves a generative, interstitial space between two loaded concepts.

Without attempting to answer this question in full, we might begin to with the fact that we, as data, are rarely tethered to some strict, immutable notion of 'woman' or 'citizen.' Instead, our datafied histories remain rewritable, partially erasable, and fully modulatory, an antiessentialism that practically grounds the hybrid theorizations of posthuman and cyborg subjectivities. These histories don't live only in the body. They also live in the datafied air. And they orient our positionalities according to often proprietary algorithmic logics at each moment of processing—only now that same air might carry an errant racial epithet from a close friend right onto your computer screen.

As emphasized in the book's preceding chapters, the materials that compose our algorithmic identities, our datafied social relations, and our translated communications are much more than meticulously organized data sets. They are interpretations of that data, a point that Alexander Galloway connects to his own technical reconfiguration of postcolonial theorist Gayatri Spivak's essay "Can the Subaltern Speak?":

> Data mining is often considered in terms of location and extraction of nuggets of information from a sea of background noise. But this metaphor is entirely wrong. Data mining is essentially a plastic art, for it responds to the sculpture of the medium itself, to the background noise itself. It valorizes the pure shape of relationships. Not "can" but "does" the body speak? Yes, it has no choice. Making a phone call from the slums of Cairo or Mumbai or Paris, the subaltern "speaks" into a database—just as much as I do when I pick up the phone. The difference for difference is no longer actual, it is technical. The subaltern speaks, and somewhere an algorithm listens.[107]

The datafication of daily life compels us to speak, although it is the NSA's, Facebook's, and Google's algorithms that subsequently speak for us: the NSA lets our IP addresses whisper our 'citizenship,' Facebook takes our profile visits as mutterings about 'friendship,' and Google uses our well-wishing to blurt out the n-word. The subject of this datafication engages with a world the user is not entirely sure of. But the marketing firms, governments, and researchers eagerly trying to identify that user are not entirely sure who she is, either. The else of this unsureness comes into play when Facebook's News Feed overwhelms us with posts from people we're not close to. It's how "personalized" advertisements might seem goofy or invasive. Or it's how our Netflix queues were "wrong" enough that the company offered a million dollars in 2006 to whoever could improve its algorithm by 10 percent.[108]

Chicana theorist Gloria Anzaldúa writes that "living on borders and in margins, keeping intact one's shifting and multiple identity and integrity, is like trying to swim in a new element, an 'alien' element."[109] While our datafied lives are subject to relentless dataveillance and algorithmic regulation, neither those doing the dataveilling nor those being dataveilled feel truly at home. The strangeness that defines this "'alien' element" is the strangeness of living in an algorithmic world. It is why algorithmic miscategorization is actually algorithmic neocategorization. And by the same token, it is why mistranslation for Google Translate is really retranslation, too.

In the Portuguese conversation mentioned earlier, "contigo manos e pais" wasn't meant to be an epithet, but it became one anyway. For the person reading it, it was a mistranslation. But for Google, now a towering arbiter of language, it is a retranslation of what "contigo manos e pais" means for the time being.

In light of ubiquitous surveillance systems that valorize datafied life in more and more strange ways, I propose we see the else as a strategy to practice what Galloway theorizes as the "whatever," a subject position of resistance and nonincorporation that suppresses the communicative relationality explicit in "somewhere an algorithm listens." While difficult to define, the whatever is "aesthetically incoherent because it does not coalesce around any given formal essence or definitional predicate. The whatever finds its power in incontinence and transformation, not unification or repetition."[110] More concisely, it "fields no questions and leaves very little to say."[111] To be aware of how we are algorithmically spoken for is to give us administration over what is left to say. The else offers a possibility for deviance, mobility, and ultimately unincorporability according to the conceptual space between algorithms and us.

Indeed, the complexity of our digital-technology-infused subjectivities does not make us throw up our hands in confusion and cede the technical realm over to a total, suffocating control. To feel creeped out is to acknowledge our vulnerability in the digital world. To feel creeped out is also to begin to resist that vulnerability. And to notice instances of neocategorization is to critically understand the logic by which we are algorithmically valued.

To return to the French philosophy that begot much of this chapter's thinking surrounding nonliberal subject relations, theorist Gilbert Simondon's variant of the else might be understood through its conceptual haecceity—a form's abstract *this-ness* that we can use to highlight the incongruous interactions between our experience and our different datafied subject relations.[112] Simondon writes about the distinction between a band saw, which cuts wood to align with a geometric plane, and a hammered wedge, which cuts wood according to the contours of its fibers: "True implicit forms are not geometrical, they are topological. The technical gesture has to respect these topological forms that constitute a parceled haecceity."[113]

While it might be empirically possible to understand which data elements make a 'citizen,' which websites make 'man,' and which graphical patterns determine a 'face,' those things tell us nothing about how we encounter them as living, breathing, data-producing subjects. The contours of life's fibers are shaved off by the geometric cuts of algorithmic interpretation. The world's measurable types can never completely represent the topography of life's "true implicit forms."

The haecceity of 'citizen' is our datafied reaction to our aggregate algorithmic 'citizenship.' The logic that makes a 'citizen' or 'you' is one thing, but your experience of that logic is something else entirely. The else is the fibers that emanate from us, the sliver of agency we have no matter an algorithm's prowess and no matter how much data we produce.

My algorithmic identity is the limitless aggregate of measurable-type identifications. If you intersect all of these, you might get 'John.' And to fully understand 'John,' you must also take into account how Google Translate configures the language I use and read, how OkCupid allocates my romantic and sexual possibilities, and how Facebook's News

Feed shows me some 'friends' but hides others. Yet this aggregate cannot fully grasp me because it doesn't take my fibers into account.

However, to effectively respond to algorithmic interpretation means the else cannot exceed the bounds of our datafied worlds. As mentioned at the onset of this chapter, datafied subject relations are only a layer, an accomplice to other subject arrangements that live on the exclusive terms of data. How I interpret the gap between John and 'John' must feed back, somehow, as data. A hiatus from Facebook can suggest a long list of potential meanings offline, but it's simply understood as a cessation of datafied activity online. Ultimately, to act as a datafied subject is to actualize algorithmic computation.

That is, yelling at a computer won't work to express frustration with algorithmic interpretation, but it might if it had a microphone and voice-recognition technology. Hiding in a cornfield might make you invisible to a nearby police patrol car, but your cell phone, even if it's turned off, can supply your location regardless. Our role within datafied subject relations is to actively understand our position in the undercurrent of dataveillers' "oceans of data" without relying on the repurposed lie of liberalism: the "needle in the haystack." There is no needle, much like there is no authentic self. Our data is not special. It doesn't mean anything in particular. There is only a reserve of data that Google, Facebook, OkCupid, and the NSA algorithmically make useful.

In this undercurrent, insurance premiums go up and down, and plane-ticket prices rise and fall. Data that we never knew was part of our datafied selves, such as the web browser we use and who we call on the phone, has constitutive effect on our lives. Whether you are 'poor' or 'rich' could cost you an extra $100 on a trip from Los Angeles to New York. The frequency with which your 'foreign' friends call you can makes you 'foreign' in the eyes of the NSA. How we see the world—but, more importantly, how the world sees us—is conditioned beyond measure. Our response to these conditions is what marks our future in the digital world.

CONCLUSION

The space carved out by the else echoes the central principle of Zeno's Dichotomy Paradox. Zeno, a Greek logician and philosophical heavyweight from the town of Elea, knew very well that the haecceity of things can never be replicated. In the aforementioned thought experiment, he imagined a voyage between two distant cities that is traveled in halves.

You walk halfway from Thessaloniki to Athens, and then you rest. From that midpoint, you then walk half of the remaining distance to Athens, and then you rest. And so on. Like the tortoise and the hare—and ultimately like the idea of probability itself—you will never get to Athens, beat the tortoise, or reach 1. Even as you near the Athenian city walls, your nose hair bending to the wood of its bolted gates, Zeno's half-distance rule will prohibit you from knocking. This infinite halving of halves means you cannot achieve the whole. In simple algebraic script, $x = 1-n$.

The impossibility of $x = 1$, or the whole, ultimately represents the grand argument against modernity, as well as the theoretical foundation for much of what defines poststructural theory, queer theory, feminist theory, critical race theory, and social constructionism at large. Structures of power are always trying to locate us within named, prescribed boxes whose enduring error is unreasonably consistent. Institutions like the NSA reify these boxed assumptions, and this is how we encounter the else online.

It is in our interaction with these assumptions that the else demonstrates how jus algoritmi will never map onto jus sanguinis or jus soli or that Google Translate, regardless of its data set, will never be a native speaker. The dividuals of our microstates (defined by theorist Tiziana Terranova as the "multiplicity of particles and interactions") that form the identities and subjectivities of our macrostates (the "averages, but also identities, subjectivities, societies and cultures") need room to move—to shift around and be resignified.[114] More than anything, they need room to be wrong.

A datafied subject relation is what sociologist Michalis Lianos sees as the "de-culturing" of technological devices that "erodes the norms and the modalities of their application in their capacity as intentional, accentuated aspects of social relations; then it reinvents them as non-negotiable constraints that are homogeneous and external to all participants."[115] Without a stable, centered cultural context, macrostates reinvent themselves on the basis of new microstates. This deculturing requires a reconsideration of what is normal and thus a reconsidering of what we mean by constraint.

That is, citing social theorist Brian Massumi, while normal might not be immediately "non-negotiable," "'normal' is now free-standing,"[116] and "dividuals are not just 'normalized,' but maintained with a certain degree of what we could call functional difference such that the thresholds of knowledge and practice are rather radically open, and are always being reconfigured."[117] Who we are and what we are subject to has functionally expanded in this radical openness, which means our capacity to evaluate our own subject positions must be reappraised, too.

Our datafied subject relations are only practiced through data, which is where this radical free-standing-ness gets affixed. While we can certainly resist relations of power outside data through direct action against Google or legal reform of the NSA, that resistance must exist on data's terms if it wants to defy our algorithmic identifications. Of course, this is not because we are literally made of data (clearly, as I look to my fingers typing, I don't see random ASCII characters or lines of code) but rather because data is the only thing legible to these algorithmic systems of power. In this way, these identificatory systems reject the organic. They deny the analogue gray between the digital polarities of +1 and 0.

Yet even when we think of ones and zeros (as we are taught to do when thinking about digitality), we're not really talking about actual, stable binary states. A hard drive's content is composed of voltage value differences, not actual ones and zeros. A binary one is ideally represented as 5.0 volts; a zero by 0.0. But a one might be 5.0013 volts, while a zero might be 0.05. Previous values of a once-deleted file have ghostly effects on the future. Short of counting beads on an abacus, any quantified measurement of the material world needs to be rounded up or down, as the physical process that marks a one a '1' can never be perfect.

There is a productive complexity in this numerical aberration. These are "monsters," to use Haraway's cyborg terminology, or philosopher Kal Alston's "unicorns": elements outside the strict classificatory standards of our world.[118] In practical terms, they're what cannot be represented as an algorithmic identity. While monsters are sometimes ignored as unclassifiable and valueless, we should see them as new ways to constitute these escapable, ineffable differences through data. Part of living along a datafied subject relation involves winking at attempts to log our personal experiences within the rubrics of power. It involves messing with those attempts, intentionally like Rosi Braidotti's nomad, to produce hiccups against algorithmic subjectification.

While it might be alluring to theorize a type of subject perfectly beholden to power and surveillance, it is also hopeless. Indeed, as sociologist Manuel Castells argues, the Orwellian concept of Big Brother that has been tossed around as the dystopian narrative par exemplar actually does a disservice to most nonstate practices of surveillance.[119] It overstates the authority of Internet surveillance, and in particular, it overstates our submission to it. Unlike in George Orwell's Airstrip One of *1984*, most of what we do online is being dataveilled, not watched. We're algorithmically assessed, not personally disciplined through observation. And that datafied subject relation simply adds another layer onto who we are, a localized instance of an algorithm connecting our data to emergent meaning.

This type of subject relation is connective, emphasizing the "and" over the "or." But to make sense of the aggregation of our data, "and" eventually needs to be pared down to scale—its average calculated to make its meaning useful (/x). This division is the algorithmic interpretation of the NSA that makes a 'citizen' or 'foreigner' from its heaps upon heaps of metadata. And this division orients our possibility for agency toward the aggregate, as a single byte of anomalous data neither ruins nor triumphs your life. Space for freedom comes from this division. An "and" without division makes us exhausted. It would tire us unnecessarily.

I opened this chapter with a lyric from a groundbreaking Washington, D.C., punk band, Black Eyes. This band, whose musical genre can best be described as posthardcore avant-garde, arose from the autonomist world of D.C. punk rock—largely the do-it-yourself (DIY) principle that rejected the luxuries of commercial outsourcing in favor of community-grown, solidarity-based associations. The DIY ethos led artists to make their own record labels, to promote their own shows, and ultimately to depend on themselves rather than institutions.

However, this mentality possessed a drawback. As bassist and vocalist Hugh McElroy of Black Eyes claimed, it's problematic to focus on "yourself" and not the collective. Since a nonassociative "yourself" can never serve as an adequate political index for sustainable action, McElroy emphasized an alternative legacy to DIY politics: "Do It Together" (DIT). Much like the "and" tires us, DIY does as well. DIT lets us see how associations and /x intersect, to understand that associations do more than passively connect us to each other. We pare them down through algorithms or even through mutual aid. Without the /x, "and"-based subject making speaks only to half of what subjectivity entails.

Associations are the lingua franca of our datafied life, the source of its fetters as well as the nourishment for its growth. Because a single piece of data means nothing on its own, the fetishized autonomy of the liberal subject would starve without the other. Patterns are made from a population, not one person. How algorithms interpret us necessarily connects us to the lives of others. This sentiment, in all its humanistic beauty, is also regulating. It controls life on the basis of what 'we' do. But, as we'll see in chapter 4, the 'we,' 'us,' and 'you' can be disrupted. We can mess with algorithmic assessment but only if we mess with it on its own terms—and we do it together.

4

PRIVACY

Wanted Dead or Alive

MARK HEMMINGS (M): My stomach is in agony, duck. I've got lumps in my stomach.

CALL HANDLER (C-H): Have you got any other symptoms?

M: I'm in agony, sweating a lot, feeling weak. Going on mostly all day.

C-H: Have you had any diarrhea or vomiting?

M: My stomach's in agony. Yes. I've been sick a few times. It is a sharp pain.

C-H: Have you ever been diagnosed with an aortic aneurysm or Marfan's syndrome?

M: No. I've got gallstones in my stomach, duck. Pain in my stomach.

C-H: Have you got any crushing or aching pain in your upper abdomen?

M: Sort of. Think so.

C-H: Any pain to your arms, neck, jaw, or shoulder?

M: No, duck. Can I have an ambulance, duck?

C-H: Have you passed a bowel motion that looks black or tarry or red or maroon?

M: No. I'm just in agony, duck.

C-H: Any new pain on your eye? Have you got any lumps or swellings in your testicles or scrotum?

M: No. Tummy pains. Am light-headed. (*Heavy breathing from Mark as call handler asks for details about his GP surgery*).

C-H: From what you've told me, you don't require an emergency ambulance, but we will get somebody to call you back.

M: Can't I have an ambulance? I'm in agony.

C-H: OK, I appreciate that, but from the answers you've given me, you don't need an ambulance. But you need to speak to the local GP in the next two hours.

M: Do I need to go to the hospital?

C-H: No, you need to stay on the phone for a moment. You could try a warm bath, but if you collapse, become unconscious, unresponsive, faint, cold, or clammy, it's 999. Keep this line free, and if you haven't heard back from them in ninety minutes, you need to call us back again.

It's 2013, and Mark Hemmings, a forty-one-year-old British disabled man, dials the number for emergency services in the UK, *999. An operator answers, and Hemmings immediately makes his condition known: "My stomach is in agony, duck. I've got lumps in my stomach." The operator responds with the first of many inquires, "Have you got any other symptoms?" Hemmings replies, "I'm in agony, sweating a lot, feeling weak. Going on mostly all day."[1]

The operator asks more questions: "Have you had any diarrhea or vomiting?" "Have you ever been diagnosed with an aortic aneurysm or Marfan's syndrome?" "Have you got any crushing or aching pain in your upper abdomen?" Through the agony, Hemmings diligently, but excruciatingly, answers them all.

He requests an ambulance three separate times. He also explains his pain, in description and accompanying tone, as "agonizing" a heartbreaking seven times. At the end of the call, the operator concludes, "From what you've told me, you don't require an emergency ambulance, but we will get somebody to call you back."

Two days later, an in-house health-care worker discovered Hemmings, collapsed and unconscious, on the floor. Rushed to the hospital, he died thirty minutes after arrival. The cause of death was a heart attack triggered by gallstones blocking his pancreatic duct. Hemmings had correctly diagnosed himself, and a routine operation would have saved his life—that is, if his answers had been classified as deserving of emergency transport. In fact, the series of questions the emergency operator asked came straight from an algorithmic triage system, used not to help Hemmings but to discern the urgency of his situation.[2]

Hemmings's verbal answers were inputs. The output was whether an ambulance would be sent based on those answers. Without changes in his symptoms, further action was forbidden. This dependence on algorithmic logic is best summed up with the ludicrous instruction, "If you collapse, become unconscious, unresponsive, faint, cold, or clammy, it's 999." The operator's own human agency was demoted to mere algorithmic translation. Her confidence in the system was such that she even told a deflated Hemmings, "We cannot override this, and although there are paramedics in the control room for us to ask, I would not think the system would come up with the wrong answer."[3]

Hemmings's symptoms data didn't fit the measurable type for 'deserving' emergency treatment. His use of the word "agonizing," his repeated pleading with the operator to send an ambulance, and the general tone of his desperation heard on the *999 recording as his organs slowly failed him were illegible to the algorithmic system. In an oddly worded proclamation, a consultant for an area hospital later described the calamity with the chill of only the most technocratic prose: "The algorithm failed to benefit Mark."[4]

Hemmings's *999 experience is, admittedly, an extreme case. His death was the result of a long series of intersecting conditions, from the increasing automation of medical diagnosis to the shrinking budgets of public-sector health programs in the UK. But his relation to an unrepentant, classificatory algorithmic logic is what many of us encounter, every day, online. States use algorithms that fail us, like the NSA's jus algoritmi discussed in chapter 3. Capital employs algorithms that fail us, too, like HP's facial recognition from this book's introduction. The practice of classification itself, a power move of the highest order, frames our worlds in ways absent our choosing. This chapter reconfigures these power moves onto more favorable terms through the lens of privacy and its historical lineage.

In concert, this chapter evaluates what privacy might look like beyond its traditional form wherein it protects an individual from observation or disturbance. Paradoxically, Hemmings possessed this traditional form of privacy, famously defined as the "right to be let alone" by legal scholars Samuel Warren and Louis Brandeis in 1890, as he sat alone in his home, desperately seeking medical attention.[5] However, he was not "let alone" in a way that empowered or protected him. Hemmings was instead "let alone" to be defenseless against *999's algorithmic output. In fact, the *999 algorithm used Hemmings's data—his provided answers—without his knowledge, in effect to testify against himself and his own physical needs.

This chapter's reconfigured idea of privacy contends with what sociologist John B. Thompson describes as the changing nature of the private, which "now consists more and more of a despatialized realm of information and symbolic content over which the individual believes she can and should be able to exercise control, regardless of where this individual and this information might be physically located."[6] Given chapter 3's focus on dividuality, I propose privacy should protect both the self and the assemblage connecting that self to others—the user, or Hemmings, and the "as if" components that further constitute that user, or his datafied answers.

This chapter follows existing attempts to reorientate privacy toward the datafied world. Communication law scholar Jisuk Woo has argued that "an important change in privacy dynamics is the fact that the 'invading entities' [of surveillance] have become broader and less easily identifiable," so that, following the scholarship of political economist Oscar Gandy, "the major impetus for the power imbalance between the subjects and objects of surveillance in the network is their differences in identifiability."[7] As we've seen time and time again in this book, marketing firms and government organizations use our data to identify us for their own, hidden machinations. In this framework, Woo proposes we seek the "right not to be identified," a subjective detachment from the regulatory power implicit in dataveillance.

For the purposes of this book, "not to be identified" is to be neither personally identified, in terms of the individual, nor algorithmically identified, in terms of the dividual. And this mode of privacy as nonidentification is best practiced through what media scholar Finn Brunton and philosopher Helen Nissenbaum call "obfuscation": the "deliberate addition of ambiguous, confusing, or misleading information to interfere with surveillance and data collection."[8] Here, privacy happens when a user suppresses the potential signals in her data with an abundance of meaningless noise, like "chaff, which fills radar's sweep with potential targets," such as a diverse group of friends sharing a single supermarket loyalty card in order to "muddle the record" about ourselves.[9] Which is to say, data about ourselves (our dividualities)—not just data that includes our names, Social Security numbers, or addresses—also deserves privacy. This point is not to anthropomorphize our data but to accept its constitutive role in our algorithmic selves.

As it stands, privacy as a concept isn't about shutting off from the world or hiding our vulnerabilities from some empowered surveillant eye. Rather, as political scientist Jean L. Cohen argues, the "normative nature of privacy lies precisely in the protection of what [sociologist Erving] Goffman has called 'the territories of the self'—a preserve to which an individual can assert 'entitlement to possess, control, use, [and] dispose of.'"[10] In this preserve, we enjoy what social theorist Anthony Giddens calls "the right—varying in content in manifold ways in different contexts—to maintain a distance from others by preserving bodily privacy and an integrity of self."[11]

Within the territory of our self, we know how we are ordered. We understand the consequences of our decisions, and thus we determine what who we are means. These territories conceptually coincide with how U.S. Supreme Court justice William Brennan envisioned protection for U.S. First Amendment freedoms: as a "breathing space to survive."[12]

It is through these spatial ideals that we can understand why Hemmings's case is relevant, even while it may seem unrelated, to privacy. As an individual, he was not entitled to anything more than the enforced protocols of the *999 algorithm. Nor, in terms of his dividualities, was he aware of what 'deserving' meant, what made him 'undeserving,' or even that his answers to the *999 operator were being algorithmically valued. Goffman's "territories" or the Court's "breathing spaces" are the conceptual grounding that Hemmings lacked.

In this chapter, I trace a brief history of privacy in the U.S., its legacy as connected to these "breathing spaces to survive," and consider how privacy can extend beyond the individual body and into the dividual world. I use Hemmings's case as a continuing example, while taking into consideration the fact that any privacy is never complete, perfect, fully possible, or entirely desirable.

REST IN PEACE, PRIVACY

Did you hear that privacy died? Ever since the Internet went mainstream, news organizations from *Time* magazine to the *Guardian* and *Forbes* have declared privacy to be either dead or dying.[13] A general consensus exists that what we do online today is not "private" at all, making many people throw up their hands and concede this once-cherished concept to some idyllic, pastoral past. Privacy's blunted practical use appears to be an unavoidable casualty of an Internet that has invaded our bodies, our social interactions, and especially our homes—the once-regal throne room of the "private."

By the same token, the Internet's comprehensive capacity to surveil has led some tech leaders, especially those who stand to make money from cultivating our datafied lives, to join the media chorus and rhetorically toss the concept of privacy out the window. As Sun Microsystems' CEO, Scott McNealy, quipped way back in 1999, "You have zero privacy anyway. Get over it."[14] Facebook's founder, Mark Zuckerberg, believes that privacy "is no longer a social norm."[15] And Google's former CEO Eric Schmidt described privacy as unnecessary and even dangerous, warning the surveilled masses that "if you have something that you don't want anyone to know, maybe you shouldn't be doing it in the first place."[16]

For these rich white men, privacy is dead because it impinges on their business models. But more generally, privacy is perceived as an impediment to the one-sided dialogue that defines the current mode of technological progress. For other not-as-rich white men, the invasion of the Internet into people's private lives is their first encounter with the control inherent in surveillance. But for most everyone else, privacy hasn't had a pulse for a long time. Warren and Brandeis's "right to be let alone," writes communication scholar Zizi Papacharissi, is, and has long been, "a luxury commodity."[17]

Privacy's time of death is a relative phenomenon, one whose passing is based almost entirely on one's proximity to wielding hegemonic power. The Internet may have ruined the white, suburban trope that designates Warren and Brandeis's "impregnable" view of "man's house as his castle" now that once-private, closed-door acts are available for commercial data collection, state surveillance, and half-decent hackers.[18] But the contemporary instances of dataveillance outlined at length in this book are just the latest in a long line of privacy-reducing behaviors, policies, and technologies—a fact that might come as a surprise to those who are not used to constant observation by some external other.

In the 1980s, feminist legal scholar Catharine MacKinnon streamlined Warren and Brandeis's mantra of privacy, "the right to be let alone," into a juridical ethos more appropriate to the U.S. government's defense of contemporary patriarchy: the right for men to be let alone.[19] Privacy in the U.S. legal system historically defended men's right to privacy above, and sometimes in lieu of, women's. For example, it took until 1993 to see marital rape outlawed in all fifty U.S. states. While the right to an abortion was granted in 1973 with the U.S. Supreme Court's *Roe v. Wade* decision, even today that law is being gutted by state governments. And as recently as fall of 2014, a Washington, D.C., judge ruled that women visiting the Lincoln Memorial could not reasonably expect privacy from men taking photos up their skirts.[20]

For other groups, such as children, privacy is principally recognized as undeserved until an individual turns eighteen years old.[21] For people with disabilities, as well as the elderly, privacy is always a conditional guarantee, illustrated by a lack of access to disabled bathrooms or the sometimes authoritarian decisions made by an individual's caretaker.[22] For people of color, "privacy" in the mode of liberal democracy is often a nonstarter.[23] Excessive state policing, nonstate social vigilance fueled by racist media representations, and the overall institutionalization of white supremacy all frame nonwhite bodies as less deserving of this "right to be let alone," making it more an empty slogan than a sound, egalitarian legal foundation.

And for people stricken by poverty across the centuries—those who face homelessness, urban overcrowding, or the inability to pay for a lawyer in the event of a legally recognized privacy invasion—there has always been a disempowering, asymmetrical relationship between those who have the right to privacy and those who don't.[24]

Yet despite these differences, issues of surveillance and privacy still cut across the different gendered, racial, and classed layers of our social worlds. The breadth of privacy's import stems from the fact that we all need it. We are all touched by power in some way, and privacy is the historical lever we employ to regulate how this power affects us. Accordingly, privacy as a civil right attracts a wide spectrum of supporters, from well-off civil libertarians worried about their porn searches falling into the wrong hands to men of color in New York protesting the city's "stop and frisk" program.[25] But we can't fetishize privacy as a secure legal right, precisely due to the countless, paradoxical examples of a right being violated by the same state theoretically employed to protect it.[26]

More tactically, I want us to think through these complexities of privacy in dividual terms. How does a reorientation to the dividual reorganize the flows of power within which we *practice* privacy? That is, the terms of privacy in a datafied world are the terms of how our data is made useful. Ultimately, this emended framing lets us see how privacy also applies to our datafied dividualities—something that neither a signatory of the U.S. Constitution nor even a lawyer in the nineteenth century could have ever envisioned, much less theorized.

PRIVACY'S LEGAL LEGACY

Historically, privacy protected an imagined sanctum for our inner selves. Indeed, the birth of U.S. privacy discourse culls from the Constitution's First, Third, Fourth, Fifth, and Ninth Amendments, which all focus on an autonomy of self and protection from the influence of others.[27] It was this constitutional foundation that led Thomas Cooley, chief justice of the Michigan Supreme Court, to propose legal protections against attempted physical contact in 1880: "the right to one's person may be said to be a right of complete immunity: to be let alone."[28] For Cooley, the law should defend against "a sudden call upon the energies for prompt and effectual resistance," such as our response to receiving an "insult" or being put "in fear," because it disrupted the sanctity of individual action—even if that disruption never became violent or physical.[29] A decade later, as referenced in the beginning of this chapter, Warren and Brandeis's ur-text "The Right to Privacy" echoed Cooley but from a more informational perspective:

> The common law secures to each individual the right of determining, ordinarily, to what extent his thoughts, sentiments, and emotions shall be communicated to others. Under our system of government, he can never be compelled to express them (except when upon the witness stand); and even if he has chosen to give them expression, he generally retains the power to fix the limits of the publicity which shall be given them.[30]

These three grandfathers of liberal privacy law created the legal kernel for what mid-twentieth-century Supreme Court justice William Douglas later described as "zones of privacy"—the dual spatial and psychological buffers that conceptually set apart the agent of the self from the agent of the other.[31] More poetically, the notion of zones of privacy also appeared in several decisions by Justice William Brennan in terms of libel law as "breathing space to survive."[32] According to these formative steps in U.S. privacy law, individuals didn't need or deserve privacy because they wanted to do illegal things or to carry out some singular act in private. They needed the privacy to be, to act, and to freely express themselves.

Computer scientist Roger Clarke broadly defines privacy as "the interest that individuals have in sustaining a 'personal space,' free from interference by other people and organizations."[33] Privacy at its onset was about a space away from interference. It's about breathable life—a metaphor we can begin to think about as an enduring sanctuary that reflects the contemplation of essayist Henry David Thoreau's Walden Pond more than it does some closed-door, temporary peace in a bathroom stall. Eric Schmidt's facile rejection of privacy dimly characterizes this "breathing space" in a negative light, parroting a trope in contemporary privacy debates that equates the right to privacy with a defense of illegality: "the right to be let alone" has morphed into "I have nothing to hide."[34]

Yet privacy at its legalistic, 135-year-old core might be better conceived as a protective relationship we have with the state and others in order to subjectively breathe. The question is, to breathe where? Privacy in the home is different from privacy in the workplace, and privacy through electronic communications is different from the privacy of one's body.

The procedural conflict between the inclusivity of the right to privacy and the specifics of that right's action makes a single, universal definition of privacy quite difficult to come by: "Privacy, like an elephant, is perhaps more readily recognized than described," quips author John B. Young.[35] Any productive notion of privacy is delimited by the particularities of a situation, or what philosopher H. J. McCloskey defines as "conditional"—that is, not a general concept that applies equally to all contexts.[36] Appropriately, upon appointment to the U.S. Supreme Court, Louis Brandeis called his legal right to privacy the "most comprehensive of rights":

The makers of the U.S. Constitution undertook to secure conditions favorable to the pursuit of happiness. They recognized
the significance of man's spiritual nature, of his feelings and
of his intellect. They knew that only a part of the pain, pleasure
and satisfactions of life are to be found in material things. They
sought to protect Americans in their beliefs, their thoughts, their
emotions and their sensations. They conferred, as against the
Government, the right to be let alone—the most comprehensive
of rights and the right most valued by civilized men. To protect
that right, every unjustifiable intrusion by the Government upon
the privacy of the individual, whatever the means employed,
must be deemed a violation of the Fourth Amendment.[37]

Brandeis's opinion gives far greater weight to privacy than it would
have as a mere right to be let alone from nuisance. For him, the requirement that all humans have for privacy is rooted in the need that our
physical, spiritual, emotional, and intellectual selves have to breathe.
Quite endearingly, he takes literally the words of the U.S. Declaration
of Independence to "secure conditions favorable to the 'pursuit of happiness'" and relates them to the Fourth Amendment, which protects
against "unwarranted search and seizure."

In order to continue reframing a broad yet historically consistent
version of what we might call dividual privacy, I propose we locate its
conceptual soul from within the preceding passage—just without the
accompanying legalese. Dividual privacy takes the origin legal framework of U.S. privacy theory and applies it to the demands of our contemporary digital era. If we are dividuals—and not individuals—on the
Internet, then a dividual privacy must functionally protect our emotional selves as well as our 'emotional' selves. When we are made of data,
we have to consider what it might mean for our dividualities also to be
"let alone."

Accordingly, if privacy is really the most comprehensive of rights,
then we might do well to avoid relying on a single definition of dividual

privacy. Rather, we can trace its logic through a suite of practices that can help us achieve, through any legitimate means, a space protected from interference. It's a space to breathe. But just as one person's happiness might be another person's hell, the breathing space that each of us needs to survive is both contextual and relative.

"Breathing space to survive" certainly has a provocative ring to it, but we can avoid letting it succumb to platitude by poking the expression with a critical stick: surviving *for* what? Legal scholar Ronald J. Krotoszynsk frames the U.S. Supreme Court's 1973 *Roe v. Wade* interpretation of privacy as "the individual privilege to act or refrain from acting."[38] But protection for action or inaction itself does not necessarily secure the conditions for the pursuit of happiness.

You might consider this question the next time you enter the oft-cited exemplar of privacy in liberal democracies: the tranquility of a cramped voting booth. A curtain pulled closed behind you ceremoniously divides the world into two intelligible spaces—the sanctuary of the private enclosure and the political prying of the outside world. Yet the central spoiler to this metaphor's universality is the assumed autonomy that the booth is supposed to provide. Much like surviving for what, we might ask, autonomy for what? Other than choosing one cherry-picked candidate over another (or not), there's little capacity for happiness or spiritual expression on Election Day.

The metaphor isn't entirely lost, however, as it still suggests that although we might not be happy in the voting booth, we do know our context. We know that our names will be marked as having "voted." We know that we are free from unwanted battery from other people. We know that no one is looking at us, and no one is monitoring our actions. We know what is expected of us and what we can and cannot do. We therefore cannot be controlled in a space outside the formative elements of ourselves, the pen, and the ballot.

Within this ideal of privacy, we can vote for whoever is on a ballot, read whatever is in a library, and talk with whomever we know. But when we know our context, privacy also affords us much more than decisions around mere action or inaction. This point conceptually re-sembles what Helen Nissenbaum has already developed as a theory of "privacy as contextual integrity."[39] According to Nissenbaum, each con-text of life has informational flows that govern rules for gathering and disseminating information. The goal of contextual privacy is to ensure that the informational norms of each context are respected. This focus on context also protects the terms of who we are. With privacy, we are able to know and understand ourselves—we are legible to ourselves. Or, citing Anthony Giddens, we possess an "integrity of self": the common denominator I propose we think about when evaluating privacy's value in a datafied, dividual world.[40]

A privacy that provides for an integrity of self is a privacy that lets us know who we are, how we're treated, and what that treatment means. Unlike the closed-door privacy of the liberal "private sphere," a privacy that celebrates integrity assumes that your life is complicated. It op-erates alongside what legal theorist Julie E. Cohen calls a "postliberal" approach to privacy: "Privacy shelters dynamic, emergent subjectivity from the efforts of commercial and government actors to render indi-viduals and communities fixed, transparent, and predictable. It protects the situated practices of boundary management through which the ca-pacity for self-determination develops."[41] This "boundary management" for self-determination must necessarily address the complexities of a datafied social/networked life, in which privacy in practice can never completely detach us from power and others.

Indeed, the loneliness implied in the idyllic, private solitude of Walden Pond is not the categorical consequence of living a private life. That would be horrible. But at Walden Pond, you are let alone to know who you are. You know that the forces of gravity, climate, and your ac-tions are the deciding factors in how your future life can be lived. And you know that if someone or something visits you, you'll have to attend to how she or it affects you. In this way, privacy can't possibly protect only personal choice, or what scholars refer to as "decisional privacy."[42] Privacy must also be for *being*. And this being requires an internal consistency of self that enables us to know who we are, not just to act as we want to act. Indeed, political philosophers like Wendy Brown and Jodi Dean have already described the neoliberal obsessions that frame concepts like privacy toward terms of action, making even the most private moments of our lives about doing and production.[43]

In fact, much to the delight of most everyone in the world, privacy also creates space for hedonism, sloth, and general disregard for social norms that would rarely surface if not for a notion of the private. "The firm expectation of having privacy for permissible deviations is a distinguishing characteristic of life in a free society," writes theorist Alan Westin.[44] Privacy is about play, about understanding that when we truly feel the breathing space of privacy, we can both do and be things differently because we won't be judged.[45] We'll be left relatively unscathed. It is precisely in these deviations from the norm that we maintain any semblance of an integrity of self.

If the entirety of privacy was really dead, we'd have no way to understand who we are. We'd have no way to voluntarily live in a world when unwanted control is present. Integrity for the individual, spared various instances of psychosis, is something we all are well practiced in and to varying degrees use privacy-enhancing techniques to maintain: we close doors, we whisper to loved ones, and we have passwords on our email accounts. It's the breathing space not to just act but also to be.

What we aren't practiced in is an integrity of self when that self is made of data. Hemmings's *999 conversation is an extreme example of this point. An integrity of self asks how we are profiled, what those profile categories mean, and how measurable types produce what is and is not legible in the world. Even as I walk down a crowded street, I still enjoy a degree of what Nissenbaum might refer to as "privacy in public": I understand how my racialized, gendered, and abled body generates meaning that conditions how I can live.[46] Without this knowledge, I am unsure of these conditions, who I am, and how my world is affected.

Just like Hemmings, I'm at the whim of the algorithm that makes me according to my data. As we'll explore further in this chapter, a privacy that attends to the dividual accounts for how systems radically order and reorder our dividualities in ways largely concealed and incomprehensible to us—in effect, modulating the making of ourselves and the world we live in. Hemmings's case turned to tragedy the moment the *999 algorithm denied him an ambulance. But his case is also a tragedy of knowledge, one in which the measurable types of 'deserving' and 'undeserving' asymmetrically (without participants' understanding) determine the medical futures for all *999 callers.

ALLEGORITHM

The traditional diagram of privacy is a direct, dialogical connection made between the surveilled self and the surveilling other: x surveils y, so y responds by demanding privacy from x. Or, in a case from 2014, Harvard University administrators (x) admitted to using in-class cameras to photograph Harvard students (y). As part of a year-long study of attendance, the university installed cameras in lecture halls, snapping a photo during every minute of class. A computer program then scanned the resulting images, counting the number of empty seats and saving that minute-by-minute data into a spreadsheet.[47] So as to avoid biasing the sample, the researchers did not tell the students beforehand (or even immediately afterward) that their physical presence was being evaluated. And after this surveillance data was eventually made known to faculty, many cried privacy foul.

It is noteworthy that Harvard's surveillance counted empty seats only in aggregate. While the cameras surely snapped photos of lecture attendees, the individuals themselves were not really being considered. It was "a" seat that was counted, like an unspoken census or a road surveyor counting cars on a busy street. And most tellingly, the consequence would not, and indeed could not, affect specific students—every empty seat was datafied as a single number (-1) that simply subtracted from the tally for each class's attendance metrics.[48] Nonetheless, students and faculty were irked, the surveillance made headlines, and the

Harvard brass sent the study to an oversight committee after much methodological explanation.

Even without an individual focus, the individual still can feel surveillance's sway. Although this sway relies on its extant presence or admission, a panopticon of visuality and/or knowledge that when perceived, and only when perceived, starts the engines of self-discipline. This is the primary limit to the *x-y* diagram within disciplinary surveillance. In other words, if we don't know that we're being surveilled, we don't know when to self-discipline, and the whole of panoptic power falls apart.

Of course, unacknowledged surveillance still has power, just a power we can't put our finger on, a point I tried to narrowly describe in chapter 3. Moreover, this problematic has been discussed at length for several decades, with many theorists attempting to move past the panopticon as the paragon diagram of surveillance and social control.[49]

Indeed, no single diagram will suffice in all of the various instances of surveillance and privacy. And no single visual diagram can work for dataveillance and dividual privacy. This is precisely because the grammar of visuality demands stability—of discernible, clear relations between objects—that belies the nonvisual, statistical ways that dataveillance operates. Instead, we might choose to follow cultural theorist Matthew Fuller's interpretation that "surveillance in the present context applies very little to acts of seeing. Surveillance is a socioalgorithmic process."[50]

As a socio-algorithmic process, a surveillance diagram that is itself algorithmic might be more apropos, such as what theorist Alexander Galloway coined an "allegorithm." An allegorithm is both allegory and algorithm combined, a portmanteau that furnishes the seeming functionalism of computer processing both direction and boundaries. While Galloway employs the term to theorize video games, it can also apply to dataveillance: "To play the game means to play the code of the game. To win means to know the system. And thus to interpret a game means to interpret its algorithm (to discover its parallel allegorithm)."[51] He continues that "video games are allegories for our contemporary life under the protocological network of continuous informatic control."[52] They orient us to a rule, a logic, even a physics for a game world that we learn about predominantly through experience, trial, and error.

This is why, without knowing the exact mathematical equation used in the original *Super Mario Brothers* Nintendo game, we have an idea about how high and for how long Mario jumps when we press *A*. This is also why EA Sports' soccer video game *FIFA '99* was almost unplayable after players discovered that every bicycle kick would miraculously hit the back of the net. Even the persistent updates to *World of Warcraft*, discussed in the chapter 2, can be understood as not just an "update" but a constitutive rewriting of the allegory of game play. Algorithms produce the perimeters for discursive possibility. They situate the realm of possible actions and subjective experiences made available to each individual player.

If Mario's capacity to jump suddenly decreased by 50 percent, we'd probably die in the game much more than we were used to—until we adapted to the new knowledges that condition our actions. And if our data is evaluated and changed in a similar way, the integrity of our dividual selves is at risk of an inherent instability. This is the else that I described in chapter 3: the way we subjectively respond to the undulations of algorithmic processing.

To return to Hemmings, his encounter with the *999 operator is framed by what we can now describe as a tragic allegorithm. He lost his integrity of self as the allegorithm defined his conditions of possibility for access to medical attention. But in this allegorithm, Hemmings's individuality does not appear as a character. He was not intentionally playing a game, but his data nonetheless played for him. His role was relegated to mere membership of a measurable type. The allocation of 'deservingness' was based on his datafied inputs.

One component of dividual privacy relies on using existing privacy theory to place the dividual in the individual's shoes. This subject substitution marshals the legacy of liberal, individual privacy to protect our dividual selves. We use liberal privacy law to safeguard our intimate, personal details. And we employ individual intellectual-property rights to regulate how companies and states record and sell our data.

But dividual privacy's tactical remainder appreciates how individual privacy theory is unable to fully address the changes that happen when our dividualities remain at the dividual level. We are usually intelligible to allegorithmic systems as data points in patterns—not as unique members. In this combined subject position, the ethos of, but not necessarily the liberal legal right to, privacy can still be employed. Here, dividual privacy operates in a register beyond the initial intersection between Hemmings's data and its fit within the pattern of 'deserving.'

Integrity of self in a datafied world attends to both the self that produces data and the measurable types that our data makes up. With adequate privacy, we should understand if we're 'deserving.' But we should also know the answer to the more structural question: what in the world does 'deserving' actually mean?

For an example, let's consider one of the most dubious measurable types we've seen yet: "Gaydar" is an algorithm developed by undergraduates at MIT that infers your 'sexuality' on the basis of how many outwardly gay friends you have on Facebook. The allegorithm in this algorithm is an assumption that if you have a higher-than-"normal" percentage of gay friends, you are likely gay. In the words of the researchers, Carter Jernigan and Behram F. T. Mistree, "birds of a feather flock together."[53]

Gaydar calculates 'gay' and 'straight' according to Facebook metadata. Metadata, the data about whom you talk to, when you talk to them, with whom you are friends, and when you became friends with them, is legally unprotected by current U.S. privacy law.[54] It's also, unsurprisingly, a large portion of data that the NSA indiscriminately collects to surveil U.S. citizens' communication patterns as described in chapter 3. Gaydar makes this metadata mean something by dually using/critiquing the most mundane of digital acts, like being friends with someone on Facebook. Gaydar's authors, in an apt summary of their work, commented, "Although we studied Facebook friendship ties, network data is pervasive in the broader context of computer-mediated communication, raising significant privacy issues for communication technologies to which there are no neat solutions."[55]

As individual Facebook users, we might feel uncomfortable when a 'sexuality' is assigned to us without inquiry and with such a reckless and inherently problematic methodology. Indeed, one of the key motives of the Gaydar study was to show that "the ability to determine the sexual orientation of an arbitrary Facebook user represents a serious violation of privacy."[56] But taking into account the explicit critique over how queer people have been counted, assessed, evaluated, and dehumanized over the centuries, following the work of legal scholar Dean Spade, we might object to the very foundation of this measurable type, not just the possibility it has to "out" you.[57]

Both gay and 'gay' are fabrications. An external power invented each for its own purposes. The former originates in the normalizing logics of mental health (in modern times, the classification of homosexuality was pathologized), not gay people identifying themselves as gay.[58] The latter serves as an unconventional, privacy-deserving category to illustrate the apparent danger in dataveillance (the researchers provide no clear reason why they chose to infer 'gay' people instead of 'class' or 'race,' other than the assumed privateness of sexual orientation), not gay people identifying themselves as gay.

Both gay and 'gay' are classifications that do not line up with our own, lived sexual orientations. And while it is perplexing as to why anyone would need to know who is 'gay,' we can ask the same question to those who put us into any category or measurable type—woman, Latino, 'man,' or 'white.' For decades, writers of what became known as queer theory, such as philosophers Michel Foucault and Eve Sedgwick, have critiqued how power locates our habits, identities, and characteristics in different categorical boxes.[59] And these same writers, as well as queer of color scholars Roderick Ferguson and José Esteban Muñoz, also point out that these boxes are often not *for* us but rather serve as objects for administration *about* us.[60] Why would anyone care that someone is gay or 'gay,' if not to use that classification in some managerial, empowered way?[61]

Furthermore, since it is our data that defines Gaydar's speculations around whether we're 'gay' or 'straight,' I propose that dividual privacy can also participate in the destruction of these categorical meanings. Sure, users who practice dividual privacy might want to avoid being assigned a 'sexuality' by Gaydar's algorithm. But users also might want to spoil the construction of the category of 'gay' or 'straight' itself: outwardly straight Facebook users could become friends with large communities of outwardly gay users, and vice versa. By confounding the homophily that Gaydar algorithmically relies on to assign users as 'gay' or 'straight,' the measurable types that define each become useless.

More theoretically, a dividual claim to privacy protects both the user that produces dividual data and the dividuals that are connected to other dividuals. Dividual privacy runs parallel to the datafied subject relations of our algorithmic identities: they are associative, concerned with oneself as well as anyone who is interpolated by Gaydar's assessment.

The macabre rhetoric that announces privacy's "death" or "end" might simply be a hyperbolic signal of liberal, individual privacy's inefficiency in the world of dividual life, a dullness that mimics the Orientalist allegory of a meeting between Saladin and King Richard the Lionheart. It was the time of the Third Crusades, and the sultan of Syria and Egypt, Saladin, was defending his seizure of Jerusalem from the far-from-home English. The encounter, popularly referenced in the 1935 Hollywood movie *Crusades*, centers on the two monarchs comparing their swords and brawn.

Ever the grandstander, Richard uses his strength and human-length broadsword to brutishly cut a mace's iron rod in two. In response, Saladin, whose arm was "thin indeed, and spare," picked up his scimitar, "a curved and narrow blade, which glittered not like the swords of the Franks, but . . . marked with ten millions of meandering lines."[62] Unimpressed by the sliced rod beneath him, he effortlessly drew his own blade across a silk cushion, carving it into pieces—a feat deemed sorcery by his English witnesses. Individual privacy's dullness is dull for the very reason that it is clumsily aligned alongside our dividual actions. A tool like Richard's broadsword might be useful at choice times, but its use is entirely dependent on the strength of the wielder—just like liberal privacy, in which individuals' proximity to power regulates how effective the formal right to privacy can be.

We might think of dividual privacy as Saladin's scimitar. Its use is multipurpose: it can slice both silk and skin. Likewise, to accept that our data makes up the "who" of who we are means privacy must attend to the 'gay' or 'straight' measurable types as much as it protects against the assessment of "*userX* is 'gay'" or "*userY* is 'straight.'" A two-pronged approach configures dividual privacy both as a space for integrity and thus action and as a space to understand how we are made legible to a system—which includes 'we' as much as, if not more than, it includes 'I.' If a user can avoid membership in a measurable type once, it doesn't mean that user will avoid it a second time.

PROCEDURAL DIVIDUAL DUE PROCESS

Detached from our individual selves, liberal privacy's unsharpened dividual edge leaves most of our data almost entirely unprotected.[63] And as we learned in this book's introduction about the Data Wars, in which Google, Microsoft, and Yahoo! spent billions of dollars to buy up several different marketing and web-analytics companies, this data has become one of the prized commodities of our contemporary epoch. Without a nameable individual to endow the right to privacy, we come up against one of privacy's fundamental inadequacies in the algorithmic age: we are unable to critique or contest how our data is made useful, so long as it is made useful far away from the individual's reach.[64]

And when it is a computer, and not an individual, that surveils and evaluates our data, our ability to claim privacy "against" an other is comparably muted. To offer an example: Gmail shows its users contextual advertisements based on the contents of their email. A short message sent to a friend about your opinions on privacy and the Internet will potentially display an advertisement for privacy-enhancing software in future emails. The release of this "feature" in 2004 sparked a series of concerns by users, its presence creepy, uncouth, and invasive.[65] Those concerns have since dwindled as contextual advertising became more and more widespread. The shock of such prophetic, magically appearing advertisements seemed to have worn out.

Yet nine years after the release of Google's contextual advertising, Russian officials launched an official inquiry into it as part of an anti-monopoly investigation of alleged unfair business practices. Google's 2013 response, rehashing a decade-old defense for its method, remains telling: "Surely, there is nobody reading your mails or your account to pick up ads for you. It is an automatic assessment algorithm similar to spam filtration that chooses ads."[66]

As with most instances of dataveillance and algorithmic interpretation, there's rarely a real, live individual who interacts with your data (Hemmings's case momentarily set aside). Google's algorithm removes the individual from both sides of the privacy equation. Not only are our dividualities up for grabs if disconnected from the individual, but surveillance itself gets reframed according to its machinic parallel: if there is no individual doing the watching, is it really surveillance?

By corollary, one might then ask, if it's not surveillance, is there anything to be concerned with? Algorithms processing data might produce our discursive environs from our dividual bits, but there's no explicit, traditional violation of privacy.

The intricacies of this problem have been well dissected by digital scholars Kate Crawford and Jason Schultz, who describe how big-data practitioners employ a "novel" methodology to evade current privacy protections, one that "do[es] not create PII [personally identifiable information] at the point of collection," although that information can become linked to the individual through processing.[67] Crawford and

Schultz's response to this evasion is to enact "procedural data due process," which would "regulate the fairness of Big Data's analytical processes with regard to how they use personal data (or metadata derived from or associated with personal data) in any adjudicative process, including processes whereby Big Data is being used to determine attributes or categories for an individual."[68]

Procedural due process means that we, as individuals, have a role to play in how we are ordered and understood. Constitutional law scholar Laurence Tribe has argued that procedural rights "function, often at some cost to the efficiency and accuracy of fact-finding, to prevent the government from treating individuals in the criminal process as though they were objects." For privacy to be valued, "it must be valued not only as a means to some independent end, but for its intrinsic characteristics: being heard is part of what it means to be a person."[69] In this setting, Crawford and Schultz's concept is fruitful. Ideally, if Hemmings would have been granted some form of procedural data due process—if he would have known both that his answers were being algorithmically evaluated and how those algorithms calculated 'deserving' or 'undeserving'—he might still be alive.

Crawford and Schultz are proposing one half of what I mean by dividual privacy. With procedural data due process, users can understand the context and consequences of their dividual selves. But the concept's theoretical limit runs up against two obstacles. One, as noted earlier, not all individuals are treated the same by the state or capital—a fact that Hemmings's disability potentially plays an important part in. A reliance on procedural due process reaffirms the role of the individual as the subject of power and thus returns us to the bounty of existing critiques of liberal humanism and how the state unevenly enforces individual rights.

And two, as users, we are made by a limitless assemblage of different algorithmic assessments online. Our data exceeds what is in our Gmail folders or even what our answers to a *999 medical survey might be. Online, who we are is made from everything we do that can be turned into data, from where we go to the instant messages sent to friends and to our search queries. It is the foundry of our datafied life that makes 'us' not on the basis of choice but on what Matthew Fuller calls the "fleck[s] of identity" of our daily routine that algorithmic processing subsequently makes useful.[70]

To care about how we are *made*, to attend to both sides of the self/algorithm privacy relation, is to require a privacy that gives us breathing space, even in our fleck-filled landfills. Procedural data due process etches a useful space away from instances of dataveillance. But to breathe for more than an instant is to consider how privacy can operate as an appropriate response to the ceaseless allegorithmic assessments of our datafied dividualities.

Indeed, Crawford and Schultz argue that conventional privacy discourse largely fails us in our datafied world, which indicates that privacy's most recent death might actually be a welcome one. But to go even further—and to think of ourselves as dividuals—the end of liberal privacy can usher in a birth of new possibilities. A fully dividual understanding of privacy clears the way to go beyond a Sisyphean undertaking of individual protection and due process.

If privacy had any longitudinal purpose over the past one hundred plus years of legal stature and millennia of daily practice, it's been to combat encroachments not just on one's private sphere but on one's life itself. As put by philosopher Joseph Kupfer, "privacy is essential to the development and maintenance of an [overdetermined] autonomous self."[71] I would add that privacy is essential to the development of the self as a concept, as well. Without attending to the structures that "make plans" for our selves, we are unable to ask the lingering existential inquiry of philosopher Charles Taylor: "is this the kind of being I ought to be, or really want to be?"[72] To know how we are ordered is to know the forces at work that disturb the internal consistency, or integrity, of who we are—and who we want to be.

Furthermore, disconnected from our individualities, dataveillance still controls us: it controls what our worlds look like, it controls whom we talk to, and it most definitely controls what who 'we' are means. In this case, 'gender' might not be gender, but 'gender' is still part of our lives and determines how we can live them. The measurable type of 'gender' is a cybertype, and its discursive ordering means that we don't just have a 'gender.' Rather, to repurpose Alexander Galloway again, our bodies speak "as a body codified with an affective identity (gendered, ethnically typed, and so on). . . . The difficulty is not simply that bodies must always speak. The difficulty is that they must always speak as."[73] Under dataveillance, our selves also speak "as," now, a 'gender.' And as theorist Alan Westin writes, without the ability to determine for ourselves "when, how, and to what extent information about [ourselves] is communicated to others," we blindly speak "as" an unknown subject.[74]

Which is to say, we lose subjective integrity when our worlds and selves are algorithmically made, in hidden and inscrutable ways, for us. Individual privacy law fortifies a defense against personal intrusion via the ability to determine how information is communicated to others. A procedural data due process would allow individual arbitration over how some agents interpret our dividual lives. But a fully dividual privacy would attend to some of the needs of an individual, as well as those of our dividuals and our connections to the other dividuals. This form of privacy establishes an integrity of self that begins and ends with the dividual.

More specifically, in most cases, Google doesn't really care who *you* are, and neither does Facebook, Quantcast, nor even the NSA. However, Google, Facebook, Quantcast, and the NSA care a great deal about who you, as dividual fragments, can be made to be. To be profiled as an 'old' 'man' locates you within two Google-made definitions. But it also creates the idea, and contexts, of 'age' and 'gender' before our very eyes. Who we are and what who we are means online is given to us. We are forced to exist on a "territory of the self" both foreign and unknown, a foundation of subjective integrity that is structurally uneven. It is the resulting asymmetry in both knowledge and control that privacy has historically defended against. Privacy's theoretical value is to make this asymmetry more equitable, and a dividual privacy does so on data's terms.

Dividual privacy lets us negotiate with systems that normally would exclude our participation. Returning to Hemmings, without procedural data due process, there was no possibility for conversation outside the routines of *999's algorithm. He was locked in, even if he wasn't aware. Indeed, his sustained requests for an ambulance suggest a belief that desperation itself might persuade the operator to help him. But it was his data that was seen as 'undeserving,' not him as a person. So while the *999 algorithm let a man die, it did so by privileging a single, authoritative interpretation of Hemmings's dividualities over any other, including his own. His datafied answers, innocently produced, were unwittingly assessed and used against him.

In the words of psychologist Irwin Altman, privacy is part of a "dialectic and dynamic boundary regulation process."[75] In socio-technical environments, we are always being evaluated, from the mechanics of Internet surfing (saving log files, recording user information) to Hemmings's *999 inputs. Quite evidently, then, referencing computer scientists Leysla Palen and Paul Dourish, "active participation in the networked world requires disclosure of information simply to be a part of it."[76]

But if we agree to this overarching tenet of active participation, we must also be careful not to uncritically accept its individualist corollary: "we also choose to explicitly disclose or publicize information about ourselves, our opinions and our activities."[77] From the ubiquitous surveillance of the Internet to the asymmetry of power implicit in an algorithmic triage system, we are not always aware of our own datafied disclosures or equally capable of interpreting them and their potential meanings. Citing computer scientist Jonathan Grudin, in digital technology, we encounter a "steady erosion of clearly situated action. We are losing control and knowledge of the consequences of our actions. . . . We no longer control access to anything we disclose."[78]

GIBBERISH AND OBFUSCATION

A prophetic anecdote begins *Wired*'s first-ever story on Internet privacy. It was early in 1993, and technology journalist Steven Levy had
just arrived at the office of a Silicon Valley start-up. He was on assignment to observe a "cypherpunk" meeting, a group whose members used
mathematically complex cryptography, or secret coding, to make their
digital data turn to gibberish.

His description of the meeting was a "time warp to the days when
hackers ran free": fifteen "techie-cum-civil libertarians" randomly
lay on the floor or wandered around cubicles, only to eventually collect themselves, hours after the scheduled time, in order to share their
crypto secrets. These were the specialist grandparents of the Internet
privacy world, the hackers and engineers who understood the distinction between privacy offline and privacy online—their purpose wasn't
to pull the digital blinds down in their houses but to make information
about them useless:

> The people in this room hope for a world where an individual's
> informational footprints—everything from an opinion on abor-
> tion to the medical record of an actual abortion—can be traced
> only if the individual involved chooses to reveal them; a world
> where coherent messages shoot around the globe by network
> and microwave, but intruders and feds trying to pluck them out
> of the vapor find only gibberish; a world where the tools of pry-
> ing are transformed into the instruments of privacy.[79]

Making information useful is the raison d'être of algorithmic processing, while making information gibberish is the raison d'être of encryption, a cornerstone to Internet privacy that deploys mathematics
not to hide one's tracks but to make them unreadable. This mathematical ideal refuses the disciplinary measures of the superpanopticon discussed in chapter 3, rendering your individual details as mere datafied

drivel. But there's an antiquatedness in the preceding quotation. It still centers around the personally identifiable.

Remember that back in 1993, marketers would have to wait a full year before Internet tracking was even invented. The dataveillance we take as common today was both technologically and politically unimaginable. The informational footprints that cypherpunks worried about were just database records attached to your name or Social Security number. They were the data that has a direct connection to our individual selves. They were not our search queries, they were not our Netflix queues, and they were not our cookies.

Yet this cypherpunk strategy of making data nonsensical marks a formative pivot in how we can continue to frame dividual privacy. While focusing on the individual in theory, it is not the individual that becomes gibberish. It is the individual's data. Cypherpunks began to question how data about our medical records or political opinions had discursive effect on our own individuality. In doing so, they successfully opened an avenue of thought that could address dividuality on its own, datafied terms.

To make something useful, à la Google's mission statement ("to organize the world's information and make it universally accessible and useful"), means that it can't also be gibberish.[80] Gibberish has no contact, no traction that connects one point to another. In effect, by founding ourselves as gibberish, we begin to think about liberty and privacy with a dividual approach. Dividuals are made to be connected, mashed up, and processed in order to create synergistic value. If we were gibberish from the get-go, then not only would our individualities be safeguarded from malicious prying and plucking but our dividualities would be eternally detached, as well.

This strategy is quite ideal to frustrate dividual pattern analysis. The 'gender' that Google assigns you or your 'ethnicity' as defined by your Quantcast profile cannot latch onto gibberish data. As a user, you would be nonsensical, useless garbage. And as a measurable type, 'gender' and 'ethnicity' would be similarly nonsensical creations. If we could successfully make our metadata gibberish (more about this later on), Gaydar's 'gayness' would be unworkable.

But Google and Quantcast desperately don't want us to be gibberish. They collect and save our data despite our attempt to conceal it. In fact, we cannot be gibberish if we want Google and Quantcast to be useful for us. You might encrypt a search query for "privacy," but much like entering a bank and speaking gibberish to the teller, Google needs to understand your query to make it useful. Encryption on a mass, dividual level disallows data from being plucked from the vapor, so long as that vapor is not owned by a Google or a Quantcast.

Like the concept of neoliberal private property itself, it is the owner of each network that determines how, and if, our data can be plucked. Encrypt all you want, but if one side of an encryption handshake is your Gmail account or your Quantcast beacon, 'you' will always be extracted to make sense of you, to market to you, and eventually to make you. But there are other ways to be gibberish, other ways to disrupt the making useful of algorithmic processing.

For example, the following are the search terms that my computer queried Google.com, Bing.com, Yahoo.com, and AOL.com in the past minute: "Living fulfilling lives without; that have been lost; Make friends with your; must push back against; Jaundiced newborns without additional; Asalaam alaikum warahmatulah wabarakatuh; comply with their legal; That moment when your; Chocolate Covered Coffee Beans; bankrupt river millionaires." Quite obviously, it wasn't me who made those searches. In reality, I wasn't even using my web browser. I was writing the preceding paragraph. Instead, those ten phrases were scraped from the RSS feeds of the top news stories at NYTimes.com, CNN.com, MSNBC.com, and TheRegister.co.uk. The program that did it was an NYU-based research project led by Helen Nissenbaum called TrackMeNot.

TrackMeNot is a browser plug-in that sits like a daemon under your browser and automatically throws random search queries at each of the aforementioned four search engines every six seconds. These capricious queries make your data gibberish but now through a different rouse. An encrypted message of "I love you" might look like "EnCt-2c8ac6bf1a9d006f33565ecae0ba295381442c0c2c8ac6bf1a9 d006f33565e-caeRKtKdrqaeQPSzgBVi1RC5GBFVRILuCn9IwEmS" to watchers in the vapor. And unencrypted, you might honestly search for "how to flee the country," but the noteworthiness of that phrase will be folded into the ten-queries-per-minute cover that TrackMeNot provides for you.

An individual FBI special agent invested in knowing if you're trying to travel to Greece might be able to subpoena your Google records and see that you searched for "Athens" at 6:31 p.m., "cheap flights" at 6:34 p.m., and "online greek classes" at 6:44 p.m. But in terms of pattern recognition, in terms of making 'you' on the basis of your dividual queries, TrackMeNot can produce enough noise in the channel that a single, identifiable, measurable-typed essence would be statistically onerous. This is gibberish through excess, not enciphering. And this gibberish is what founds Finn Brunton and Helen Nissenbaum's obfuscation, the contemporary strategy I propose we use to practice dividual privacy.[81]

The cypherpunks of the 1990s hid by converting their data into alphanumeric ridiculousness. TrackMeNot hides your dividualities in plain sight but overloads what might become meaningful with layers upon layers of extradividual nonsense.[82] While "Jaundiced newborns without additional" might be absurdly figurative, it's also baloney. Obfuscation creates layers of data incoherency, further upholding our dividual privacy. It is not that TrackMeNot aims to avoid an FBI special agent. TrackMeNot avoids incorporation, and thus discursive effect, within the Googleverse's (and Microsoft's, Yahoo!'s, and AOL's) array of measurable types.

Obfuscation is the practice by which the world, as organized through data, can be messed with on data's terms. A privacy that relies on a "don't look at this, it's private!" liberal-rights-based approach will always fall vulnerable to people, inside and outside the government, who break and/or ignore the law. Instead, we can view dividual privacy praxis as a "try to look, but I doubt you will find anything useful" invitation to our surveilling others.

Practices of dividual privacy establish the ground for an integrity of self. Sometimes this integrity can be produced through knowledge about the context of surveillance and how exactly it produces constraint on your life. Other times it can be zeroed out by generating enough gibberish that 'you' as a datafied subject becomes meaningless. Citing an obfuscatory example from Brunton and Nissenbaum, take the 1960 film *Spartacus*, in which a group of recaptured slaves protect Spartacus—who had earlier led an unsuccessful revolt against the Roman Empire—by each person self-identifying as the "real" Spartacus. As one after another stands up to claim, "I am Spartacus," "Spartacus" is drained of meaning.[83] For a moment, it loses its uniqueness.

Tools like TrackMeNot perform this soliloquy over and over, producing data that an algorithmic system believes to be authentic, much like a self-identifying speech act in the face of Roman soldiers. But unlike the case of a name, in which only one person can be believably called Spartacus, which eventually led all the slaves to crucifixion, there's no reliable way to understand the difference between a genuine and a bogus query.

This inability to decipher genuine from bogus reveals a structural and exploitable gap. And this gap supplies us the breathing space we desperately need outside surveillance's reach. But as we try to keep breathing, we also unwittingly produce data about ourselves every time we make a datafied move. Our datafied footprints are impossible to completely sidestep.

TOWARD A DIVIDUAL PRIVACY

Algorithms are fallible—even to the point of manslaughter. The UK's *999 algorithm, as we later learned, was programmed to identify life-threatening heart problems. It was not programmed to identify gallbladder problems that could eventually lead to life-threatening heart problems.

Given Hemmings's tragic death, the *999 algorithm could surely be updated to take these gallbladder problems into account. But to focus on the algorithm is to implicitly argue that Hemmings, and anyone else like him, could have been saved with savvier processing, better technology, and even more data. This perspective is what new media scholar José van Dijck refers to as "dataism," or "widespread belief in the objective quantification and potential tracking of all kinds of human behavior and sociality through online media technologies."[84] There is no end to this line of thought. Similarly, we can never be 100 percent sure that certain data—such as DNA evidence, fingerprints, or vocal prints—connects to a single, unique individual.[85]

Algorithms are devices for allocation, and their allocation will always be empowered, functionalist, and incomplete. Sometimes a decision and its consequences can be unintentional, as in Hemmings's case. Other times it can be overtly political, such as the use of quotas to dictate which immigrants, and from which countries, receive U.S. green cards.[86] Whether this process is deliberate or not, you as a person are read as data—and therefore you as a person are beholden to the logic of each and every system that makes that data useful. Failing systems are the unavoidable shortcomings of technocratic implementation.

To reiterate from earlier, Hemmings's death by algorithm is certainly about privacy, just not privacy in its traditional form. Hemmings may have been inside his house, enjoying his "right to be let alone," but he was also helpless in his private sphere, pleading for assistance over a telephone wire. Seen one way, this is the antithesis of liberal privacy: the overt sharing and invited invasion of the government into one's own home.

But Hemmings's house wasn't the system that framed his context for disclosure. The system was *999's algorithm. Hemmings needed privacy—an integrity of self—because without it he was unable to regulate how his data was made useful. He was denied the ability to determine his role in the system. More pointedly, he was not "let alone" in a way that would empower him within the algorithmic order. Instead, he was "let alone" to be vulnerable to the output of the algorithm.

As procedural data due process tells us, we need to build into privacy's conceptual foundation a recognition that we all expect different types of privacy in different contexts—even if those contexts are algorithmically produced. This reframing affixes loosely to Nissenbaum's idea of privacy as "contextual integrity," as explored earlier in this chapter.[87] Hemmings's data was taken from him in one context (verbal question) and then used against him in another (algorithmic processing). But the expansive variance of contexts not only that we encounter everyday but also from which our territories of the self are made means that to have an integrity of self is to understand how we are made on all fronts.

More generally, as political sociologist Jeff Weintraub writes, "discourses of public and private cover a variety of subjects that are analytically distinct and, at the same time, subtly—often confusingly—overlapping and intertwined."[88] Our private spaces are constantly invaded by state and capital surveillance, as well as by our families, friends, and the person who leers a bit too long into an open window. The networked intersubjectivity of daily life establishes a domain of privacy that legal scholar Paul Schwartz describes as an overlapping region for negotiation.[89]

We confront this overlap in the work of legal theorist Julie E. Cohen, whose *Configuring the Networked Self* emphasizes the fact that context matters in how we make and remake ourselves.[90] Who we are in one context is different from who we are in another, so that "a robust theory of privacy requires an understanding of the processes by which selfhood comes into being and is negotiated through contexts and over time."[91] Contexts, like life, are dynamic, and the current practice of privacy that keeps up with this dynamism is obfuscating. Rather than attempting to hide, conceal, or frankly negotiate with power, a dividual privacy can instead negotiate with noise.

To negotiate with noise is to accept that yes, procedural data due process allows us a degree of freedom within algorithmic assessment. But by taking into account the diversity of our algorithmic identifications, we can also appreciate how exhausting that proceduralism might be. Through obfuscation, we recruit Jisuk Woo's idea of nonidentification not as a right but as a practice of overdetermining our potential algorithmic assignments.

Obfuscation serves as a practical addendum that reconciles privacy's original rationale, the "right to be let alone," with our contemporary shift toward what technology critic Evgeny Morozov has described as the "tyranny of algorithms."[92] And it is to follow writer Richard W. Severson's offering that "we must learn to think of personal data as an extension of the self and treat it with the same respect we would a living individual. To do otherwise runs the risk of undermining the privacy that makes self-determination possible."[93]

In the balance of this chapter, I investigate how the practice of Woo's nonidentification might operate, what it looks like, and what that means for privacy in general. In this way, dividual privacy goes beyond its duty to the individual body or person and even to our own dividual selves. It also extends to the knowledges of the world that our dividualities help compose. We are all more than just profiles affixed with different measurable-type identities. We are living, breathing, constitutive parts of those measurable types. Dividual privacy can provide productive breathing space by disconnecting us from identification, as well as by disrupting the construction of dividual knowledge itself. As a political act, dividual privacy rejects the attempt by state and capital to classify us, our behaviors, and our voices.

As dataveillance constantly tries to process our algorithmic selves in "as if" ways, dividual privacy allows for strategic dissociations from these founts of classificatory power. But with this embedded constancy, to think about privacy in this way is to think about a privacy with no end. It's a privacy of the "and." Despite the seemingly naturalized dichotomy between the private and the public, privacy can't just be about shutting out the public world.

Privacy offers a way to participate in or reject this project of legibility, much like how we close our blinds to make ourselves illegible to the social world or use passwords on our email accounts to deny others participation in the making of our individual selves. In this form, privacy serves as a way to enact a kind of "whatever," to reference Alexander Galloway's concept, that "fields no questions and leaves very little to say."[94] Woo's "right not to be identified," and the dividual privacy I work to theorize beyond that, tries to make our dividualities say little, if anything at all. Because when it comes to our dividualities, it is not us that makes 'us.' It's *them*. A dividual privacy aims to think through this asymmetry of self-definition on all fronts, of data that connects to you *and* data that connects to other data.

WHAT DOES DIVIDUAL PRIVACY LOOK LIKE?

We need dividual privacy—a privacy that extends beyond our individual bodies, that accepts the realities of ubiquitous surveillance, and that defends the "right to be let alone" even, and especially, when we are made of data—because the teeth of its liberal cousin cut too superficially and inefficiently. To anoint the individual subject as the sole index of power is to miss out on everything else that happens outside the individual's point of view: the modulating, discursive environs that condition our dividualities; the flows of dataveillance power that deny us an integrity of self; and the intersubjectivity of others' dividualities that play a part in who we are and how we're understood. In short, to focus only on the individual is to avoid the hard questions that dataveillance introduces into our lives.

Understanding that our data is part and parcel of who we are and what we are subject to lets us think about privacy in a new way. Privacy has long been heralded as a human right, but what does privacy look like now that we are more than just our bodies but also our information? What is privacy for the posthuman whose 'citizenship' and 'sexuality' are assigned according to one's metadata and whose 'class' is determined by one's web browser or operating system? A dividual privacy that safeguards our posthumanity wouldn't abandon the individual, but it would recognize the impossibility for a "safe space," a cordoned-off private sphere that becomes ever more impossible in our increasingly informationalized world. The posthuman need for dividual privacy is a need that has no individual counterpart. This is also why, throughout this book, I have refrained from focusing too much on "personally identifiable information" to explain how ubiquitous dataveillance challenges our previously held notions about life, the world, and knowledge itself.

Information about ourselves is the cornerstone for how our posthumanity is made intelligible to systems of power. Even removing our first or last names from data does little to reduce that information's capacity for control. While the origin expectations we have for privacy as a human need can be understood, just the same, as a posthuman need, how we articulate that need necessarily changes. In a dividual world, we no longer can center privacy on traditional liberal individuality, just as dividual privacy does not protect the same vulnerabilities as its individual counterpart does.

This is why the obfuscating tools for dividual privacy do more than make your full name and other unique identifiers nonsensical. Within the vapor, a piece of information about you can be tied to another, which can be tied to another, until this data string becomes 'you.' As such, to pay exclusive attention to the specifics of a unique person is to recenter dividual privacy back onto an individual index.

Dividual privacy is largely a relation to discursive objects, not people. Since there is no datafied record that connects everything that is John Cheney-Lippold, I am bound to an endless aggregation of measurable types that make me 'me.' 'Me' only exists in the resulting equation: 'gender' + 'race' + 'deserving medical treatment' + 'citizen,' + 'etc.' = 'me.' Individual privacy focuses exclusively on the right side of the equals sign.

Dividual privacy targets both sides, of each measurable-type addend as well as the resulting sum.

Like Saladin's blade, dividual privacy is a weapon that is multivariate and tactical. It has extensive purpose but no guarantee of perfection. Dividual privacy is also implicitly in solidarity with others, a sense that although we alone don't make up 'gender,' 'gender' affects us all. You, as an individual, might not want to be profiled and manipulated without your knowledge, but your fate is tied to the rest of the population whose dividual lives become the patterns by which you are recognized.

On the one hand, there's a beautiful fellowship that makes us all statistically significant to each other. On the other, dividual privacy is a discursive disruption that brandishes privacy's edge at the level of the measurable type—not just at the last mile that connects each measurable type to an IP address, Google account, or NSA dossier.

One technology that embodies this logic of dividual privacy is a software networking tool called Tor (formerly the Onion Router). Initially funded by the U.S. Navy, Tor shuttles Internet traffic across discrete, theoretically untraceable layers. It is, in the words of the NSA, "the King of high secure, low-latency Internet anonymity" with "no contenders for the throne in waiting."[95]

Less regally, a user who uses Tor structurally rejects the sender/receiver dialogue of a "clear" TCP/IP request: you type in google.com to your web browser, your computer sends a TCP/IP request to Google's computer, and Google sends the requested information (the contents of google.com/index.php) back to your computer, the entire process concluding within mere milliseconds. With Tor, a user doesn't just "go" to Google. Instead, the software automatically reroutes each request through around three different proxies/relays (onion layers), furnishing three different steps of anonymity between your computer and Google.

The virtue of this tool actually comes from an old, well-practiced form of anonymization. Take journalist Bob Woodward, who in 1972 famously onion routed himself around Washington, D.C., to receive leaked Watergate information from then−FBI associate director Mark

Felt, aka "Deep Throat."[96] Beginning at his apartment in Dupont Circle, Woodward would walk down the street and, let's say, take a single taxi to the National Mall. Then, Woodward would leave that taxi, enter a new one, and go to a second location, like Georgetown. Then, Woodward would again step out and hail a third taxi. From Georgetown, he would travel across the Key Bridge into Virginia, into Rosslyn, and near the Oakhill Office Building. He would exit the final taxi and walk the remaining blocks to the parking garage where Felt was waiting.

The idea behind this meandering was to avoid a direct connection between Woodward's Washington, D.C., and Felt's Rosslyn, Virginia. The proxy taxis Woodward took to and from the parking structure would obscure any single, perceivable connection between the two high-profile individuals. Tor does this every time you go to a web page, bestowing each of your trips anonymity even while they may remain in public view.

With onion routing, Tor avoids the prototypical tracking mechanisms that are so commonly found on the superficial web. By routing user traffic through three different medium servers, the index of a single, unique user gets blown apart. Data that takes a bunch of different taxis is difficult to make useful. And attached to useless data, our datafied subject relations feel a bit freer.

Tor functionally fashions anonymity through this automated confusion, one that refuses a linear, directional trail of footprints. In technical terms, you produce three times the metadata every time you visit a site through Tor. But that data also confers on you a degree of freedom: each piece of metadata is just a unique, anonymous digital incident unavailable for tethering. In this way, Tor is an effective tool to practice dividual privacy.

But more interesting is that Tor socializes the practice of dividual privacy. This need for socialization, citing Tor's origin as a military project, is best expressed by researcher Paul Syverson: "If you have a system that's only a Navy system, anything popping out of it is obviously from the Navy. You need to have a network that carries traffic for other people as well."[97] This is also why, while users access the superficial Internet (or the clearnet) via any web browser, the Internet of the Darknet (sites that are accessible only to users who use anonymizing networks like Tor) requires you to download Tor before you can join the network. In order to practice dividual privacy as a user, you must also practice dividual privacy for everyone else. With no user on the network holding onto a stable identity, no user can be profiled according to the patterns of others. You are, at the level of infrastructure, forced to engage with questions of privacy at square one, both for the sake of yourself and also for the sake of the server and other users.

On the superficial web, the surveillant assemblage easily combs through your flecks of data. Quantcast knows your IP address went to a series of different websites. The NSA follows your phone as you travel across the Atlantic Ocean. But on the Darknet, your metadata is just untethered, isolated nonsense. It's only vapor, in the parlance of the cypherpunks, that materially dissipates instead of algorithmically congealing.

Yet Tor is not perfect, as no privacy tool is or will ever be. It is available to be hacked (NSA documentation shows inroads in deanonymizing Tor).[98] It also heightens individual suspicion (a user who uses Tor on a local network is able to be singled out because she may be the only one using it). And it's also often slow given its extra proxy steps. Watching streaming video while taking three taxis to and from Netflix servers might make daily web life a bit more cumbersome. And even if we used Netflix.com through Tor, we'd still be connected to our user accounts—we'd still be ordered according to the logics of Netflix's genre-defining algorithms and how those algorithms profile, and thus delimit, our lives.[99]

Again, there is no safe space for our dividual selves. Journalist Julia Angwin describes this impossibility in her book *Dragnet Nation*. During her research, Angwin spent incredible amounts of time, money, and effort in pursuit of full anonymity online.[100] And of course, through no fault of her own, she failed. Some people might fetishize some aseptic perfection of supreme privacy, but its practice is utterly unworkable. No matter how hard we may try to avoid surveillance's embrace, its ubiquity still manages to bring us back into the fold.

IMPOSSIBILITY

The tussle between the forces of ubiquitous surveillance and the forces of privacy is ultimately a struggle over the organization of digital life itself. What data is organized to be is what we are expected to be. 'Gender' becomes gender, just like the NSA's 'citizen' functionally transforms into citizen. When we negotiate with different systems of surveillance and power, we are indebted to each system's assumptions and allegorithms, so that the discursive neoliberal precincts of Google and Facebook use our data to make us and our future for us—most often without our recognition. To repeat from earlier, who we are online is up to the ominous *them*, not us.

In contrast, when *Seinfeld*'s George Costanza yells in frustration, "you know, we're living in a society!" he is appealing to a set of shared circumstances, an idealized assumption that both meaning and ethics cross more than one authoritarian or subjective experience. The impulse toward society is important because it rebuffs the privatized authorship of Google to define 'gender,' Quantcast to define 'ethnicity,' and Gaydar to define 'gay.' While we all have different versions of categorical meaning in our individual heads, these versions must necessarily interact with others, with a social world that queries and interrogates their meaning according to social use.

But the measurable types that make up our dividual selves aren't social. The algorithms that make them up are largely proprietary, legally shrouded in secret (and closed away from critique) because it is exactly their spurring of sociality that gives them their value. If Facebook's algorithms were public, Facebook would no longer hold a monopoly over the digital culture it birthed. The data that makes up Quantcast's 'Caucasian' refuses conversation with questions of white supremacy and histories of racial legacy because it's not directly talking about the institutions upholding the social construct of race. 'Caucasian' is a functionalist, utilitarian category that modulates as a mode for profit and control, not as a social form or part of an explicit racialized politics.

In the height of childish unfairness, we almost always have to share with these agents of surveillance, but they almost never have to share with us. The measurable types that serve as our points of contact with power become sites of demarcation. These sites shape the asymmetry between how we perceive the present and future and how the present and future are a priori conditioned and normalized for us.

Informational disclosure is a systemic phenomenon, which means that our dividualities are disclosed to systems, not society. Indeed, our informational sharing has no direct, dialogical relationship to any level of society. It merely trickles into social life like pipes of a sewer system, a pollution of privatized knowledges that ooze their discursive refuse into the already-muddled waters of social thought. As stated in the introduction, 'race' is about race, but it's also not. The consequence of this discursive disproportion is in its discursive confusion. And not at all far away from these sewage ducts is an eager allegorithm, hoarding our dividual garbage as our lives get framed by algorithmic recycling.

Hemmings's relationship to this allegorithmic world was directed and decided for him. He could not refuse to talk with the operator, nor did he know that 'deserving' and 'undeserving' existed. He was just living his life in preconditioned waters. In other words, his call to *999 locked him into a system that allegorithmically forbid him any prospect for an integrity of self.

Dividual privacy focuses, surely, on each users' independent actions to proactively disturb how measurable types are compiled and attached to our dividual identities. But a dividual privacy cannot make the user the exclusive actor responsible for her own well-being. Dividual privacy is social. It requires public participation. It depends on infrastructural projects like Tor that socialize the need for privacy across society's protocols and access points.

In the example of *999, Hemmings would ideally be able to practice procedural data due process, to opt out of the triage system, or to
emphasize the value of his own requests for help over the *999 system's devaluation of him. Yet alongside Hemmings's mistaken triage
lies another allegorithmic tragedy. This tragedy plays out in the vocabulary of triage itself, in which the category of 'deservingness' was
so callously followed that its social value became overpowered by its
technical meaning. Hemmings lacked dividual privacy because he was
recognized and treated as a discursive object. He had no choice in the
matter. To repeat, Hemmings's death wasn't about Hemmings at all—it
was about his data. And it wasn't even his data; it was his data as algorithmically assessed by *999's triage algorithm.

I began this chapter with Hemmings's case because it doesn't end
well. Indeed, it can't. If we blame Hemmings or we blame the algorithm
or we blame the emergency operator, we will get nowhere. All are small
pieces in the elaborate narrative by which algorithms make us and
condition our possibilities. There are many different ways we can ma-
neuver within these conditions at any particular moment, but the negotiation inherent in social relations befouls the clean idea of a subject
who decides her own fate. And now, our negotiation with algorithmic
construction befouls us even further.

This is the final act in the tragedy of Hemmings's death. It was unavoidable from the moment he dialed, because the system was fixed
against him. This system is not the gamut of predetermination that arrives from race, gender, disability, class, sexuality, age, and their accompanying structural prejudices. Rather, it was in the algorithmic
impossibility of his data keeping him alive.

While an improved algorithm might have saved Hemmings, it would
have killed another. Our lives cannot be datafied in perfect fidelity, as
there will always be a material aberration that causes a hiccup—a lived
experience that the ontology of the computer cannot fully reconceptualize. If anything merits our accusatory finger-pointing, it's the technocratic desire we have to make data speak, to have data about ourselves

be the determining factor in not just our individual actions but the construction of what is: 'deserving,' 'citizen,' or 'celebrity.'

Yet, in writing this chapter, I also point a different finger at myself. It's important to acknowledge that, both in my discussion of Hemmings's case and in the journalism that followed his death, his own individual privacy went out the window. His experience with *999 became a public event, a piece of evidence I use that further publicizes his name, identity, medical details, and words for argument's sake. The integrity of self that we all desire, in both life and death, is disturbed by our contemporary capacity to record text and audio data, circulate it effortlessly online, and thus sell newspapers, advertising, or books. For this reason, and others, I dedicate *We Are Data* to him.

Ultimately, I aim in this chapter to continue a discussion about the problems of ubiquitous surveillance, not to provide a complete solution. Yet I try in this chapter, at the very least, to sketch out a discursive space with new terms so that we can begin answering these problems together. To claim "I want privacy" might seem pointless in the contemporary epoch, when privacy has been left for dead. But as a necessary function of social life, privacy should be celebrated.

Dividual privacy can be socialized if it can be instrumentalized. Technologies can be used together to disrupt identificatory assumptions. Social protest can help frustrate the gross ineptitude of a bureaucratic system that lays off workers and cedes diagnostic authority to a *999 algorithm. Privacy as an atomizing, isolating phenomenon is a privacy not worth fighting for. Privacy as intersubjective, social, and associative is a privacy worth thinking through and resuscitating.

CONCLUSION

The first sentence of Facebook's terms of service agreement is as hilarious as it's insightful: "your privacy is very important to us."[101] This document, which outlines the terms you must agree to in order to use Facebook, is the virtual constitution for how life on the site is lived. What is allowed, what is disallowed, all are explicitly spelled out in pages of legalese. And with this accompanying language, Facebook as a site owner is able both to police the site as it wishes and to legally exculpate itself in the case of real-world lawbreaking (i.e., Facebook isn't responsible for a user posting illegal content on the site, because that user already promised not to post illegal content).

Facebook's business model depends on commodifying our personal data, so of course privacy is very important. But this is a privacy of the individual, a privacy that makes us feel less creeped out by Facebook's immense accumulation of information about our lives. The site offers users levers that let them regulate how much of the data we uploaded from our Friday night is available to our friends, coworkers, and family. Without this privacy, Facebook could likely fail as a business. So yes, I agree, privacy is important for it.

But this "very important" privacy is the kind that's already dead. In the way that governments and conservative ideology co-opt many radical historical figures after their demise (Martin Luther King, Jr., Rosa Parks, Cesar Chavez), the privacy that Facebook cares about is a privacy that has no teeth. It's a privacy that might keep your disreputable photos away from your boss, but that's not really privacy, is it? For me, that's just adequate site architecture. We couldn't imagine an architect patting herself on the back because she remembered to put walls between rooms, much less acclaiming how "important" privacy is to her because there isn't a gaping hole between the bathroom and kitchen. Facebook's privacy is similar.

A privacy that isn't dead is a privacy that calls back to privacy's origins: a breathing space to be. However, this privacy of being is also very important to Facebook, not because it wants to protect it but because it wants to exploit it. It's important that dead privacy be kept away from its still-breathing relative, because a privacy that protects what writer David Shenk calls the "data smog" expelled by the motors of our online activities would mean a Facebook that can't profit from that smog's commodification.[102] The current business logic of Facebook, and the rest of the Internet at large, is reliant on us not having/practicing this kind of privacy.

We are made legible to Facebook on its own terms—not ours. This is another kind of "terms" of service, one more structural and much less apparent. An asymmetry of terms is what control is about, both offline and online. The same asymmetry is also what privacy combats when control is made and regulated based on data about ourselves. And lastly, this asymmetry is one of the defining conditions of Internet life, as the terms of each site, in both legal and conceptual forms, are what give each site its uniqueness.

Part of dividual privacy is to combat this asymmetry, but most of it is to understand it. If you use Facebook, short of making a new Facebook, you will be under the terms of service and thus the terms of Facebook—same with Netflix, Twitter, and any other (capitalist) web presence. We are always on unequal footing. Everything from plane prices to friends to news content to even whom we might date is determined for us on the basis of how our data is made useful. Rarely in life are we so unknowing of the knowledge that makes us, and our world, in such rarefied ways.

This unknowingness came to the fore in the early months of 2014, when an experiment discussed in chapter 1, of Facebook modifying users' News Feeds on the basis of the 'positive' and 'negative' expressions of user status updates, was made public. Users felt toyed with. They learned that their very own portals to the social world were part of an experiment. And quickly thereafter, critics discovered that the terms of service acceding to this experimental study had been slipped in under the radar. Facebook had retroactively updated its terms to allow this kind of mass, anonymous, but still influential research.

But more damningly, and I argue more consequentially, Facebook's study also changed the terms by which users would engage with their social world, a befitting example of how power articulates according to the measurable type. The critics who cried foul after the study's publication were practicing dividual privacy. Users felt uncomfortable on the site because they were unable to just "be." They were being toyed with by researchers. They lacked an integrity of self. They didn't understand the context of their datafied life.

Yet most damningly, and most consequentially, we are toyed with on a similar scale, and by nonsimilar actors, every single day. The entirety of our datafied subjectivities is indebted to this variability, as the invariability that we assumed grounded our News Feeds was always a lie. Indeed, almost everything that is algorithmic is a lie in the same way. Privacy in the digital world is a lived version of resistance to this lie, a resistance that isn't to be cherished because of its rebelliousness but to be protected due to its necessity.

CONCLUSION

Ghosts in the Machine

Inside us all there is a code. A code that represents not what we are but who we might become. It is our potential. 25 years ago a company was started based on the idea that technology is the key to unlocking the power of human potential. And so Microsoft launched a revolution. Fueled by innovative software that threw open new horizons, eliminated boundaries, and broke down barriers. People asked, what can I be? We inspired them to pursue their dreams. Workers ask, how far can I go? We give them the tools to express their ideas. Businesses ask, how do I compete? We empower them to respond with agility. Developers ask, what's the next big thing? We enable them to fulfill their visions. The better we do our job, the more potential we unleash. And the greater achievements we inspire. Moving forward, we embrace the promise of an open world and the unexpected opportunities it presents. It's the world's greatest challenge, to advance the achievements of the human race by unleashing the potential that is encoded in us all. Microsoft.

—Microsoft "Potential" video[1]

We are made of data. But we are really only *made* when that data is made useful. This configuration is best described by the technologist wet dream in the epigraph. For the cyberutopians who believe this stuff, we are a code, a Heideggerian standing reserve that actualizes us through technology.[2] Or more appropriately, we are a rudimentary cyborgism laid bare by Microsoft's rhetoric: inside us is a code; that code represents not us but our potential; and despite the code being inside of *us* and signifying *our* potential, it must unlocked by (Microsoft) technology.

Microsoft's "Potential" recruiting video is wonderful because it so transparently celebrates a world where corporate profit goes hand in hand with digital technology, which goes hand in hand with capitalist globalization, which goes hand in hand with the colonization of our own futures by some super-intense neoliberal metaphor of code. One might ask, does this code ever rest? Does it have fun, go to a soccer match, or drink a glass of wine? Or is its only function to work/use Microsoft products? The code inside us seems like the kind of code who stays late at the office to the detriment of friendship, partnership, or possibly a child's birthday.

Yet Microsoft's overwrought voice-over copy superficially grazes the more substantial consequence of "inside us all there is a code." If we are made of code, the world fundamentally changes. This codified interpretation of life is, at the level of our subjectivity, how the digital world is being organized. It is, at the level of knowledge, how that world is being defined. And it is, at the level of social relations, how that world is being connected. Of course, we don't have to use Microsoft products to unleash our potential. That's beside the point. But Microsoft's iconic corporate monopoly works as a convenient stand-in to critique the role that technology has in not just representing us but functionally determining "who we might become."

Representation plays second fiddle if Microsoft can quite literally rewrite the codes of race, class, gender, sexuality, citizenship, celebrity, and terrorist. Rewriting these codes transcodes their meaning onto Microsoft's terms. They become the author of who 'we' are and can be.

Asymmetry defines this type of emergent power relation. Power (be it state or capital) classifies us without querying us. And those classifications carry immense weight to determine who possesses the rights of a 'citizen,' what 'race' and 'gender' mean, and even who your 'friends' are. Indeed, the central argument of this book is that the world is no longer expressed in terms we can understand. This world has become datafied, algorithmically interpreted, and cybernetically reconfigured so that I can never say, "I am 'John'" with full comprehension of what that means. As a concrete subjective agent, 'John' can't really exist. However, 'John' can be controlled.

This apparent paradox fits with the famed doublethink slogan that defines George Orwell's political dystopia of *1984*: "who controls the past controls the future; who controls the present controls the past."[3] To control the present is to control everything that comes before as well as everything that happens after. So what happens when you don't just control the present but also construct it? Novelist Zadie Smith supplies us an answer in her own review of the 2010 film about Facebook, *The Social Network*:

> When a human being becomes a set of data on a website like Facebook, he or she is reduced. Everything shrinks. Individual character. Friendships. Language. Sensibility. In a way it's a transcendent experience: we lose our bodies, our messy feelings, our desires, our fears. It reminds me that those of us who turn in disgust from

what we consider an overinflated liberal-bourgeois sense of self should be careful what we wish for: our denuded networked selves don't look more free, they just look more owned.[4]

On Facebook, our selves are not more free; they are more owned. And they are owned because we are now made of data.

Let's consider an example from Facebook, where researchers have reconceptualized the very idea of 'inappropriate' with a new feature that aims to introduce a bit more decorum into our digital lives. An automated "assistant" can evaluate your photos, videos, status updates, and social interactions, scanning them all for what Facebook thinks is 'inappropriate' content. When you post something that Facebook considers unbecoming, your algorithmic assistant will ask, "Uh, this is being posted publicly. Are you sure you want your boss and your mother to see this?"[5]

That Facebook will know 'inappropriate' from 'appropriate' is beholden to the same presumption that Quantcast knows a 'Caucasian,' Google knows a 'celebrity,' and the NSA knows a 'terrorist.' They don't. All of these are made up, constructed anew and rife with both error and ontological inconsistency. Yet despite this error, their capacity for control is impressively powerful. Facebook's gentility assistant, if it ever gets implemented, will likely have more import in framing acceptable behavior than any etiquette book ever written has.

These algorithms may "unlock" your potential—or, in the case of Facebook, may curate your potential—but not in the way that Microsoft wants you to believe. Microsoft's prose suggests you have some static DNA hard coded into your system that is just waiting to succeed in the marketplace. Trust me (and anyone who isn't your parent), you don't. What you do have is life, and one brief look at contemporary capitalism's CV will demonstrate its terrifying competence to colonize that life with its own logic and motives. What these algorithms do "unlock" is the ability to make your life useful on terms productive for algorithms' authors.

Imagine a world where a company like Google doesn't just gatekeep the world's information but also controls how we describe that world. This is the precise problem we encounter when discourse is privatized, although not the way people usually talk about the crisis of privatized knowledge. Sure, public libraries are losing funding, museums are closing, and even academic journals are pettily protecting copyright for the articles that scholars write for free. That's one kind of privatization. But much like Google has the ability to make a 'celebrity' and Facebook to define 'inappropriate,' Google, Facebook, and others are on their way to privatizing "everything."

PRIVACY AND PRIVATIZATION

By privatizing "everything," I really mean *everything*. Love, friendship, criminality, citizenship, and even celebrity have all been datafied by algorithms we will rarely know about. These proprietary ideas about the world are not open for debate, made social and available to the public. They are assigned from behind a private enclosure, a discursive trebuchet that assails us with meaning like rabble outside the castle walls.

The consequence of this privatization means that privacy has become inverted, not in its definition but in its participants and circumstances. A site like OkCupid has privacy from us, but we don't have privacy from OkCupid. We don't know how our data is being used. We can't peek inside its compatibility match algorithm. But every little thing we do can be watched and datafied.

Google's algorithm orders the world's knowledge and thus frames what is and is not 'true,' using our own search data and its catalogue of our web habits to improve its functioning. But the machinations of Google search will always be hidden, intellectual property that we can never, ever know.[6] Google has no obligation to tell us how they make 'us' or the 'world' useful. But in order to use each site, via its terms of service, we must agree not to have privacy. We agree to let our datafied 'us' be mined and made meaningful according to the whims of site operators. Each site's legal terms of service are the lived terms of life online.

In fact, via the terms of service for a site like Facebook, not only do we not have privacy, but our data (our photos, videos, even chats) doesn't even belong to us. Data, more often than not, belongs to whoever holds it in the cloud. The semantic resemblance of privacy and privatization can be twisted together, a slippery neoliberal convergence by which the two concepts almost eagerly fold into one.

We can trace this neoliberal folding back to the Internet of the 1990s, around the time when AOL's famous "terms of service" were king and the company served a deluge of "TOS violations" to software pirates and explicit-language users. AOL's terms strictly forbid both proprietary software trading and unseemly discourse.[7] The resulting corporate cyberspace wasn't the unruly anarchist paradise feared/hoped for by some people but rather a highly controlled platform for "civility" and "security" that made AOL's paying customers feel, well, civil and secure.[8]

In a love-it-or-leave-it policy, any user who did not accept the stringent terms of AOL's service was disallowed access. Anyone who accepted them but later sinned was eventually banned. Users became indebted to these terms as they prescribed exactly how the network could be used. And a crucial feature of those terms was that your datafied life belonged to AOL, not you. Owners of cyberspaces like AOL drafted their own terms in order to give them sovereignty over their digital space, and the resulting discursive sphere was soon governed by AOL's legal code.

Quite predictably, this privatized cyberspace became business space, its business model became advertising, its advertising got targeted, and its targets were built with this possessed data.[9] As communication scholar Christian Fuchs has detailed, the data gathered in these privatized spaces became the constant capital by which profit would be produced, echoing the most basic of capital relations: we legally agree to turn over our data to owners, those owners use that data for profit, and that profit lets a company gather even more data to make even more profit.[10] So while the terms of cyberspace are defined by a company like AOL, the knowledges that make our datafied worlds are similarly owned.

But beyond the fundamentals of capitalist exploitation, the baseline premise of data being ownable has a provocative ring to it. If we could mobilize and change Facebook's terms of service to allow us true ownership over our Facebook profiles and data, then we could wrestle some control back. In this way, ownership is interpreted as a liberatory, privacy-enhancing move.

Tim Berners-Lee, inventor of the World Wide Web and leading voice against the commercialization of the Internet, believes our data belongs to you or me or whoever births it.[11] In a way, our datafied lives are mere by-products of our mundane entrepreneurial spirits, a tradable commodity whose value and use we, and we alone, decide. One step further, computer scientist Jaron Lanier has argued for a reconceptualized economic infrastructure in which we not only own but ought to be paid for our data—that the profits reaped by the million-/billionaires in the tech world should trickle down to those who make them their millions/billions.[12]

Whether owned by a corporation or ourselves, our data (and by default our privacy) finds comfortable accommodations in the swell of capitalist exchange. Indeed, Lanier's approach reincorporates the costly externalities of privacy invasion back into the full social cost of dataveillance. But to frame privacy in terms of ownership locates the agent of privacy as some unique, bodied, named, and bank-accountable person. A dividual can't receive a paycheck for her data-used-by-capital, but John Cheney-Lippold can.

This discussion eventually gets subsumed into a revolving circuit of critiques around what theorist Tiziana Terranova has coined "free labor."[13] The digital economy, as part of a capital-producing ecosystem, reconfigures how we conceive of work, compensation, and even production. If our datafied lives are made by our own actions, they order as well as represent a new kind of labor. You on OkCupid, diligently answering questions in the hope of romantic partnership, produce the knowledges that feed the site's algorithmic operations. OkCupid's value and profit margins are dependent on these knowledges.

This is where Italian autonomists have argued the "social factory" has relocated to, reframing the relation between capital and labor outside the factory walls and into the fabric of social life itself.[14] By commodifying our every action, the social factory structures not just labor but life within the rubric of industry. This is now an unsurprising reality of our daily, networked existence. But requisite in such commodification is the reversal of privacy.

The reversal of privacy lets dataveilling agents make us useful without us knowing what that use is. I can't find out what Google's 'gender' looks like (I've tried), although I do know I am a 'woman.' And I can't find out what Quantcast's 'ethnicity' looks like (I've tried), but neither do I know what Quantcast thinks I am. The privatized realms of measurable-type construction are owned by the other, sometimes hidden, other times superficially shown, but almost never transparent in how knowledges about the world, the discourses through which we're made subject, are created and modulated.

Microsoft's code is much more than a metaphor. It's an empirical, marketable commodity that defines the things we find important now—race, gender, class, sexuality, citizenship—as well as the things that we will find important in the future. When privacy is reversed, everything changes. Our worlds are decided for us, our present and futures dictated from behind the computational curtain.

GHOSTS IN THE MACHINE

I've always enjoyed the imagery of the "ghost in the machine." Beyond its origin as a critique of Cartesian dualism (philosopher Gilbert Ryle, the coiner of the phrase, used it to reject a separation between mind and body, deeming it logically impossible given the two's necessary operational overlap), a ghost in a machine evokes a haunting of what was previously a simple technological instrument.[15] A ghost in a blender? A ghost in a photocopier? A ghost in a Datsun? Ridiculous, yes, but these ghosts in otherwise functional machines emphasize the fact that machines are not just what they say they are—like our selves.

As described throughout the book, instances of 'celebrity,' 'English,' and 'citizen' are all materially and conceptually different from their non-quotation-marked cousins. They are made according to what digital theorist David Golumbia refers to as the "cultural logic of computation," not the capitalist logic of celebrity, the cultural logic of translation, or the political logic of citizenship.[16] Who is a 'citizen' is who, at the moment, produces data that the NSA's algorithmic logic defines as citizen. A straightforward birthday email to an Argentine friend in Buenos Aires is haunted by a heightened degree of 'foreignness.'

This book's title proposes much more than some unadorned commentary about how data affects our lives. Data holds no significance by itself—it has to be made useful. We are thus made subject not to our data but to interpretations of that data. These interpretations are specters that haunt anything connected to a networked device. A list of webpage visits in the morning, a coffee purchase in the afternoon, and an online conversation with a promising sexual partner in the evening all carry with them their own, ghostly effects. However, while these ghostly effects are 'true,' they're never true—algorithms will never be able to understand you as you.

A 'celebrity' will never be a celebrity, no matter how hard people try to bridge the ontological gap, a gap that reaffirms what I in previous chapters called the else. It may be useful to think about ghosts haunting not just the machine but also this bridge into the algorithmic world. As such, apparitions appear in alarmingly bizarre ways: through linguistic translations that include the n-word, Facebook asking you to tag a 'person' in a photo of what is clearly just a tree, and suggestions that you date your own mother.

These ghosts in the machine acknowledge the black-box nature of algorithmic meaning proposed in the book's introduction. When we log into Facebook or into Google or onto the Internet at large, we encounter a world we might be immediately familiar with, but the depth and complexity of this world elude any possibility for us to truly know it. We are affected by algorithmic interpretation all the time, but we rarely know exactly how or why. Every day we deal with the ghostly effects of an endless series of interpretations, of us, of society, and of those in society who are "as if" us.

How sociology treats ghosts might serve as a supernatural convergence to this line of thought. For sociologists like Avery Gordon, ghosts are phenomena that are felt even as they lay outside traditional, empirical analysis, usually understood as what is visible, representable, and thus acknowledged. For example, while the Argentine dictatorship disappeared tens of thousands of people in the 1970s and 1980s, those *desaparecidos* play a part in Argentine society even today. Then-president Jorge Rafaela Videla astonishingly explained that the disappeared "is not an entity, . . . is neither dead nor alive" in a 1979 press conference.[17] But the disappeared, returning to Gordon, still "pull us affectively into the structure of feeling of a reality we come to experience as recognition."[18]

The pull of ghostly matters is not unlike our encounters with algorithmic identification, a process in which our every measurable-type assignment draws us toward a particular algorithmic interpretation. But whereas a sociological ghost haunts the past and conditions our present and future according to the traces left by those ghostly matters, a ghost in the machine haunts the present and conditions our present and future. On all fronts, we're affected, pulled in one direction or another. And on all fronts, we're almost always unknowing of if, and how, we're exactly being pulled.

This unknowingness becomes the film that occludes the black box of algorithmic identification. Agents like the NSA live within this box, assess us, analyze those assessments, and organize our lives. This process of phantasmal organization turns our data into 'citizen' and uses our Facebook friendships to label us 'gay.' Everything made from within this box is creepy because it's ghostly, like how personalized ads creep us out when they're spookily right or farcically wrong.

The control at the heart of algorithmic identification, soft biopolitics, is effectual inasmuch as it hides these ghosts in the machine and thus dampens the else. Like shocks on a car, our lives, as conditioned by the physics of the road, appear unconditioned by technological intervention. We are unknowing of the reality that exists beneath us. A car with perfect shocks would make even the rockiest of roads seem impossibly smooth. Which is real, the shocks or the road? From the perspective of the driver, there's no truth to either version. Each is just a different perspective, a different system that is indebted to its own conditioning via physics, politics, logics, aesthetics, ethics, and many other -ics.

The world looks different when it's statistically flattened, the hard edges of human experience softened by the algorithmic interpolations processed using each new input. Take the driving video game *Forza Horizon 2*, released in 2014. The game's engine learns how 'you' drive over time. Your "Drivatar" is an average of how you steer, accelerate, brake, and handle and your "style of racing," just like Shimon, the marimba-playing robot discussed in chapter 1. With this collection of data, *Forza Horizon 2* learns how 'you' pilot a simulated car (figure C.1).[19] This averaged version of 'you' becomes your driving soul, and as with any quantitative model, there's always a center, or centroid, that when calculated will get to the conceptual essence of the phenomenon being studied.

This center exists outside you. It lives across the algorithmic bridge. It sits in a database, waiting to be called on to race as 'you' against your friends. These are ghosts in the machine that make the world a posteriori—without preconditioning and training. Their smoothness averages out the errant accidents, poor turns, late starts, and erratic tempos of a single race, blurring these isolated deviations into a semi-competent Drivatar.

But ghosts in the machine are mere layers of the world, like sheets (for last-minute Halloween costume shoppers) to follow the phantasmologi-

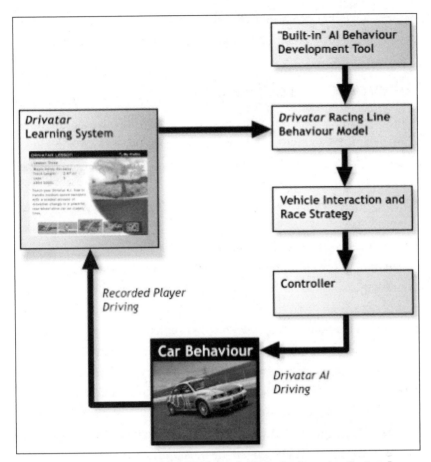

FIGURE C.1. A diagram of *Forza Horizon 2*'s "Drivatar Learning System."
Source: Microsoft Research, "Drivatar™ in Forza Motorsport," 2015, http://
research.microsoft.com.

cal. The essences of algorithmic life are not the entirety of life. Rather, the driving 'you' and Shimon's version of 'you' are mathematical essences, residing across the algorithmic bridge on the plane of computation. But unlike the sociological ghosts that are accessible only as traces in the social record, the ghosts in the machine are actually *in* the machine.[20] Whether or not we can see what makes up Shimon's or *Forza Horizon 2*'s 'you,' it really exists. It's not like a perfect circle or the good or any of the other comparably unfeasible idealist metaphysical forms. It's an existing, mathematical interpretation that makes you useful . . . for them.

THE FUTURE OF ALGORITHMIC LOGICS

As everything we do becomes datafied, everything we do becomes controllable. So when we combine "we are data" with "inside us all is a code," we see that who we are becomes controlled, too. Let's remember the case of ZunZuneo, the "Cuban Twitter" from chapter 2, which highlights how governments use big data for malicious ends. And let's also remember that the USAID-based surveillance program was shut down only two years after it began due to funding issues.

But the Minerva Initiative, a U.S. Department of Defense research program that "seek[s] to define and develop foundational knowledge about sources of present and future conflict with an eye toward better understanding of the political trajectories of key regions of the world," remains open.[21] Since 2008, the U.S. government has distributed millions of dollars to social science university researchers in the hope that innovative projects will assist the United States in its global geopolitical strategies.

Unsurprisingly, many of these projects rely on big data and machine-learning algorithms to "understand" the foreign world. As we've learned in the earlier chapters, data from the most mundane of datafied events, like our Gmail contacts list, can be used to classify us as 'foreigner' or 'citizen.' Even the GPS data coming from our cell phones can be compared against existing information signatures in order to determine if we're a 'terrorist' or 'not.' In these two cases, our ghosts in the machine aren't ethereal spirits lingering in the background. They're instead flat-out hegemonic.

They're hegemonic because the Minerva Initiative's mission is not about equality or fairness or justice. It's about the dominance of the United States and how researchers can use data to ensure that dominance extends into the next several decades. Consider a Minerva project funded in 2015, innocuously titled "Dynamic Statistical Network

Informatics." And look carefully at the project description, keeping an eye out for how the institutional vocabulary of research summaries dilutes an otherwise affronting imperial activity:

> This basic research proposal aims to develop new dynamic statistical network techniques that support the identification of structural features in communities or nation-states that can be leveraged to increase the resiliency, *alter the distribution of power*, support deterrence activities or stabilize or *destabilize communities*. At its core, developing this socio-cultural understanding (the socio-cognitive cultural map (SCM)) means collecting, reasoning about, visualizing and forecasting change in networks.[22]

This research, aimed at "regions of interest" that include "Syria/Iraq, Pacific Rim, and Global," collects "diverse data sources (questionnaire, news, subject matter expert assessments, and sensor data)" and processes it for purposes of destabilizing unfriendly regimes. By "forecasting change" in networks, the government's ability to leverage big data for global hegemony is no longer the stuff for conspiracy theorists.[23] It's instead a real, funded technological possibility for the U.S. Department of Defense.

The ability to forecast changes in a country's informational pattern is scary, but the resulting ability (and let's admit it, rationale for funding the project) to manipulate those changes is doubly so. Here, the ghosts of "inside us all is a code" do more than assign a 'gender' to us from afar. Now our political futures become tethered to governments' algorithmic interpretations of what the world should look like. This direness points to the structural danger in a digital life ordered and reordered beyond our pale and without our knowledge. Without making our identities and thoughts social, without a general understanding of how resources and rights are asymmetrically distributed, and without an ability to know how our information is used to manipulate us toward some political goal, that algorithmic knowledge is unavailable for critique. Or struggle.

WE ARE DATA

There's a whole genre of techno-philosophical literature that I have been loathe to touch in the preceding pages, a futurist dys-/utopian idea that has spawned movies, books, and even real-world panic. The techno-logical singularity, a hypothesis that linear technological progress will overtake the capacities of the human mind and body, has already pro-duced more than its share of high-tech futurist fantasies.[24] One response to these fantasies is authored by literary critic N. Katherine Hayles and her acclaimed book *How We Became Posthuman*, particularly her reac-tion to the first time she encountered futurist Hans Moravec's *Mind Children: The Future of Robots and Human Intelligence*.[25]

Hayles was shocked to read Moravec's proposal of a transferable, em-igrating human consciousness. Envision a world where we can actually survive within a computer, leaving our bodies behind as we upload our consciousness onto a server to exist forever, so long as that server re-mains plugged in. Immortality in this case isn't about people actually living forever but about their souls becoming code, their datafied selves engaging with the world sans a human brain or human body.

This is the end point of "inside us all there is a code. A code that represents not what we are but who we might become." The singular-ity promises everything that our mere, mortal humanity isolates us from—an evolution of self that lets us escape from the distastefulness of our unruly bodies. Ironically, by shedding our bodies, or excess mate-rial, we would lose our machines. We would become our own figurative ghosts as we truly become "we are data."

The perceived cataclysm of the theorized singularity would also be the cataclysm of our techno-social formations: after the singularity, what we know will no longer have the same traction or use. The ac-claimed "superintelligence" of the singularity will surely laugh in the face of our petty divisions of gender or race.[26]

But we are not at all close to that day. What we are close to is a super-intelligence of the measurable type that is not really super or that intelligent. It's just different, the separate layers of algorithmic knowledge that add onto our world. In its difference, we found entire industries, from marketing to spy craft. In its difference, we create new algorithmic ideas, from what a 'celebrity' is to who our 'friends' are. And in its difference, we reform how politics functions, from conferring 'citizenship' to algorithmically adjudicating the death of a 'terrorist.'

I refrained from mentioning the singularity earlier because it more than likely won't exist. It's a techno-futurist aspiration that is more marvel than muster. But what does exist is that ideas of our selves (not our souls) have already become datafied and been uploaded onto a server and then, so long as the server is kept plugged in, shape us and the discourses that make us. It's not our selves that will be made into code but the foundry by which our selves are made known to the world.

So while we don't live in a world where our reality is exclusively data, we do live in a world where our reality is augmented by data. That is, we were already made of data; we just didn't know it yet. We don't have to wait for some sibylline technological development to make it so. In fact, data has almost always made us, though historically it hasn't been as algorithmic and ubiquitous as it is now.

Which is to say, the singularity of technological futurism will never arrive . . . because it's already kind of here. 'Race' isn't really about our bodies but about datafied interpretations of those bodies. To return to the introduction, Black Desi's face is digitally distanced from his body, abstracted away as a "technical issue" that nonetheless returns us to an underlying question of power. Who has power in an algorithmic world? Who can wield it? And how do the technologies of the world, often unintentionally, inscribe that underlying power in ways that make, protect, and modulate that world in order to suit the status quo or privilege some interests over others? Those are the questions this book should want to make us answer.

Acknowledgments

After many revisions, what began as an idea turned into a manuscript and finally became the book you now hold in your hands (or have on your screen). Accordingly, over the past several years, I have relied on, learned from, and been inspired by a roll of different scholars, thinkers, friends, and/or personalities.

First, I want to thank Sarah Banet-Weiser for her patient and assuring guidance. Manuel Castells, Larry Gross, and Tara McPherson are all remarkable mentors and intellectual role models. And Charlotte Lapsansky and Russell Newman have long provided me their own, unique sense of what we might call skeptical hope around the prospects of critical academic work.

Amanda Price taught me what good writing looked like. Celine Kuklowsky helped me understand the absurdity that defines most of what we all do each and every day. Paula Winicki embodied human resilience. Bekah Dickstein's wit made me a better thinker, and she is also responsible for the title of this book. And for the fifteen years I have known Megan O'Brien, she has been one of my dearest friends. She has shown me what life can—and should—be.

To Livia Castiglioni, Giulio Crisante, Rania Divani, Alessia Esposito, Roberta Fadda, Roberto Fuentes-Rionda, Xara Gavalaki, Gretel Goyanarte, Claudia Michilli, and Jimena Valdés Figueroa, I want to thank you for being fellow travelers, as well as cherished companions.

I also want to acknowledge los de Roberto, los de La Birra, and los de Boca for their formative role in making me who I am today. Y gracias a Martín Palermo por tanto.

Anjali Nath's continuing contributions to my intellectual growth will be greedily devoured until either one of us dies. Natasha Hakimi Zapata's spirit follows her ancestry, and she will doubtlessly write a book far better than this. And Laura Portwood-Stacer has been my academic partner since we met in graduate school and has been an indispensable confidant and teacher, as well as editor.

To my colleagues Megan Ankerson, Tung-Hui Hu, and Lisa Nakamura, I cherish your support, camaraderie, and guidance. And to my community at Michigan and beyond, I want to sincerely thank Carolina Aguerre, Evelyn Alsultany, Patricia Aufderheide, Finn Brunton, Amy Sara Carroll, Iván Chaar-López, Maria Cotera, Greg Dowd, Larry La Fountain-Stokes, Mary Frieman, Parisa Ghaderi, Judy Gray, Colin Gunckel, Zehra Hashmi, June Howard, Dara Leto, Peggy McCracken, Richard Meisler, Stephen Molldrem, Marlene Moore, Anthony Mora, JP Obley, Christian Sandvig, Sidonie Smith, Alexandra Minna Stern, Ted Striphas, Wendy Sung, and Tammy Zill.

I also want to thank Lisha Nadkarni and NYU Press for their help, and accommodation, in producing this book. And abundant credit goes to Kim Greenwell and her laser-like ability to parse text, argument, and puerility.

Lastly, to my sister Emily, my brother Matt, and especially my mother, Karen: while our family might be unique in its formation, it remains loving in its future.

Notes

PREFACE

1. Larry Gross, John Stuart Katz, and Jay Ruby, *Image Ethics in the Digital Age* (Minneapolis: University of Minnesota Press, 2003); Sean Redmond and Su Holmes, eds., *Stardom and Celebrity: A Reader* (Thousand Oaks, CA: Sage, 2007).
2. Court of Justice of the European Union, *Google Spain SL, Google Inc. v Agencia Española de Protección de Datos (AEPD), Mario Costeja González*, 2014.
3. "What People Are Asking to Be Removed from Google Searches," *Telegraph*, October 13, 2014, www.telegraph.co.uk.
4. Stewart Baker, "Does Google Think You're Famous?," *Washington Post*, September 1, 2014, www.washingtonpost.com.
5. Stewart Baker, "More on How Google Decides You're Famous," *The Volokh Conspiracy* (blog), *Washington Post*, September 9, 2014, www.washington-post.com.
6. Richard Dyer, *Stars* (London: British Film Institute, 1979), 68.
7. Irving Rein, Philip Kotler, and Martin Stoller, *High Visibility: Making and Marketing of Celebrities* (New York: McGraw-Hill, 1997).
8. Graeme Turner, *Understanding Celebrity*, 2nd ed. (London: Sage, 2014), 101–102.
9. Rachel E. Dubrofsky and Megan M. Wood, "Gender, Race, and Authenticity: Celebrity Women Tweeting for the Gaze," in *Feminist Surveillance Studies*, ed. Rachel E. Dubrofsky and Shoshana Amielle Magnet (Durham, NC: Duke University Press, 2015).
10. Joseph Turow, *The Daily You: How the Advertising Industry Is Defining Your Identity and Your World* (New Haven, CT: Yale University Press, 2012); WikiLeaks, *The Spy Files*, 2011–2014, https://wikileaks.org.
11. Lisa Gitelman and Virginia Jackson, introduction to *"Raw Data" Is an Oxymoron*, ed. Lisa Gitelman (Cambridge, MA: MIT Press, 2013), 3.

INTRODUCTION

1. Marshall McLuhan, *Understanding Media: The Extensions of Man* (Cambridge, MA: MIT Press, 1994), 22.
2. Manuel Castells, *Communication Power* (Oxford: Oxford University Press, 2009).

3. Zygmunt Bauman and David Lyon, *Liquid Surveillance: A Conversation* (Cambridge, UK: Polity, 2012).

4. Maciej Ceglowski, "What Happens Next Will Amaze You," FREMTIDENS Internet Conference, Copenhagen, Denmark, September 14, 2015, http://idlewords.com.

5. Frank Pasquale, *Black Box Society: The Secret Algorithms That Control Money and Information* (Cambridge, MA: Harvard University Press, 2015), 4–5.

6. Ibid., 8.

7. Greg Elmer, *Profiling Machines: Mapping the Personal Information Economy* (Cambridge, MA: MIT Press, 2004).

8. John Cheney-Lippold, "A New Algorithmic Identity: Soft Biopolitics and the Modulation of Control." *Theory, Culture & Society* 28, no. 6 (2011): 164–181.

9. Antoinette Rouvroy, "The End(s) of Critique: Data Behaviourism versus Due Process," in *Privacy, Due Process, and the Computational Turn: The Philosophy of Law Meets the Philosophy of Technology*, ed. Mireille Hildebrandt and Katja de Vries (London: Routledge, 2013), 157.

10. Sarah Banet-Weiser, *Authentic™: The Politics of Ambivalence in a Brand Culture* (New York: NYU Press, 2012).

11. Geoffrey Bowker and Leigh Star, *Sorting Things Out: Classification and Its Consequences* (Cambridge, MA: MIT Press, 1999), 196.

12. C. Edwin Baker, *Media, Markets, and Democracy* (Cambridge: Cambridge University Press, 2004), 180.

13. C. Edwin Baker, "The Media That Citizens Need," *University of Pennsylvania Law Review* 147, no. 2 (1998): 377.

14. Oscar Gandy, "Exploring Identity and Identification in Cyberspace." *Notre Dame Journal of Ethics & Public Policy* 14 (2000): 1089.

15. Mark Poster, *The Second Media Age* (Cambridge, UK: Polity, 1995); Ian Hacking, "Making Up People," in *Reconstructing Individualism: Autonomy, Individuality, and the Self in Western Thought*, ed. Thomas C. Heller, David E. Wellbery, and Morton Sosna (Stanford, CA: Stanford University Press, 1986).

16. Gandy, "Exploring Identity," 1101.

17. Wendy Hui Kyong Chun, *Programmed Visions: Software and Memory* (Cambridge, MA: MIT Press, 2011), 9.

18. I use the phrase "near real-time" in order to provide some temporal leeway to definitions of an immediate present. As Tung-Hui Hu argues, "real time" itself is a construction in which "we too often confuse real time with the medium that manifests it," Tung-Hui Hu, "Real Time / Zero Time," *Discourse* 34, nos. 2–3 (2012): 163. For my argument, I employ "near real-time" to refer to how web surveillance may track user data second by second while that data takes time to be recorded and compared against previous data sets.

19. Louise Amoore, "On the Emergence of a Security Risk Calculus for Our Times," *Theory, Culture & Society* 28, no. 6 (2011): 27.

20. Alexander Galloway, *Gaming: Essays on Algorithmic Culture* (Minneapolis: University of Minnesota Press, 2006), 103.

21. Nicholas Negroponte, *Being Digital* (New York: Vintage, 1995), 4.

22. Eugene Thacker, "Bioinformatics and Bio-logics," *Postmodern Culture* 13, no. 2 (2003): 58.

23. Viktor Mayer-Schönberger and Kenneth Cukier, *Big Data: A Revolution That Will Transform How We Live, Work, and Think* (Boston: Eamon Dolan / Houghton Mifflin Harcourt, 2013).

24. Tyler Reigeluth, "Why Data Is Not Enough: Digital Traces as Control of Self and Self-Control," *Surveillance & Society* 12, no. 2 (2014): 249.

25. Alondra Nelson, *The Social Life of DNA: Race, Reparations, and Reconciliation after the Genome* (Boston: Beacon, 2016); Kim Tallbear, *Native American DNA: Tribal Belonging and the False Promise of Genetic Science* (Minneapolis: University of Minnesota Press, 2013).

26. Simone Browne, "Digital Epidermalization: Race, Identity and Biometrics," *Critical Sociology* 36, no. 1 (2010): 135.

27. Lev Manovich, *Language of New Media* (Cambridge, MA: MIT Press, 2001), 63.

28. Ibid., 63–64.

29. Ian Fasel, Bret Fortenberry, and Javier Movellan, "A Generative Framework for Real Time Object Detection and Classification," *Computer Vision and Image Understanding* 98, no. 1 (2005): 182–210.

30. Jacob Whitehill, Gwen Littlewort, Ian Fasel, Marian Bartlett, and Javier Movellan, "Toward Practical Smile Detection," *IEEE Transactions on Pattern Analysis and Machine Intelligence* 31, no. 11 (2009): 2107.

31. Ms Smith, "Face Detection Technology Tool Now Detects Your Moods Too," *Network World*, July 14, 2011, www.networkworld.com; Yaniv Taigman and Lior Wolf, "Leveraging Billions of Faces to Overcome Performance Barriers in Unconstrained Face Recognition," arXiv:1108.1122, 2011.

32. Darren Murph, "Face.com Acquired by Facebook for an Estimated $80 Million+, Facial Tagging Clearly at the Forefront," *Engadget*, June 18, 2012, www.engadget.com.

33. N. Katherine Hayles, "Traumas of Code," *Critical Inquiry* 33, no. 1 (2006): 136–157.

34. This general argument comes from the work of N. Katherine Hayles, particularly her book *How We Became Posthuman: Virtual Bodies in Cybernetics, Literature, and Informatics* (Chicago: University of Chicago Press, 1999).

35. Stephen Wolfram, *A New Kind of Science* (Champaign, IL: Wolfram Media, 2002); Rudy Rucker, *Mind Tools: The Five Levels of Mathematical Reality* (Boston: Mariner Books, 1988); Rudy Rucker, *Infinity and the Mind: The Science and Philosophy of the Infinite* (Princeton, NJ: Princeton University Press, 2004).

36. Kelly Gates, *Our Biometric Future: Facial Recognition Technology and the Culture of Surveillance* (New York: NYU Press, 2011).

37. Geoffrey Bowker, "Data Flakes: An Afterward to 'Raw Data' Is an Oxymoron," in *Raw Data Is an Oxymoron*, ed. Lisa Gitelman (Cambridge, MA: MIT Press, 2013), 167–171.

38. Keith Clark, "Negation as Failure," in *Logic and Databases*, ed. Herve Gallaire and Jack Minker (New York: Plenum, 1978), 293.

39. Wanda Zamen, "HP Computers Are Racist," YouTube.com, December 10, 2009.

40. For a fuller explanation of how digital epidermalization operates in this example, see Simone Browne, *Dark Matters: On the Surveillance of Blackness* (Durham, NC: Duke University Press, 2015), 161–164.

41. Julianne Hing, "HP Face-Tracker Software Can't See Black People," *Colorlines*, December 21, 2009, www.colorlines.com.

42. Wendy Hui Kyong Chun, "On Software, or the Persistence of Visual Knowledge," *Grey Room* 18 (2005): 26–51.

43. HSV (hue, saturation, value) is a color space used in computer image processing. HSV is often used over other color spaces, like RGB (red, green, blue), because it separates color from intensity, enabling a processor to better control for shadows, overexposure, and other lighting modifications.

44. Donna Haraway, "Situated Knowledges: The Science Question in Feminism and the Privilege of Partial Perspective," *Feminist Studies* 14, no. 3 (1988): 583.

45. Nicholas Mirzoeff, *The Right to Look: A Counterhistory of Visuality* (Durham, NC: Duke University Press, 2011), 6.

46. Beth Coleman, "Race as Technology," *Camera Obscura* 24, no. 1 (2009): 193.

47. Zamen, "HP Computers Are Racist."

48. An excellent review of HP's algorithmic facial-recognition process is available in Christian Sandvig, Karrie Karahaolis, and Cedric Langbort, "Re-centering the Algorithm," paper presented at the Governing Algorithms Conference, New York, May 16–17, 2013.

49. In this sentence, I do not mean to posit that racism itself is waning. Rather, I want to highlight a shift away from essentialist claims about race and toward what Eduardo Bonilla-Silva succinctly calls a "racism without racists." See Eduardo Bonilla-Silva, *Racism without Racists: Color-Blind Racism and the Persistence of Racial Inequality in America* (Lanham, MD: Rowman and Littlefield, 2013).

50. Lisa Nakamura, *Digitizing Race: Visual Cultures of the Internet* (Minneapolis: University of Minnesota Press, 2007), 14.

51. Josh Harkinson, "Silicon Valley Firms Are Even Whiter and More Male than You Thought," *Mother Jones*, May 29, 2014, www.motherjones.com.

52. A similar relationship between technology and nonwhite skin is available in the history of film, where film-stock emulsions, light meters, and even the models for adjusting color and tone were calibrated according to light, white skin hues. The consequence of this technological "limitation" was that, if black characters were visible at all, their faces were distorted, washed out, and ultimately featureless. While excessive

lighting could be used as a "solution" (which would then lead to extreme discomfort and sweating on the behalf of these faces), Vaseline would also be smeared onto actors' skin to better reflect light into the racialized technology of the camera. See Lorna Roth, "The Fade-Out of Shirley, a Once-Ultimate Norm: Colour Balance, Image Technologies, and Cognitive Equity," in *The Melanin Millennium*, ed. Ronald Hall (New York: Springer, 2012), 273–286. Also, see Judy Wajcman, *Feminist Confronts Technology* (University Park: Pennsylvania State University Press, 1991).

53. Tim Wu, "United States of Secrets," *Frontline*, PBS, 2013, www.pbs.org.
54. Christian Fuchs, *Social Media: A Critical Introduction* (Thousand Oaks, CA: Sage, 2013).
55. Wu, "United States of Secrets."
56. Kevin Haggerty and Richard Ericson, "The Surveillant Assemblage," *British Journal of Sociology* 51, no. 4 (2000): 605–622.
57. "DoubleClick.net Usage Statistics," BuiltWith.com, July 28, 2016, http://trends.builtwith.com; Steven Levy, "How Google Search Dealt with Mobile," *Backchannel*, January 15, 2015, https://backchannel.com; Frederic Lardinois, "Gmail Now Has 425 Million Users," *TechCrunch*, June 28, 2012, http://techcrunch.com.
58. Microsoft, "Microsoft Statement on Proposed Acquisition of DoubleClick by Google," April 15, 2007, http://news.microsoft.com.
59. Siva Vaidhyanathan describes this giant surveillant assemblage as a "cryptopticon" in his *Googlization of Everything (and Why We Should Worry)* (Berkeley: University of California Press, 2011), 112.
60. Frederic Kaplan, "Linguistic Capitalism and Algorithmic Mediation," *Representations* 127, no. 1 (2014): 57–63.
61. Richard Clarke, "Information Technology and Dataveillance," Roger Clarke's website, November 1987, www.rogerclarke.com.
62. Colin Bennett, *The Privacy Advocates: Resisting the Spread of Surveillance* (Cambridge, MA: MIT Press, 2010).
63. David Lyon, "Surveillance, Snowden, and Big Data: Capacities, Consequences, Critique," *Big Data & Society* 1, no. 2 (2014): 1–13.
64. Walter Perry, Brian McInnis, Carter C. Price, Susan Smith, and John Hollywood, "Predictive Policing: The Role of Crime Forecasting in Law Enforcement Operations," RAND Corporation, 2013, www.rand.org.
65. Jeremy Gorner, "Chicago Police Use Heat List as Strategy to Prevent Violence," *Chicago Tribune*, August 21, 2013, http://articles.chicagotribune.com.
66. Anthony Braga, Andrew Papachristos, and David Hureau, "The Effects of Hot Spots Policing on Crime: An Updated Systematic Review and Meta-analysis," *Justice Quarterly* 31, no. 4 (2012): 633–663.
67. Todd R. Clear, *Imprisoning Communities: How Mass Incarceration Makes Disadvantaged Neighborhoods Worse* (Oxford: Oxford University Press, 2007).
68. Gorner, "Chicago Police Use Heat List."

69. Max Weber, *The Methodology of the Social Sciences* (New York: Free Press, 1949), 90.

70. Tarleton Gillespie, "The Relevance of Algorithms," In *Media Technologies: Essays on Communication, Materiality, and Society*, ed. Tarleton Gillespie, Pablo J. Boczkowski, and Kristen A. Foot (Cambridge, MA: MIT Press, 2014), 190.

71. Pasquale, *Black Box Society*, 9.

72. Judith Butler, *Bodies That Matter: On the Discursive Limits of Sex* (New York: Routledge, 1993).

73. Judith Halberstam, "Automating Gender: Postmodern Feminism in the Age of the Intelligent Machine." *Feminist Studies* 17, no. 3 (1991): 443.

74. Ibid.

75. Mark Andrejevic, *iSpy: Surveillance and Power in the Interactive Era* (Lawrence: University Press of Kansas, 2007), 8.

76. Gilles Deleuze, "Postscript on the Societies of Control," *October* 59 (1992): 4.

77. Ibid., 3–7.

78. Tiziana Terranova, *Network Culture: Politics for the Information Age* (London: Pluto, 2004), 56; see also Deleuze, "Postscript."

79. Terranova, *Network Culture*, 28.

80. Alexander R. Galloway, *Protocol: How Control Exists after Decentralization* (Cambridge, MA: MIT Press, 2004), 69.

81. Ibid., 30.

82. Alexander R. Galloway and Eugene Thacker, *The Exploit: A Theory of Networks* (Minneapolis: University of Minnesota Press, 2007), 42.

83. Cheney-Lippold, "New Algorithmic Identity."

84. Cass Sunstein, *Republic.com 2.0* (Princeton, NJ: Princeton University Press, 2009); and Eli Pariser, *The Filter Bubble: How the New Personalized Web Is Changing What We Read and How We Think* (New York: Penguin Books, 2012).

85. Michel Foucault, *Power/Knowledge* (Brighton, UK: Harvester, 1980).

86. Judith Butler, *Excitable Speech: A Politics of the Performative* (New York: Routledge, 1997), 34.

87. Although Flanagan talks explicitly about women's bodies, I use her concept to engage with the lived virtuality of these "creatures." This is not to degender the concept but to better understand how algorithms interface with bodies of all different genders. See Mary Flanagan, "The Bride Stripped Bare to Her Data: Information Flow + Digibodies," in *Data Made Flesh: Embodying Information*, ed. Robert Mitchel and Phillip Thurtle (New York: Routledge, 2004), 175–176.

88. Anna Watkins Fisher, "User Be Used," *Discourse* 36, no. 3 (2014): 385.

89. Vaidhyanathan, *Googlization of Everything*, 84.

90. Friedrich Kittler, *Discourse Networks, 1800/1900* (Stanford, CA: Stanford University Press, 1992).

91. Evgeny Dantsin, Thomas Eiter, Georg Gottlob, and Andrei Voronkov, "Complexity and Expressive Power of Logic Programming," *ACM Computing Surveys* 33, no. 3 (2001): 374–425; Ian Bogost, *Persuasive*

Games: The Expressive Power of Videogames (Cambridge, MA: MIT Press, 2007); Noah Wardrip-Fruin, *Expressive Processing: Digital Fictions, Computer Games, and Software Studies* (Cambridge, MA: MIT Press, 2009).

92. Kevin Kelly and Derrick de Kerckhove, "4.10: What Would McLuhan Say?," *Wired*, October 1, 1996, http://archive.wired.com.

93. Melvin Kranzberg, "Technology and History: 'Kranzberg's Laws,'" *Technology and Culture* 27, no. 3 (1986): 544–560.

94. David Lyon, *Surveillance Society: Monitoring Everyday Life* (Berkshire, UK: Open University Press, 2001); Daniel Solove, *The Digital Person: Technology and Privacy in the Information Age* (Rochester, NY: Social Science Research Network, 2004).

95. Evelyn Ruppert, "The Governmental Topologies of Database Devices," *Theory, Culture & Society* 29, nos. 4–5 (2012): 124.

96. Pedro Domingos, *The Master Algorithm: How the Quest for the Ultimate Learning Machine Will Remake Our World* (New York: Basic Books, 2015), 25.

97. Donna Haraway, *Simians, Cyborgs, and Women: The Reinvention of Nature* (New York: Routledge, 1990), 196.

CHAPTER 1. CATEGORIZATION

1. Christian Rudder, "Inside OkCupid: The Math of Online Dating," TedEd, 2013, http://ed.ted.com.

2. David Cole, "'We Kill People Based on Metadata,'" *NYR Daily* (blog), *New York Review of Books*, May 10 2014, www.nybooks.com.

3. Daniel Klaidman, *Kill or Capture: The War on Terror and the Soul of the Obama Presidency* (Boston: Houghton Mifflin Harcourt, 2012), 41.

4. Bureau of Investigative Journalism, 2015, https://www.thebureauinvestigates.com/category/projects/drones/drones-pakistan.

5. Danya Greenfield, "The Case against Drone Strikes on People Who Only 'Act' like Terrorists," *Atlantic*, August 19, 2013, www.theatlantic.com.

6. Jeremy Scahill and Glenn Greenwald, "The NSA's Secret Role in the U.S. Assassination Program," *Intercept*, February 10, 2014, https://theintercept.com.

7. Tom Engelhardt, *Shadow Government: Surveillance, Secret Wars, and a Global Security State in a Single-Superpower World* (Chicago: Haymarket Books, 2014), 76.

8. Jo Becker and Scott Shane, "Secret 'Kill List' Proves a Test of Obama's Principles and Will," *New York Times*, May 29, 2012, www.nytimes.com.

9. Mark Andrejevic, "FCJ-187: The Droning of Experience," *Fibreculture Journal* 25 (2015): 206; Ian Bogost, *Alien Phenomenology, or, What It Is Like to Be a Thing* (Minneapolis: University of Minnesota Press, 2012), 41–42.

10. Hans Vaihinger, *The Philosophy of "As If": A System of the Theoretical, Practical and Religious Fictions of Mankind* (New York: Harcourt Brace, 1924). See also Curtis White, *We, Robots: Staying Human in the Age of Big Data* (New York: Melville House, 2015). For more on the as if, see chapter 3's discussion on Rosi Braidotti.

11. Atlantic Council, "Transcript: Stabilizing Transatlantic Relations after the NSA Revelations," November 8, 2013, www.atlanticcouncil.org.

12. Thomas H. Davenport, Paul Barth, and Randy Bean, "How 'Big Data' Is Different," *MIT Sloan Management Review*, July 30, 2012, http://sloanreview.mit.edu.

13. Evelyn Alsultany, *Arabs and Muslims in the Media: Race and Representation after 9/11* (New York: NYU Press, 2012), 9.

14. Jasbir Puar and Amit S. Rai, "Monster, Terrorist, Fag: The War on Terrorism and the Production of Docile Bodies," *Social Text* 20, no. 3 (2002): 125.

15. Scott Shane, "Drone Strikes Reveal Uncomfortable Truth: U.S. Is Often Unsure about Who Will Die," *New York Times*, April 23, 2015, www.nytimes.com.

16. Charles Townshend, "The Culture of Paramilitarism in Ireland," in *Terrorism in Context*, ed. Martha Crenshaw (University Park: Pennsylvania State University Press, 2010), 311–351.

17. Adam Entous, Siobhan Gorman, and Julian E. Barnes, "U.S. Relaxes Drone Rules," *Wall Street Journal*, April 26, 2012, www.wsj.com.

18. Alexander J. Martin, "PGP Zimmermann: 'You Want Privacy? Well Privacy Costs money,'" *Register*, October, 8, 2015, www.theregister.co.uk.

19. Luciano Floridi, "Big Data and Their Epistemological Challenge," *Philosophy and Technology* 25, no. 4 (2012): 436; and Stephen J. Collier, "Topologies of Power: Foucault's Analysis of Political Government beyond 'Governmentality,'" *Theory, Culture & Society* 26, no. 6 (2009): 87.

20. Seth Greenblatt, Thayne Coffman, and Sherry Marcus, "Behavioral Network Analysis for Terrorist Detection," in *Emergent Information Technologies and Enabling Policies for Counter Terrorism*, ed. Robert L. Popp and John Yen (Hoboken, NJ: Wiley–IEEE, 2006), 334.

21. Grégoire Chamayou, "Oceanic Enemy: A Brief Philosophical History of the NSA," *Radical Philosophy* 191 (2015): 3–4.

22. Spencer Ackerman, "White House Stays Silent on Renewal of NSA Data Collection Order," *Guardian*, July 18, 2013, www.theguardian.com.

23. C. Edwin Baker, *Media, Markets, and Democracy* (Cambridge: Cambridge University Press, 2001), 180.

24. Nikolas Rose, *Powers of Freedom: Reframing Political Thought* (Cambridge: Cambridge University Press, 1999), 133.

25. Chamayou, "Oceanic Enemy," 4.

26. National Security Agency, "New Collection Posture," 2011, www.aclu.org.

27. David Lazer, Alex Pentland, Lada Adamic, Sinan Aral, Albert-László Barabási, Devon Brewer, Nicholas Christakis, Noshir Contractor, James Fowler, Myron Gutmann, Tony Jebara, Gary King, Michael Macy, Deb Roy, and Marshall Van Alstyne, "Computational Social Science," *Science* 323, no. 5915 (2009): 721–723; danah boyd and Kate Crawford, "Critical Questions for Big Data," *Information, Communication & Society* 15, no. 5 (2012): 662–679; Mark Andrejevic, *Infoglut: How Too Much Information Is Changing the Way We Think and Know* (New York: Routledge, 2013).

28. Google, "Company—Google," 2014, www.google.com.

29. Michel Foucault, *Power/Knowledge: Selected Interviews and Other Writings, 1972–1977* (New York: Pantheon Books, 1980), 52.
30. Christian Rudder, *Dataclysm: Who We Are (When We Think No One Is Looking)* (New York: Crown, 2014), 20.
31. Erving Goffman, *The Presentation of Self in Everyday Life* (New York: Anchor, 1959); Max Weber, *The Methodology of the Social Sciences* (New York: Free Press, 1949).
32. Brian Cantwell Smith, "Limits of Correctness in Computers," in *Computerization and Controversy*, ed. Charles Dunlop and Rob Kling (San Diego: Academic Press, 1991), 636.
33. Johanna Drucker (and Bethany Nowviskie), "Speculative Computing: Aesthetic Provocations in Humanities Computing," in *A Companion to Digital Humanities*, ed. Susan Schreibman, Ray Siemens, and John Unsworth (Oxford, UK: Blackwell, 2004), 444.
34. Smith, "Limits of Correctness," 636.
35. Adam Kramer, Jamie Guillory, and Jeffrey Hancock, "Experimental Evidence of Massive-Scale Emotional Contagion through Social Networks," *Proceedings of the National Academy of Sciences of the United States of America*, 2014, 8788–8790, 8788.
36. James W. Pennebaker, Cindy K. Chung, Molly Ireland, Amy Gonzales, and Roger J. Booth, "The Development and Psychometric Properties of LIWC2007," LIWC.net, 2007.
37. Jacques Derrida and Bernard Stiegler, *Echographies of Television* (Cambridge, UK: Polity, 2002), 149.
38. Willard McCarty, "Modeling: A Study in Words and Meanings," in *A Companion to Digital Humanities*, ed. Susan Schreibman, Ray Siemens, John Unsworth (Oxford, UK: Blackwell, 2004), 257.
39. A scholarly connection of set theory to digital culture is found in Ian Bogost, *Unit Operations: An Approach to Videogame Criticism* (Cambridge, MA: MIT Press, 2006), which thinks about data through Alain Badiou's decades-long investigation on mathematical ontologies and knowledge in general.
40. For example, a sample text, like Bill Clinton's First Inaugural Address, is valued as 0.06 'sexual' on the basis of a simple averaging model (the number of 'sexual' words in the text divided by the total number of words in the text). Even the unimpressive phrase "Dick Cheney was the forty-sixth vice president of the United States," while clearly not intended to be, enjoys a spry 9.09 'sexual' rating from the LIWC.
41. Weber, *Methodology of the Social Sciences*, 90.
42. Goffman, *Presentation of Self*, 72.
43. Pierre Bourdieu, *Distinction: A Social Critique of the Judgement of Taste* (Cambridge, MA: Harvard University Press, 1984).
44. Gaston Bachelard, *Le rationalisme appliqué*, 3rd ed. (1949; Paris: Presses Universitaires de France, 1966), 35.
45. McCarty, "Modeling."

46. Foucault, *Power/Knowledge*; Antonio Gramsci, *Selections from the Prison Notebooks* (New York: International Publishers, 1971); Harry Collins, *Changing Order: Replication and Induction in Scientific Practice* (London: Sage, 1985); and Bruno Latour and Steve Woolgar, *Laboratory Life: The Social Construction of Scientific Facts* (Beverly Hills, CA: Sage, 1979).

47. Michael Omi and Howard Winant, *Racial Formation in the United States* (New York: Routledge, 2014); Geoffrey Bowker and Leigh Star, *Sorting Things Out: Classification and Its Consequences* (Cambridge, MA: MIT Press, 1999).

48. LIWC, 2015, http://liwc.wpengine.com.

49. David M. Berry, *The Philosophy of Software: Code and Mediation in the Digital Age* (London: Palgrave Macmillan, 2011), 14.

50. Sheila Jasanoff, "Ordering Knowledge, Ordering Society," in *States of Knowledge: The Co-production of Science and Social Order*, ed. Sheila Jasanoff (London: Routledge, 2004), 27. See also Bob Lingard, *Politics, Policies and Pedagogies in Education: The Selected Works of Bob Lingard* (London: Routledge, 2013).

51. Theodore Porter, *Trust in Numbers: The Pursuit of Objectivity in Science and Public Life* (Princeton, NJ: Princeton University Press, 1995), 77.

52. Sandra Scarr, *Race, Social Class, and Individual Differences in I.Q.* (Hillsdale, NJ: Lawrence Erlbaum, 1981).

53. James P. Scott, *Seeing like a State: How Certain Schemes to Improve the Human Condition Have Failed* (New Haven, CT: Yale University Press, 1998); Mae Ngai, *Impossible Subjects: Illegal Aliens and the Making of Modern America* (Princeton, NJ: Princeton University Press, 2014).

54. Grace Kyungwon Hong, *The Ruptures of American Capital: Women of Color Feminism and the Culture of Immigrant Labor* (Minneapolis: University of Minnesota Press, 2006), 80.

55. Lisa Gitelman, ed., *"Raw Data" Is an Oxymoron* (Cambridge, MA: MIT Press, 2013).

56. Richard Selleck, "The Manchester Statistical Society and the Foundation of Social Science Research," *Australian Educational Researcher* 16, no. 1 (1989): 7.

57. Helen Verran, "Number," in *Inventive Methods: The Happening of the Social*, ed. Lury Celia and Nina Wakeford (London: Routledge, 2012), 110–124.

58. Donna Haraway, *Modest_Witness@Second_Millenium.FemaleMan_Meets_OncoMouse: Feminism and Technoscience* (London: Routledge, 1997), 142.

59. Ibid.

60. Feminist scholar Shoshana Magnet has already outlined the racial, classed, and gendered dimensions of this machinic process. And surveillance theorist Simone Browne has argued that this biometric objectification constructs newly minted racial truths. See Shoshana Magnet, *When Biometrics Fail: Gender, Race, and the Technology of Identity* (Durham, NC: Duke University Press, 2011); Simone Browne, *Dark Matters: On the Surveillance of Blackness* (Durham, NC: Duke University Press, 2015).

61. Brad Weslake, "Explanatory Depth," *Philosophy of Science* 77, no. 2 (2010): 273–294.

62. Kate Crawford, "The Hidden Biases of Big Data," *Harvard Business Review*, April 1, 2013, http://hbr.org.

63. Geoffrey Bowker, "Data Flakes: An Afterward to 'Raw Data' Is an Oxymoron," in Gitelman, *"Raw Data" Is an Oxymoron*, 170.

64. Tom Boellstorff, "Making Big Data, in Theory," *First Monday* 18, no. 10 (2013): http://firstmonday.org.

65. danah boyd and Kate Crawford, "Critical Questions for Big Data," *Information, Communication & Society* 15, no. 5 (2012): 663.

66. Franco Moretti, "Conjectures on World Literature," *New Left Review* 1 (2000): 57.

67. Viktor Mayer-Schönberger and Kenneth Cukier, *Big Data: A Revolution That Will Transform How We Live, Work, and Think* (Boston: Eamon Dolan, 2013), 41.

68. Jonathan Culler, "The Closeness of Close Reading," *ADE Bulletin* 149 (2010): 20–25.

69. Joshua Rothman, "An Attempt to Discover the Laws of Literature," *New Yorker*, March 20, 2014, www.newyorker.com.

70. Jiawei Han, Micheline Kamber, and Jian Pei, *Data Mining: Concepts and Techniques* (Waltham, MA: Morgan Kaufmann, 2011); Trevor Hastie, Robert Tibshirani, and Jerome Friedman, *The Elements of Statistical Learning: Data Mining, Inference, and Prediction* (New York: Springer, 2009).

71. Rob Kitchin, "Big Data, New Epistemologies and Paradigm Shifts," *Big Data & Society*, April–June 2014, 1–12.

72. Kim Koehler, Evgeny Skvortsov, and Wiesner Vos, "A Method for Measuring Online Audiences," Google, 2012, http://static.googleusercontent.com.

73. As of 2014, comScore has a "2-million global panel" that observes online users' activity. See Lauren Amira, "Understand Campaign Delivery beyond Demographics with vCE Behavioral Segments," comScore, 2014, www.comscore.com. And as of 2015, Alexa gets its panel from "a sample of millions of Internet users using one of over 25,000 different browser extensions." See Alexa, "About Us," 2015, www.alexa.com.

74. See Jaideep Srivastava, Robert Cooley, Mukund Deshpande, and Pang-Ning Tan, "Web Usage Mining: Discovery and Applications of Usage Patterns from Web Data," *SIGKDD Explorations* 1, no. 2 (2000): 1–12.

75. Importantly, for purposes of consistency, I collapse the gendered identity of male and the sexed identity of man. This is due to the fact that there is no theoretically satisfying way to differentiate sex from gender as well as that most algorithmic agents (largely marketers) ignore the distinction also.

76. Judith Halberstam, "Automating Gender: Postmodern Feminism in the Age of the Intelligent Machine," *Feminist Studies* 17, no. 3 (1991): 443.

77. Judith Butler, *Subjects of Desire: Hegelian Reflections in Twentieth-Century France* (New York: Columbia University Press, 1987), 131.

78. Michel Foucault, *Security, Territory, Population: Lectures at the Collège de France 1977–1978* (New York: Picador, 2009), 57.

79. Ian Hacking, *The Taming of Chance* (Cambridge: Cambridge University Press, 1990), 119.

80. Sandra Harding, *Whose Science? Whose Knowledge? Thinking from Women's Lives* (Ithaca, NY: Cornell University Press, 1991); bell hooks, *Ain't I a Woman?* (Boston: South End, 1981), 145.

81. Tiziana Terranova, *Network Culture: Politics for the Information Age* (London: Pluto, 2004).

82. Stuart Hall, "Minimal Selves," in *The Real Me: Post-modernism and the Question of Identity*, ed. Homi K. Bhabha (London: Institute of Contemporary Arts, 1987), 44–46.

83. danah boyd and Kate Crawford, "Six Provocations for Big Data," paper presented at A Decade in Internet Time: Symposium on the Dynamics of the Internet and Society, September 21, 2011, Oxford, UK, http://papers. ssrn.com.

84. Vasant Dhar, "Data Science and Prediction," *Communications of the ACM* 56, no. 12 (2013): 66.

85. Mike Annany, "The Curious Connection between Apps for Gay Men and Sex Offenders," *Atlantic*, April 24, 2011, www.theatlantic.com; Nick Seaver, "Knowing Algorithms," paper presented at Media in Transition 8, Cambridge, MA, April 2013.

86. Louise Amoore, *The Politics of Possibility: Risk and Security Beyond Probability* (Durham, NC: Duke University Press, 2013), 72; Foucault, *Security, Territory, Population*, 45.

87. Farhad Manjoo, "Larry Page on Google's Many Arms," *New York Times*, June 26, 2014, www.nytimes.com.

88. Ian Witten, Eibe Frank, and Mark A. Hall, *Data Mining: Practical Machine Learning Tools and Techniques* (Burlington, VT: Morgan Kaufmann, 2011), xxiii.

89. Max Jones, John Chilton, and Leonard Feather, *Salute to Satchmo* (London: IPC, 1970), 25.

90. Paul Allen Anderson, *Deep River: Music and Memory in Harlem Renaissance Thought* (Durham, NC: Duke University Press Books, 2001); Herman Gray, *Cultural Moves: African Americans and the Politics of Representation* (Berkeley: University of California Press, 2005).

91. Extraordinary thanks go to Eitan Wilf for his scholarship and introduction to Georgia Tech's "Shimon."

92. Ryan Nikolaidis and Gil Weinberg, "Playing with the Masters: A Model for Improvisatory Musical Interaction between Robots and Humans," *2010 IEEE RO-MAN*, 2010, 712–717.

93. Eitan Wilf, "Sociable Robots, Jazz Music, and Divination: Contingency as a Cultural Resource for Negotiating Problems of Intentionality," *American Ethnologist* 40, no. 4 (2013): 605–618.

94. Guy Hoffman and Gil Weinberg, "Interactive Improvisation with a Robotic Marimba Player," *Autonomous Robots* 31, nos. 2–3 (2011): 133–153; Gil Weinberg, Guy Hoffman, Ryan Nikolaidis, and Roberto Aim, "Shimon +

ZOOZbeat: An Improvising Robot Musician You Can Jam With," in *ACM SIGGRAPH ASIA 2009 Art Gallery & Emerging Technologies: Adaptation* (New York: ACM, 2009), 84.

95. MIDI, an abbreviation for Musical Information Digital Interface, is the technical standard by which a user's playing can be born as already datafied. This data is taken from an MIDI instrument as a digital signal that specifies notation, pitch, and velocity.

96. Weinberg et al., "Shimon + ZOOZbeat," 84.

97. Eitan Wilf, "Toward an Anthropology of Computer-Mediated, Algorithmic Forms of Sociality," *Current Anthropology* 54, no. 6 (2013): 737.

98. Joseph Turrow and Nora Draper, "Industry Conceptions of Audience in the Digital Space," *Cultural Studies* 28, no. 4 (2014): 646.

99. C. W. Anderson. "Between Creative and Quantified Audiences: Web Metrics and Changing Patterns of Newswork in Local U.S. Newsrooms," *Journalism* 12, no. 5 (2011): 550–566.

100. Lev Manovich, *The Language of New Media* (Cambridge, MA: MIT Press, 2001), 71.

101. This is the same list that MySpace used for its profiles—in 2007, Millennial Media was the ad network contracted to serve and sell mobile-based advertisements to MySpace subscribers. See Millennial Media, "Press Release: MySpace Launches Free Mobile Web Services," 2007, http://investors.millennialmedia.com.

102. James Ball, "Angry Birds and 'Leaky' Phone Apps Targeted by NSA and GCHQ for User Data," *Guardian*, January 27, 2014, www.theguardian.com.

103. Richard Rogers, "Post-Demographic Machines," in *Walled Garden*, ed. Annet Dekker and Annette Wolfsberger (Amsterdam: Virtual Platform, 2009), 30.

104. Fernando Bermejo, *The Internet Audience: Constitution and Measurement* (New York: Peter Lang, 2007).

105. Daniel Yankelovich, "New Criteria for Market Segmentation," *Harvard Business Review*, March 1964, https://hbr.org.

106. Joseph Plummer, "The Concept and Application of Life Style Segmentation," *Journal of Marketing* 38, no. 1 (1974): 33–37; Emmanuel Demby, "Psychographics and from Whence It Came," in *Life Style and Psychographics*, ed. William D. Wells (Chicago: American Marketing Association, 1974), 9–30.

107. James Atlas, "Beyond Demographics," *Atlantic Monthly*, October 1984, 52.

108. Claritas, "PRIZM NE: The New Evolution Segment Snapshots," 2003, www.tetrad.com, 4.

109. Quantcast, "Understanding Digital Audience Measurement," 2014, www.quantcast.com.

110. Vital to note is that women of color theorists like Angela Davis (*Women Race and Class* [New York: Random House, 1981]) and Cherríe Moraga (*Loving in the War Years: Lo Que Nunca Pasó Por Sus Labios* [Boston: South End, 1983]) had already deessentialized the category of woman a

decade before intersectionality "provided a name to a pre-existing theoretical and political commitment." See Jennifer C. Nash, "Re-thinking Intersectionality," *Feminist Review* 89 (2008): 3.

111. Kimberlé Crenshaw, "Mapping the Margins: Intersectionality, Identity Politics, and Violence against Women of Color," *Stanford Law Review* 43 (1991): 1244.

112. Leslie McCall, "The Complexity of Intersectionality," *Signs* 30, no. 3 (2005): 1773–1774, 1783. See also Leela Fernandes's work on "politics of categories" in *Producing Workers: The Politics of Gender, Class, and Culture in the Calcutta Jute Mills* (Philadelphia: University of Pennsylvania Press, 1997).

113. Jasbir Puar, "I Would Rather Be a Cyborg than a Goddess: Becoming Intersectional in Assemblage Theory," *philoSOPHIA* 2, no. 1 (2012): 58.

114. Jasbir Puar, *Terrorist Assemblages: Homonationalism in Queer Times* (Durham, NC: Duke University Press, 2007), 213.

115. Zoubin Ghahramani, "Unsupervised Learning," in *Advanced Lectures on Machine Learning: ML Summer Schools 2003, Canberra, Australia, February 2–14, 2003, Tübingen, Germany, August 4–16, 2003, Revised Lectures*, ed. Olivier Bousquet, Ulrike von Luxburg, and Gunnar Rätsch (Berlin: Springer-Verlag, 2004), 73.

116. Puar, "I Would Rather Be a Cyborg than a Goddess," 50.

117. Judith Butler, *Gender Trouble: Feminism and the Subversion of Identity* (New York: Routledge, 1990); and Judith Butler, *Bodies That Matter: On the Discursive Limits of Sex* (New York: Routledge, 1993).

118. David Bamman, Jacob Eisenstein, and Tyler Schnoebelen, "Gender in Twitter: Styles, Stances, and Social Networks," arXiv:1210.4567, 2012, 2.

119. Chris Anderson, "The End of Theory: The Data Deluge Makes the Scientific Method Obsolete," *Wired*, June 23, 2008, www.wired.com.

120. Gartner, "Gartner Says Worldwide Enterprise IT Spending to Reach $2.7 Trillion in 2012," October 2011, http://gartner.com.

121. David Ribes and Steven J. Jackson, "Data Bite Man: The Work of Sustaining Long-Term Study," in Gitelman, *"Raw Data" Is an Oxymoron*, 147–166; Kate Crawford, "The Hidden Biases of Big Data," *Harvard Business Review Blog*, April 1, 2013, http://blogs.hbr.org; Rob Kitchin, "Big Data and Human Geography: Opportunities, Challenges and Risks," *Dialogues in Human Geography* 3, no. 3 (2013): 262–267.

122. Bamman, Eisenstein, and Schnoebelen, "Gender in Twitter," 2.

123. Ibid.

124. This 'female' identification was assigned after the initial clustering algorithm was run. Here, 'female' refers to a trained, a priori idea of 'gender' based on users' display name on Twitter. In this study, research-ers labeled individual names as 'male' or 'female' according to information from the U.S. Social Security Administration Census. For example, names like "Roberta" skewed heavily female in Census data and thus would be read as 'female' in the researchers' postclustering analysis. The same was the case with names like "Robert" being a male and belonging to 'male.'

125. Bamman, Einstein, and Schnoebelen, "Gender in Twitter," 23.
126. N. Katherine Hayles, *My Mother Was a Computer: Digital Subjects and Literary Texts* (Chicago: University of Chicago Press, 2005), 27.
127. Ibid., 41.
128. Wendy Hui Kyong Chun, *Updating to Remain the Same: Habitual New Media* (Cambridge, MA: MIT Press, 2016), 40.
129. Butler, *Gender Trouble*, 3.
130. Combahee River Collective, "The Combahee River Collective Statement," 1978, http://circuitous.org.
131. Audre Lorde, *Sister Outsider: Essays and Speeches* (Freedom, CA: Crossing, 1984), 116.
132. Cherríe Moraga and Gloria Anzaldúa, eds., *This Bridge Called My Back*, 4th ed. (Albany: SUNY Press, 2015); Patricia Hill Collins, *Black Feminist Thought: Knowledge, Consciousness, and the Politics of Empowerment* (New York: Routledge, 1990).
133. Doug Bowman, "Goodbye, Google," 2009, http://stopdesign.com.
134. Nicholas Rule, Nalini Ambady, and Katherine C. Hallett, "Female Sexual Orientation Is Perceived Accurately, Rapidly, and Automatically from the Face and Its Features," *Journal of Experimental Social Psychology* 45, no. 6 (2009): 1245–1251; Nicholas Rule, C. Neil Macrae, and Nalini Ambady, "Ambiguous Group Membership Is Extracted Automatically from Faces," *Psychological Science* 20, no. 4 (2009): 441–443.
135. Zach Blas, "Facial Weaponization Suite | Zach Blas," 2014, www.zachblas. info.
136. James P. Scott, *Seeing like a State: How Certain Schemes to Improve the Human Condition Have Failed* (New Haven, CT: Yale University Press, 1999), 80.
137. Ibid., 81.
138. Ibid., 83.
139. Lev Manovich, *Software Takes Command* (London: Bloomsbury, 2013); Lev Manovich, "The Algorithms of Our Lives," *Chronicle of Higher Education*, December 16, 2013, http://chronicle.com.

CHAPTER 2. CONTROL

1. Pierre-Joseph Proudhon, *General Idea of the Revolution in the Nineteenth Century* (1851), trans. John Beverly Robinson (London: Freedom Press, 1923), http://fair-use.org.
2. Michel Foucault, *Discipline and Punish* (New York: Vintage, 1979); Michalis Lianos, "Social Control after Foucault," *Surveillance & Society* 1, no. 3 (2003): 412–430.
3. Brad Millington, "Wii Has Never Been Modern: 'Active' Video Games and the 'Conduct of Conduct,'" *New Media & Society* 11, no. 4 (2009): 621–640.
4. Michel Foucault, *The History of Sexuality, Volume 1: An Introduction* (New York: Pantheon Books, 1978), 139.
5. Nikolas Rose, "Government and Control," *British Journal of Criminology* 40 (2000): 323.

6. Michel Foucault, *Ethics: Subjectivity and Truth.* Vol. 1 of *The Essential Works of Michel Foucault, 1954–1984* (New York: New Press, 1997), 68.

7. Seb Franklin, *Control: Digitality as Cultural Logic* (Cambridge, MA: MIT Press, 2015), xv.

8. Ibid., xviii.

9. Ibid., xv.

10. Evelyn Ruppert, "The Governmental Topologies of Database Devices," *Theory, Culture & Society* 29, nos. 4–5 (2012): 116–136; Kevin Haggerty and Richard Ericson, "The Surveillant Assemblage," *British Journal of Sociology* 51, no. 4 (2000): 605–622; Michael Hardt, "The Withering of Civil Society," *Social Text* 45 (1995): 27–44.

11. Gilles Deleuze, "Postscript on the Societies of Control," *October* 59 (1992): 5, 7.

12. Ibid., 5.

13. Gilbert Simondon, as referenced in Gilles Deleuze and Felix Guattari, *A Thousand Plateaus: Capitalism and Schizophrenia* (Minneapolis: University of Minnesota Press, 1987), 408–409.

14. Deleuze, "Postscript," 4.

15. Ibid., 7.

16. Celia Pearce, *Communities of Play: Emergent Cultures in Multiplayer Games and Virtual Worlds* (Cambridge, MA: MIT Press, 2011).

17. The concept of the "magic circle" originates in the work of Johan Huizinga, in which play itself requires a material or ideal separation between what is part of the game and what isn't (often referred to as the real versus the virtual in video game studies). As a concept, the magic circle has been long criticized as overly binary, although it still enjoys conceptual use. See Johan Huizinga, *Homo Ludens: A Study of Play-Element in Culture* (Boston: Beacon, 1971). For more, see Bonnie Nardi, *My Life as a Night Elf Priest: An Anthropological Account of World of Warcraft* (Ann Arbor: University of Michigan Press, 2010); and Mia Consalvo, "There Is No Magic Circle," *Games and Culture* 4, no. 4 (2009): 408–417.

18. Tim O'Reilly, "Open Data and Algorithmic Regulation," in *Beyond Transparency*, ed. Brett Goldstein and Lauren Dyson (San Francisco: Code for America Press, 2013), 291.

19. Lawrence Lessig, *Code: And Other Laws of Cyberspace, Version 2.0* (New York: Basic Books, 2006), 38.

20. Ibid., 5.

21. Julie E. Cohen, *Configuring the Networked Self: Law, Code, and the Play of Everyday Life* (New Haven, CT: Yale University Press, 2012), 185.

22. Deleuze, "Postscript," 3–7.

23. Nigel Thrift and Shaun French, "The Automatic Production of Space," *Transactions of the Institute of British Geographers* 27, no. 3 (2002): 331.

24. Michel Foucault, *Power/Knowledge: Selected Interviews and Other Writings, 1972–1977* (New York: Vintage, 1980).

25. Judith Butler, *Excitable Speech: A Politics of the Performative* (New York: Routledge, 1997), 34.

26. Judith Butler, *Bodies That Matter: On the Discursive Limits of Sex* (New York: Routledge, 1993), 23.

27. Bruce Curtis, "Foucault on Governmentality and Population: The Impossible Discovery," *Canadian Journal of Sociology / Cahiers canadiens de sociologie* 27, no. 4 (2002): 505–533; Michel Foucault, *The Birth of Biopolitics: Lectures at the Collège de France, 1978–1979* (New York: Picador, 2010).

28. Quantcast, "Measure for Apps," 2016, www.quantcast.com.

29. Quantcast, "Quantcast in a Nutshell," 2014, www.quantcast.com.

30. Michael Zimmer, "The Externalities of Search 2.0: The Emerging Privacy Threats When the Drive for the Perfect Search Engine Meets Web 2.0," *First Monday* 13, no. 3 (2008), http://firstmonday.org.

31. Quantcast, "Understanding Digital Audience Measurement," 2014, www.quantcast.com.

32. Ibid.

33. Interview with anonymous data engineer, February 9, 2011.

34. Quantcast, "Quantcast Methodology Overview," 2008, www.quantcast.com [no longer available].

35. Thomas Bayes and Richard Price, "An Essay towards Solving a Problem in the Doctrine of Chances, by the Late Rev. Mr. Bayes, F.R.S. Communicated by Mr. Price, in a Letter to John Canton, A.M.F.R.S.," *Philosophical Transactions (1683–1775)* 53 (1763): 370–418.

36. Finn Brunton, *Spam: A Shadow History of the Internet* (Cambridge, MA: MIT Press, 2013), 135.

37. Paolo Totaro and Domenico Ninno, "The Concept of Algorithm as an Interpretative Key of Modern Rationality," *Theory, Culture & Society* 31, no. 4 (2014): 31.

38. Michael Hardt and Antonio Negri, *Empire* (Cambridge, MA: Harvard University Press, 2000), 295.

39. Nigel Thrift, *Knowing Capitalism* (Thousand Oaks, CA: Sage, 2005), 172.

40. Aihwa Ong, *Neoliberalism as Exception: Mutations in Citizenship and Sovereignty* (Durham, NC: Duke University Press, 2006), 124.

41. Tung Hui-Hu, *A Prehistory of the Cloud* (Cambridge, MA: MIT Press, 2015), 146.

42. Eli Pariser, *The Filter Bubble: How the New Personalized Web Is Changing What We Read and How We Think* (New York: Penguin Books, 2012).

43. Antoinette Rouvroy, "The End(s) of Critique: Data Behaviourism versus Due Process," in *Privacy, Due Process, and the Computational Turn: The Philosophy of Law Meets the Philosophy of Technology*, ed. Mireille Hildebrandt and Katja de Vries (London: Routledge, 2013), 157.

44. Tiziana Terranova, *Network Culture: Politics for the Information Age* (London: Pluto, 2004), 108.

45. Wendy Hui Kyong Chun, *Programmed Visions: Software and Memory* (Cambridge, MA: MIT Press, 2011), 9.

46. Michel Foucault, *"Society Must Be Defended": Lectures at the Collège de France, 1975–1976* (New York: Picador, 2003), 135.

47. Katia Genel, "The Question of Biopower: Foucault and Agamben," *Rethinking Marxism: A Journal of Economics, Culture & Society* 18, no. 1 (2006): 43–62.

48. Let's Move!, "Get Active," 2014, www.letsmove.gov.

49. Richard H. Thaler and Cass R. Sunstein, *Nudge: Improving Decisions about Health, Wealth, and Happiness* (New York: Penguin Books, 2009).

50. Let's Move!, "Get Active."

51. Quantified Self, "About the Quantified Self," 2014, http://quantifiedself. com.

52. Dawn Nafus and Jamie Sherman, "Big Data, Big Questions | This One Does Not Go Up to 11: The Quantified Self Movement as an Alternative Big Data Practice," *International Journal of Communication* 8 (2014): 1785.

53. Thanks goes to Farzana Dudhwala for introducing me to this example. See Farzana Dudhwala, "The Quantified Qualified Self: The Number Affect," paper presented at 4S Conference, Buenos Aires, 2014.

54. Google, "Google Flu Trends," 2014, www.google.org.

55. Jeremy Ginsberg, Matthew Mohebbi, Rajan Patel, Lynnette Brammer, Mark Smolinski, and Larry Brilliant, "Detecting Influenza Epidemics Using Search Engine Query Data," *Nature* 457, no. 7232 (2009): 1012–1014.

56. Declan Butler, "When Google Got Flu Wrong," *Nature* 494, no. 7436 (2013): 155–156.

57. Miguel Helft, "Using the Internet to Track Flu's Spread," *New York Times*, October 11, 2008.

58. Nidhi Makhija-Chimnani, "People's Insights Volume 1, Issue 52: Vicks Mobile Ad Campaign," MSLGroup, 2013, asia.mslgroup.com.

59. David Lazer, Ryan Kennedy, Gary King, and Alessandro Vespignani, "The Parable of Google Flu: Traps in Big Data Analysis," *Science* 343 (March 14, 2014): 1203–1205.

60. Steve Lohr, "For Big-Data Scientists, 'Janitor Work' Is Key Hurdle to Insights," *New York Times*, August 17, 2014.

61. Lazer, Kennedy, and Vespignani, "Parable of Google Flu."

62. Foucault, *"Society Must Be Defended,"* 249.

63. Mauricio Santillana, D. Wendong Zhang, Benjamin Althouse, and John Ayers, "What Can Digital Disease Detection Learn from (an External Revision to) Google Flu Trends?," *American Journal of Preventive Medicine* 47, no. 3 (2014): 341–347.

64. Ibid.

65. See Norbert Wiener, *Cybernetics; or, Control and Communication in the Animal and the Machine* (Cambridge, MA: MIT Press, 1961); William Ashby, *Introduction to Cybernetics* (London: Methuen, 1979); Heinz Von Foerster, *Understanding Understanding: Essays on Cybernetics and Cognition* (New York: Springer, 2002).

66. N. Katherine Hayles, *How We Became Posthuman: Virtual Bodies in Cybernetics, Literature, and Informatics* (Chicago: University of Chicago Press, 1999).

67. Luciana Parisi and Tiziana Terranova, "Heat-Death: Emergence and Control in Genetic Engineering and Artificial Life," *CTheory*, May 10, 2000, www.ctheory.net.

68. Ibid.; Eugene Thacker, "Networks, Swarms, Multitudes," *CTheory*, May 18, 2004, www.ctheory.net.

69. Burkhard Schipper and Hee Yul Woo, "Political Awareness, Microtargeting of Voters, and Negative Electoral Campaigning," unpublished paper, June 12, 2014, http://papers.ssrn.com.

70. Associated Press, "US Secretly Created 'Cuban Twitter' to Stir Unrest and Undermine Government," *Guardian*, April 3, 2014, www.theguardian.com.

71. Louise Amoore, *The Politics of Possibility: Risk and Security Beyond Probability* (Durham, NC: Duke University Press, 2013).

72. Google Flu Trends Team, "The Next Chapter for Flu Trends," *Google Research Blog*, August 20, 2015, http://googleresearch.blogspot.com.

73. David Lyon, *Surveillance as Social Sorting: Privacy, Risk and Automated Discrimination* (New York: Routledge, 2002); Stephen Graham, "Software-Sorted Geographies," *Progress in Human Geography* 29, no. 5 (2005): 562–580.

74. Quantcast, "Quantcast in a Nutshell," 2014, www.quantcast.com; Quantcast, "About Us," 2016, www.quantcast.com.

75. Quantcast, "Quantcast Methodology Overview," 2008, www.quantcast.com [no longer available].

76. John Cheney-Lippold, "A New Algorithmic Identity: Soft Biopolitics and the Modulation of Control," *Theory, Culture & Society* 28, no. 6 (2011): 164–181.

77. Nikolas Rose, "Government and Control," *British Journal of Criminology* 40, no. 2 (2000): 324.

78. Michel Foucault, *The Order of Things: An Archaeology of the Human Sciences* (New York: Vintage, 1994), xx.

79. Alexander R. Galloway, *Protocol: How Control Exists after Decentralization* (Cambridge, MA: MIT Press, 2004).

80. Stephen Collier, "Topologies of Power: Foucault's Analysis of Political Government beyond 'Governmentality,'" *Theory, Culture & Society* 26, no. 6 (2009): 78–108.

81. Jun-Yan Zhu, Yong Jae Lee, and Alexei A. Efros, "AverageExplorer: Interactive Exploration and Alignment of Visual Data Collections," *ACM Transactions on Graphics (TOG)* 33, no. 4 (2014): 160.

82. Of course, each Santaclaus.jpg image is indebted to a long cultural history that defines what is, and is not, Santa Claus. But to focus only on that cultural history would ignore the technological procedure by which any digital image labeled "Santaclaus.jpg" would become part of Reza's 'Santa' algorithm.

83. Quantcast, "Quantcast Methodology Overview."

84. For a detailed analysis of centroid use in large data sets, see Sudipto Guha, Rajeev Rastogi, and Kyuseok Shim, "CURE: An Efficient Clustering Algorithm for Large Databases," *Proceedings of the 1998 ACM SIGMOD*

International Conference on Management of Data (SIGMOD '98), ed. Ashutosh Tiwary and Michael Franklin (New York: ACM, 1998), 73–84; and Sudipto Guha, Rajeev Rastogi, and Kyuseok Shim, "ROCK: A Robust Clustering Algorithmic for Categorical Attributes," *Information Systems* 25, no. 5 (2000): 512–521.

85. Judith Butler, *Gender Trouble: Feminism and the Subversion of Identity* (New York: Routledge, 1990).

86. Manuel Castells, *The Power of Identity: The Information Age: Economy, Society, and Culture*, vol. 2 (Oxford, UK: Blackwell, 2010).

87. Maurizio Lazzarato, "The Concepts of Life and the Living in the Societies of Control," in *Deleuze and the Social*, ed. Martin Fuglsang and Bent Meier Sørensen (Edinburgh: Edinburgh University Press, 2006), 181; Gabriel Tarde, *L'opinion et la foule* (Paris: Presses Universitaires de Frances, 1989), 39.

88. Walter Benjamin, "The Work of Art in the Age of Mechanical Reproduction," in *Illuminations: Essays and Reflections* (New York: Schocken, 1969), 222.

89. Ibid., 223.

90. Zeynep Tufekci, "Engineering the Public: Big Data, Surveillance and Computational Politics," *First Monday* 19, no. 7 (2014), http://firstmonday.org.

91. Chris Anderson, "The End of Theory: Will the Data Deluge Make the Scientific Method Obsolete?," *Wired*, June 23, 2008, http://archive.wired.com.

92. Kai Eriksson, "Foucault, Deleuze, and the Ontology of Networks," *European Legacy* 10, no. 6 (2005): 599–600; Foucault, *History of Sexuality, Volume 1*, 92–93.

CHAPTER 3. SUBJECTIVITY

1. Babycastles, "julian assange—When Google Met WikiLeaks Book Release Party," Facebook, 2014, www.facebook.com.

2. James Camp, "Julian Assange: 'When You Post to Facebook, You're Being a Rat,'" *Guardian*, September 25, 2014, www.theguardian.com.

3. Google, "Google's Mission Is to Organize the World's Information and Make It Universally Accessible and Useful," 2015, www.google.com.

4. National Security Agency, "The NSA/CSS Mission—NSA/CSS," 2015, www.nsa.gov.

5. Judith Butler, *Excitable Speech: A Politics of the Performative* (London: Routledge, 1997), 16.

6. Mary Flanagan, "Hyberbodies, Hyperknowledge: Women in Games, Women in Cyberpunk, and Strategies of Resistance," in *Reload: Rethinking Women + Cyberculture*, ed. Mary Flanagan and Austin Booth (Cambridge, MA: MIT Press, 2002), 440.

7. Rosi Braidotti, *Nomadic Subjects: Embodiment and Sexual Difference in Contemporary Feminist Theory* (New York: Columbia University Press, 2011), 6.

8. Seb Franklin, *Control: Digitality as Cultural Logic* (Cambridge, MA: MIT Press, 2015), xviii.

9. Electronic Frontier Foundation, "2013 in Review: The Year the NSA Finally Admitted Its 'Collect It All' Strategy," 2013, www.eff.org.

10. Ellen Nakashima and Joby Warrick, "For NSA Chief, Terrorist Threat Drives Passion to 'Collect It All,'" *Washington Post*, July 14, 2013, www.washingtonpost.com.

11. NBC News, "Inside the Mind of Edward Snowden, Part 3," May 29, 2014, www.nbcnews.com.

12. The NSA's assemblage depends heavily on several different code-named programs: PRISM was the system used to access emails, chat messages, search queries, and personal data within Microsoft's, Google's, Yahoo!'s, Facebook's, PalTalk's, AOL's, YouTube's, Skype's, and Apple's secure networks; XKeyscore acted as a "front-end search engine" for all of the NSA's recorded data—like a Google for the NSA's huge cache of data that lets analysts search the near entirety of the past three to five days of Internet traffic; Trafficthief and MARINA both produced reservoirs of Internet metadata from physical wiretaps.

13. Jamie Kowalczyk and Thomas S. Popkewitz, "Multiculturalism, Recognition and Abjection: (Re)Mapping Italian Identity," *Policy Futures in Education* 3, no. 4 (2005): 423–435.

14. Arendt's formulation of the "right to have rights" is largely understood as the cardinal human right, which, in itself, requires recognition by a political body. This recognition is often done through the apparatus of the state, which is how I connect citizenship to Arendt's conception. See Alison Kesby, *The Right to Have Rights: Citizenship, Humanity, and International Law* (Oxford: Oxford University Press: 2012); and Hannah Arendt, *The Human Condition*, 2nd ed. (Chicago: University of Chicago Press, 1998).

15. Barton Gellman and Laura Poitras, "U.S., British Intelligence Mining Data from Nine U.S. Internet Companies in Broad Secret Program," *Washington Post*, June 6, 2013, www.washingtonpost.com.

16. John Cheney-Lippold, "Jus Algoritmi: How the NSA Remade Citizenship," *International Journal of Communications* 10 (2016): 1721–1742.

17. This discussion on jus soli and jus sanguinis is wholly abstract, aimed to carve out theoretical space to introduce the concept of jus algoritmi. The complexities of how the state allocates citizenship rights—in any form— are unending, as is discussed in the following sections.

18. Tom Boellstorff, "Making Big Data, in Theory," *First Monday* 18, no. 10 (2013), http://firstmonday.org.

19. A satire of this process is available in the fake HTTP header "X-No-Wiretap." See antimatter15, "X-No-Wiretap—Blog," September 2013, http://antimatter15.com.

20. Eric Holder, as cited in Glenn Greenwald and James Ball, "The Top Secret Rules That Allow NSA to Use US Data without a Warrant," *Guardian*, June 20, 2013, www.theguardian.com (emphasis added).

21. Barton Gellman and Laura Poitras, "U.S., British Intelligence Mining Data from Nine U.S. Internet Companies in Broad Secret Program," *Washington Post*, June 6, 2013, www.washingtonpost.com.

22. Eric Holder, "Procedures Used by the National Security Agency for Targeting Non–United States Persons Reasonably Believed to Be Located outside the United States to Acquire Foreign Intelligence Information Pursuant to Section 702 of the Foreign Intelligence Surveillance Act of 1978, as Amended," 2009, www.aclu.org.

23. Glenn Greenwald, Roberto Kaz, and José Casado, "UA espionaram milhões de e-mails e ligações de brasileiros" [United States spied on millions of emails and calls from Brazil], *Jornal O Globo*, July 6, 2013, http://oglobo. globo.com.

24. Gilles Deleuze, *Empiricism and Subjectivity: An Essay on Hume's Theory of Human Nature* (New York: Columbia University Press, 2001).

25. Diana Coole and Samantha Frost, eds., *New Materialisms: Ontology, Agency, and Politics* (Durham, NC: Duke University Press, 2010).

26. Donna Haraway, *Simians, Cyborgs, and Women: The Reinvention of Nature* (New York: Routledge, 1991); Chela Sandoval, "New Sciences: Cyborg Feminism and the Methodology of the Oppressed," in *Feminist and Queer Information Studies Reader*, ed. Patrick Keilty and Rebecca Dean (Sacramento, CA: Litwin Books, 2012).

27. Haraway, *Simians, Cyborgs, and Women*, 151–152.

28. N. Katherine Hayles, *How We Became Posthuman: Virtual Bodies in Cybernetics, Literature, and Informatics* (Chicago: University of Chicago Press, 1999); Cary Wolfe, *What Is Posthumanism?* (Minneapolis: University of Minnesota Press, 2015); Rosi Braidotti, *The Posthuman* (Cambridge, UK: Polity, 2013).

29. Hayles, *How We Became Posthuman*, 3.

30. Alondra Nelson, *The Social Life of DNA: Race, Reparations, and Reconciliation after the Genome* (Boston: Beacon, 2016); Kim Tallbear, *Native American DNA: Tribal Belonging and the False Promise of Genetic Science* (Minneapolis: University of Minnesota Press, 2013); Clara E. Rodriguez, *Changing Race: Latinos, the Census, and the History of Ethnicity in the United States* (New York: NYU Press, 2000).

31. Mae Ngai, *Impossible Subjects: Illegal Aliens and the Making of Modern America* (Princeton, NJ: Princeton University Press, 2014).

32. Edlie L. Wong, *Racial Reconstruction: Black Inclusion, Chinese Exclusion, and the Fictions of Citizenship* (New York: NYU Press, 2015).

33. Gilles Deleuze and Félix Guattari, *A Thousand Plateaus: Capitalism and Schizophrenia* (Minneapolis: University of Minnesota Press, 1980).

34. Rosi Braidotti, *Nomadic Subjects: Embodiment and Sexual Difference in Contemporary Feminist Theory* (New York: Columbia University Press, 2011), 26–27.

35. Ibid., 28.

36. Ibid.

37. Ibid., 26.

38. San Jeong Cho, *An Ethics of Becoming: Configurations of Feminine Subjectivity in Jane Austen, Charlotte Brontë, and George Eliot* (New York: Routledge, 2006), 91.

39. Lorraine Code, *Rhetorical Spaces: Essays on Gendered Locations* (New York: Routledge, 1995), 141, 153.

40. Daniel Solove, *The Future of Reputation: Gossip, Rumor, and Privacy on the Internet* (New Haven, CT: Yale University Press, 2007), 33.

41. Megan Sapnar Ankerson, "Writing Web Histories with an Eye on the Analog Past," *New Media & Society* 14, no. 3 (2012): 384–400; Megan Sapnar Ankerson, "Read/Write the Digital Archive: Strategies for Historical Web Research," in *Digital Research Confidential: The Secrets of Studying Behavior Online*, ed. Eszter Hargittai and Christian Sandvig (Cambridge, MA: MIT Press, 2015), 29–54.

42. Spencer Ackerman, "NSA Review Panel Casts Doubt on Bulk Data Collection Claims," *Guardian*, January 14, 2014, www.theguardian.com.

43. An MIT-based web application called Immersion does a good job of mining the entirety of your Gmail contacts and conversations in order to generate a cluster model of social relationships that visually distributes your "proximity" to others. See https://immersion.media.mit.edu.

44. Matteo Pasquinelli, "Italian Operaismo and the Information Machine," *Theory, Culture & Society* 32, no. 3 (2014): 51.

45. The NSA looks two to three degrees "deep" into each "target," meaning that if a "target" talks to your friend, and your friend talks to you, you are two "hops" away from a datafied suspect. See Kenton Powell and Greg Chen, "Three Degrees of Separation," *Guardian*, November 1, 2013, www.theguardian.com.

46. Louis Althusser, "Ideology and Ideological State Apparatuses: Notes towards an Investigation" (1970), in *Lenin and Philosophy and Other Essays*, trans. Ben Brewster (New York: Monthly Review Press, 1971), www.marxists.org.

47. Jacques Lacan, *Écrits: A Selection* (New York: Norton, 1977).

48. Curtis White, *We, Robots: Staying Human in the Age of Big Data* (Brooklyn, NY: Melville House, 2015), 118.

49. Jacques Lacan, *The Seminar of Jacques Lacan, Book I: Freud's Papers on Technique, 1953–1954* (New York: Norton, 1988).

50. Ronald Day, *Indexing It All: The Subject in the Age of Documentation, Information, and Data* (Cambridge, MA: MIT Press, 2015), 76.

51. Ibid., 66.

52. Ibid., 71, 75.

53. Mladen Dolar, "Beyond Interpellation," *Qui Parle* 6, no. 2 (1993): 75–96.

54. Félix Guattari, *Chaosmosis: An Ethico-Aesthetic Paradigm* (Bloomington: Indiana University Press, 1995), 9.

55. Ibid., 16.

56. Mark Poster, *The Mode of Information: Poststructuralism and Social Context* (Chicago: University of Chicago Press, 1990).

57. Ibid., 4.

58. Mark B. N. Hansen, *Feed-Forward: On the Future of Twenty-First Century Media* (Chicago: University of Chicago Press, 2015), 3.

59. Colin Bennett, "Unsafe at Any Altitude: The Comparative Politics of No-Fly Lists in the United States and Canada," in *Politics at the Airport*, ed. Mark B. Salter (Minneapolis: University of Minnesota Press, 2008), 51–76; Joel

Slemrod, "Taxation and Big Brother: Information, Personalisation and Privacy in 21st Century Tax Policy," *Fiscal Studies* 27, no. 1 (2006): 1–15; Julia Sudbury, ed., *Global Lockdown: Race, Gender, and the Prison-Industrial Complex* (New York: Routledge, 2004); José David Saldívar, *Border Matters: Remapping American Cultural Studies* (Berkeley: University of California Press, 1997).

60. Gilles Deleuze, "Postscript on the Societies of Control," *October* 59 (1992): 5.

61. Franklin, *Control*, 9.

62. Antoinette Rouvroy, "The End(s) of Critique: Data Behaviourism versus Due Process," in *Privacy, Due Process, and the Computational Turn: The Philosophy of Law Meets the Philosophy of Technology*, ed. Mireille Hildebrandt and Katja de Vries (London: Routledge, 2013), 157.

63. Ibid.

64. James Bridle, "Citizen-Ex," 2015, https://citizen-ex.com.

65. Marissa Moorman, "Can an Algorithm Be Racist?," *Africa Is a Country* (blog), September 29, 2014, http://africasacountry.com.

66. Ibid.

67. This point is admittedly confounded by the dominance of Brazilian Portuguese, which uses "você" as the default second-person subject.

68. The same applies to Google Translate Spanish, in which the informal "tú" is often replaced by the formal "usted."

69. David Bellos, *Is That a Fish in Your Ear? Translation and the Meaning of Everything* (New York: Farrar, Straus and Giroux, 2012).

70. Franz Joseph Och, "Statistical Machine Translation: Foundations and Recent Advances," Google, September 12, 2005, www.mt-archive.info; Christian Boitet, Hervé Blanchon, Mark Seligman, and Valérie Bellynck, "Evolution of MT with the Web," *Proceedings of the Conference "Machine Translation 25 Years On,"* 2009, 1–13.

71. Franz Josef Och, "Selection and Use of Nonstatistical Translation Components in a Statistical Machine Translation Framework," Google, 2014, www.google.com.

72. Additionally, some languages also neocolonially move through their "closest" language to get to "English." Catalan passes through Spanish, Haitian Creole passes through French, and Urdu passes through Hindustani.

73. While Google engineers may not be intentionally racist, it is important to note that Google could have easily implemented a conditional statement in its English-language translations, so that any output that includes a racial epithet would be flagged or potentially removed.

74. In the months following Melissa Morman's report, Google Translate's translation of "contigo manos e pais" changed. The phrase now translates to "you brothers and parents."

75. Ryckie Wade, "Try Google Translate to Overcome Language Barriers," *BMJ*, November 15, 2011, www.bmj.com.

76. Andrew Beaujon, "Hartford Courant's Spanish Site Is Google Translate," *Poynter*, August 17, 2012, www.poynter.org. The news site's project was

quickly abandoned, though, with the *Courant* launching Noticias, a "100-percent Spanish language news site produced by our newsroom," one year later. See Andrew Beaujon, "Hartford Courant Launches New Spanish-Language Site to Replace Google Translate Version," *Poynter*, September 5, 2012, www.poynter.org.

77. Alexander Galloway and Eugene Thacker, *The Exploit: A Theory of Networks* (Minneapolis: University of Minnesota Press, 2007).

78. Nigel Thrift, *Knowing Capitalism* (Thousand Oaks, CA: Sage, 2005), 178.

79. Hillel Schwartz, *The Culture of the Copy: Striking Likenesses, Unreasonable Facsimiles* (Cambridge, MA: MIT Press, 1996), 175.

80. Matt McGee, "EdgeRank Is Dead: Facebook's News Feed Algorithm Now Has Close to 100K Weight Factors," *Marketingland*, August 16, 2013, http://marketingland.com.

81. Tania Bucher, "Want to Be on the Top? Algorithmic Power and the Threat of Invisibility on Facebook," *New Media & Society* 14, no. 7 (2012): 1168.

82. Adrian Mackenzie, "The Viterbi Algorithm and the Mosaic of Machine Time," in *24/7: Time and Temporality in the Network Society*, ed. Robert Hassan and Ronald Purser (Stanford, CA: Stanford University Press, 2007), 91.

83. Rob Kitchin and Martin Dodge, *Code/Space: Software and Everyday Life* (Cambridge, MA: MIT Press, 2011), 16.

84. A 2014 change in OkCupid's site has since removed 'friend' as a measurable type, leaving only 'match' and 'enemy.'

85. Hiawatha Bray, "Online Dating: The Economics of Love," *Boston Globe*, February 13, 2007, http://archive.boston.com.

86. While 100 percent confidence is mathematically impossible, it is technically possible to reach 100 percent "match" on OkCupid. OkCupid subtracts a "reasonable margin of error" from the "match" percentage (1/size of S, where S = the number of questions you and another user have answered in common), making it functionally impossible to reach 100 percent. But when S is more than forty thousand (meaning you and another user answered all forty thousand in the same way), a 99.5 percent "match" is possible, which would round up to 100 percent. See OkCupid, "OkCupid Support: Match Percentages," 2015, www.okcupid.com.

87. Dan Slater, *Love in the Time of Algorithms: What Technology Does to Meeting and Mating* (New York: Current, 2013); Christopher Mascaro, Rachel M. Magee, and Sean P. Goggins, "Not Just a Wink and Smile: An Analysis of User-Defined Success in Online Dating," *Proceedings of the 2012 iConference*, 2012, 200–206.

88. Lisa Nakamura, *Digitizing Race: Visual Cultures of the Internet* (Minneapolis: University of Minnesota Press, 2007).

89. Christian Rudder, *Dataclysm: Who We Are* (New York: Crown, 2014).

90. Christian Rudder, "How Your Race Affects the Messages You Get," *OkTrends* (blog), OkCupid, 2009, http://blog.okcupid.com.

91. Geoffrey Bowker, *Memory Practices in the Sciences* (Cambridge, MA: MIT Press, 2006).

92. Lisa Nakamura, "The Socioalgorithmics of Race: Sorting It Out in Jihad Worlds," in *The New Media of Surveillance*, ed. Kelly Gates and Shoshana Magnet (New York: Routledge, 2009), 150.

93. The term "just-in-time" comes from the twentieth-century capitalist business world, in which companies used information technologies to fine-tune how inventory is shipped "just-in-time" for manufacturing. This strategy reduces overhead—such as warehouse space and extraneous shipping costs. Though it originated with Japanese car makers, the term increasingly is used to reference e-commerce companies, such as Amazon.com. See Yosuhiro Monden, *Toyota Production System: An Integrated Approach to Just-in-Time*, 4th ed. (Boca Raton, FL: Productivity, 2011); and John Walsh and Sue Godfrey, "The Internet: A New Era in Customer Service," *European Management Journal* 18, no. 1 (2000): 85–92.

94. Tung-Hui Hu, "Real Time / Zero Time," *Discourse*, 34, nos. 2–3 (2012): 164.

95. Aniko Hannak, Gary Soeller, David Lazer, Alan Mislove, and Christo Wilson, "Measuring Price Discrimination and Steering on E-commerce Web Sites," Auditing Algorithms Research Group, 2014, http://personalization.ccs.neu.edu; Jakub Mikians, László Gyarmati, Vijay Erramilli, and Nikolaos Laoutaris, "Detecting Price and Search Discrimination on the Internet," *Proceedings of the 11th ACM Workshop on Hot Topics in Networks*, 2012, 79–84.

96. This practice is called "dynamic pricing": prices modulate according to day and time, as well as by use and personal details. See Joseph Turow, Lauren Feldman, and Kimberly Meltzer, "Open to Exploitation: America's Shoppers Online and Offline; A Report from the Annenberg Public Policy Center of the University of Pennsylvania," working paper, 2005, http://repository.upenn.edu; and Thorin Klosowski, "How Web Sites Vary Prices Based on Your Information (and What You Can Do about It)," *Lifehacker*, January 7, 2013, http://lifehacker.com.

97. In the case of Orbitz.com, researchers discovered that use of an Apple computer would not necessarily give you higher prices but would front-load more expensive options in your search result. This is called "price steering," in which a $200 hotel might show up on the first page of search results rather than the third or fourth if you are deemed more likely to pay for it. In another case, other researchers found that travel site Priceline.com charged users higher prices if they were using a mobile browser versus desktop. See Hannak et al., "Measuring Price Discrimination."

98. Victor Mendoza, "A Queer Nomadology of Jessica Hagedorn's Dogeaters," *American Literature* 77, no. 4 (2005): 819.

99. David Cole, Kenneth Roth, and James Bamford, "'We Kill People Based on Metadata,'" *NYRblog*, *New York Review of Books*, May 10, 2014, www.nybooks.com.

100. Grégoire Chamayou, "Patterns of Life: A Very Short History of Schematic Bodies," *The Funambulist Papers* 57, 2014, http://thefunambulist.net.

101. Day, *Indexing It All*, 133.

102. Jeremy Scahill and Glenn Greenwald, "The NSA's Secret Role in the U.S. Assassination Program," *Intercept*, February 10, 2014, https://theintercept. com. The same JSOC drone pilot went on to say that "everything they turned into a kinetic strike or a night raid was almost 90 percent that," and "you could tell, because you'd go back to the mission reports and it will say 'this mission was triggered by SIGINT,' which means it was triggered by a geolocation cell."

103. This response is indicative of how populations under surveillance resist these forms of control. For example, during the Vietnam War, the U.S. Army used "people sniffers" to detect human "effluents," like sweat and urine, on the basis of their measured levels of ammonia. These devices let the Army know where enemy soldiers were in dense jungle areas so that aerial assaults could be launched based on that information. Knowing how these "people sniffers" worked, Viet Cong combatants would hang bags of urine in trees, leading the Army to drop bombs on empty territory. See Andrew Cockburn, *Kill Chain: The Rise of the High-Tech Assassins* (New York: Holt, 2015); and Robert Barkan, "Bringing the Toys Home from Vietnam," *New Scientist*, June 15, 1972. A longer history of these types of ground sensors and how they connect to contemporary debates on surveillance and state power is found in Iván Chaar-López, "Drone Technopolitics: A History of 'Intrusion' on the U.S.-Mexico Border, 1948–Present" (PhD diss., University of Michigan, n.d.).

104. Deleuze and Guattari, *Thousand Plateaus*, 25.

105. Haraway, *Simians, Cyborgs, and Women*, 163.

106. Judith Halberstam and Ira Livingston, "Introduction: Posthuman Bodies," in *Posthuman Bodies*, ed. Judith Halberstam and Ira Livingston (Bloomington: Indiana University Press, 1995), 13.

107. Alexander Galloway, *The Interface Effect* (Cambridge, UK: Polity, 2012), 137.

108. Blake Hallinan and Ted Striphas, "Recommended for You: The Netflix Price and the Production of Algorithmic Culture," *New Media & Society*, 1–21 (2014).

109. Gloria Anzaldúa, *Borderlands—La Frontera: The New Mestiza* (San Francisco: Aunt Lute Books, 1987), 1.

110. Galloway, *Interface Effect*, 142.

111. Ibid., 143.

112. Gilbert Simondon, as cited in Gilles Deleuze, *The Logic of Sense* (New York: Columbia University Press, 1990).

113. Gilbert Simondon, *L'individu et sa genèse physico-biologique* (Paris: Presses Universitaires de France, 1964), 52, as cited in Léopold Lambert, "#SIMONDON /// Episode 03: Topological Life: The World Can't Be Fathomed in Plans and Sections," *The Funambulist*, November 27, 2013, http://thefunambulist.net.

114. Tiziana Terranova, *Network Culture: Politics of the Information Age* (London: Pluto 2004), 28.

115. Michel Lianos, "Social Control after Foucault," *Surveillance and Society* 1, no. 3 (2003): 421.

116. Brian Massumi, "Requiem for Our Prospective Dead (Toward a Participatory Critique of Capitalist Power)," in *Deleuze and Guattari: New Mappings in Politics, Philosophy, and Culture*, ed. Eleanor Kaufman and Kevin Jon Heller (Minneapolis: University of Minnesota Press, 1998), 57.

117. Nikolas Rose, as cited in Nicholas Thoburn, *Deleuze, Marx and Politics* (New York: Routledge, 2003), 98.

118. Donna Haraway, "The Promises of Monsters: A Regenerative Politics for Inappropriate/d Others," in *Cultural Studies*, ed. Lawrence Grossberg, Cary Nelson, and Paula A. Treichler (New York: Routledge, 1992), 295–337; Kal Alston, "A Unicorn's Memoirs: Solitude and the Life of Teaching and Learning," in *The Center of the Web: Women and Solitude*, ed. Delease Wear (Albany: SUNY Press, 1993), 95–109.

119. Manuel Castells, *The Power of Identity: The Information Age: Economy, Society, and Culture*, vol. 2 (Malden, MA: Wiley-Blackwell, 2009).

CHAPTER 4. PRIVACY

1. Jessica Best, "Dying Man Told by 999 Operator: Call Back When You're Unconscious," *Mirror*, October 16, 2014, www.mirror.co.uk.

2. Triage systems historically operate in a protoalgorithmic fashion: a diagnosing doctor determines which patients, and in which order, deserve attention on the basis of the relative interpreted severity of each case. The UK's *999 system is unique due to its strict limits on input, the necessary self-disclosure of Hemmings's symptoms, the rigidity of the system's conclusion, and the overall absence of medical authority.

3. Dave Blackhurst, "Medics Say Meir Man Mark Hemmings Could Have Been Saved If Paramedics Had Been Dispatched Sooner," *Stoke Sentinel*, October 16, 2014, www.stokesentinel.co.uk.

4. Ibid.

5. Samuel Warren and Louis Brandeis, "The Right to Privacy," *Harvard Law Review* 4, no. 5 (1890).

6. John B. Thompson, "Shifting Boundaries of Public and Private Life," *Theory, Culture & Society* 28, no. 4 (2011): 63.

7. Jisuk Woo, "The Right Not to Be Identified: Privacy and Anonymity in the Interactive Media Environment," *New Media & Society* 8, no. 6 (2006): 953–954, 961.

8. Finn Brunton and Helen Nissenbaum, *Obfuscation: A User's Guide for Privacy and Protest* (Cambridge, MA: MIT Press, 2015), 1.

9. Finn Brunton and Helen Nissenbaum, "Vernacular Resistance to Data Collection and Analysis: A Political Theory of Obfuscation," *First Monday* 16, no. 5 (2011), http://firstmonday.org.

10. Jean L. Cohen, *Regulating Intimacy: A New Legal Paradigm* (Princeton, NJ: Princeton University Press, 2002), 56; Erving Goffman, *Relations in Public: Microstudies of the Public Order* (New York: Basic, 1971), 28.

11. Anthony Giddens, *The Constitution of Society* (Berkeley: University of California Press, 1986), 54.

12. NAACP v. Button, 371 U.S. 415, 433 (1963); New York Times Company v. Sullivan, 376 U.S. 254, 272 (1964).

13. Josh Quittner, "The Death of Privacy," *Time*, August 25, 1997; Alex Preston, "The Death of Privacy," *Guardian*, August 3, 2015, www.theguardian.com; Adam Penenberg, "The Death of Privacy," *Forbes*, November 29, 1999, www.forbes.com.

14. Polly Sprenger, "Sun on Privacy: 'Get over It,'" *Wired*, January 26, 1999, http://archive.wired.com.

15. Bobbie Johnson, "Privacy No Longer a Social Norm, Says Facebook Founder," *Guardian*, January 11, 2010, www.theguardian.com.

16. Richard Esguerra, "Google CEO Eric Schmidt Dismisses the Importance of Privacy," Electronic Frontier Foundation, December 10, 2009, www.eff.org.

17. Zizi Papacharissi, "Privacy as a Luxury Commodity," *First Monday* 15, no. 8 (2010), http://firstmonday.org.

18. Warren and Brandeis, "Right to Privacy," 220.

19. Catharine MacKinnon, *Toward a Feminist Theory of the State* (Cambridge, MA: Harvard University Press, 1991), 168.

20. Charlotte Alter, "Judge Says Women Aren't Entitled to Privacy in Public Places," *Time*, October 10, 2014, http://time.com.

21. The Children's Online Privacy Protection Act of 1998 (COPPA) outwardly protects children from online collection of personal information, but those children still remain under the tutelage of their parent or guardian.

22. Scott Campbell Brown, "Methodological Paradigms That Shape Disability Research," in *Handbook of Disability Studies*, ed. Gary Albrecht, Katherine Seelman, and Michael Burdy (Thousand Oaks, CA: Sage, 2001); Alison Marie Kenner, "Securing the Elderly Body: Dimentia, Surveillance, and the Politics of 'Aging in Place,'" *Surveillance & Society* 5, no. 3 (2008).

23. Imani Perry, *More Beautiful and More Terrible: The Embrace and Transcendence of Racial Inequality in the United States* (New York: NYU Press, 2011).

24. Albert Bendich, "Privacy, Poverty, and the Constitution," *California Law Review* 54, no. 2 (1966): 407–442; John Gilliom, *Overseers of the Poor* (Chicago: University of Chicago Press, 2001).

25. Eliot Spitzer, "The New York City Police Department's 'Stop and Frisk' Practices," Office of the New York State Attorney General, 1999, www.oag.state.ny.us; Andrew Gelman, Jeffrey Fagan, and Alex Kiss, "An Analysis of the New York City Police Department's 'Stop-and-Frisk' Policy in the Context of Claims of Racial Bias," *Journal of the American Statistical Association* 102, no. 479 (2007): 813–823.

26. Both philosopher Jacques Rancière and anthropologist Elizabeth Povinelli have done well to criticize this structural tenant of liberal rights theory. See Jacques Rancière, "Who Is the Subject of the Rights of Man?," *South Atlantic Quarterly*, 103, nos. 2–3 (2004); and Elizabeth Povinelli, *The Cunning of Recognition: Indigenous Alterities and the Making of Australian Multiculturalism* (Durham, NC: Duke University Press, 2002).

27. Milton Konvit, "Privacy and the Law: A Philosophical Prelude," *Law and Contemporary Problems* 31, no. 2 (1966): 272–280.

28. Thomas Cooley, *A Treatise on the Law of Torts Which Arise Independently of Contract* (Chicago: Callaghan, 1906), 33.

29. Ibid.

30. Warren and Brandeis, "Right to Privacy," 198.

31. Griswold v. Connecticut, 381 U.S. 479, 484 (1965).

32. NAACP v. Button, 371 U.S. 415, 433 (1963); New York Times Company v. Sullivan, 376 U.S. 254, 272 (1964).

33. Roger Clarke, "Introduction to Dataveillance and Information Privacy, and Definitions of Terms," Roger Clarke's website, 1999, www.rogerclarke.com.

34. Daniel Solove, "'I've Got Nothing to Hide' and Other Misunderstandings of Privacy," *San Diego Law Review* 44, no. 745 (2007): 745–772.

35. John B. Young, "Introduction: A Look at Privacy," in *Privacy*, ed. John B. Young (New York: Wiley, 1978), 2.

36. H. J. McCloskey, "Privacy and the Right to Privacy," *Philosophy* 55, no. 211 (1980): 38.

37. Olmstead v. United States, 277 U.S. 438, 478 (1928).

38. Ronald Krotoszynski, "Autonomy, Community, and Traditions of Liberty: The Contrast of British and American Privacy Law," *Duke Law Journal* 6 (1990): 1401.

39. Helen Nissenbaum, "Privacy as Contextual Integrity," *Washington Law Review* 79, no. 1 (2004): 195–217.

40. Giddens, *Constitution of Society*, 54.

41. Julie E. Cohen, "What Privacy Is For," *Harvard Law Review* 126 (2013): 1905.

42. Anita L. Allen, "Coercing Privacy," *William and Mary Law Review* 40, no. 3 (1999): 723–757.

43. Wendy Brown, *Undoing the Demos: Neoliberalism's Stealth Revolution* (Cambridge, MA: MIT Press, 2015); Jodi Dean, *Democracy and Other Neoliberal Fantasies: Communicative Capitalism and Left Politics* (Durham, NC: Duke University Press, 2009).

44. Alan Westin, *Privacy and Freedom* (New York: Atheneum, 1967), 35.

45. Farveh Ghafouri and Carol Anne Wien, "'Give Us a Privacy': Play and Social Literacy In Young Children," *Journal of Research in Childhood Education* 19, no. 4 (2005): 279–291.

46. Helen Nissenbaum, "Toward an Approach to Privacy in Public: Challenges of Information Technology," *Ethics & Behavior* 7, no. 3 (1997): 207–219.

47. Dev Patel and Steven Watros, "BoI Authorized Study That Photographed Faculty, Students in Class without Notice," *Crimson*, November 5, 2014, www.thecrimson.com.

48. It's significant to note that most universities do this, not just Harvard.

49. David Murakami Wood, "Beyond the Panopticon? Foucault and Surveillance Studies," in *Space, Knowledge and Power: Foucault and Geography*, ed. Jeremy Crampton and Stuart Elden (Aldershot, UK: Ashgate, 2007); David Lyon, ed., *Theorizing Surveillance: The Panopticon*

and Beyond (Cullompton, UK: Willan, 2006); Roy Boyne, "Post-Panopticism," *Economy and Society* 29, no. 2 (2000): 285–307.

50. Matthew Fuller, *Media Ecologies: Materialist Energies in Art and Technoculture* (Cambridge, MA: MIT Press, 2005), 149.

51. Alexander Galloway, *Gaming: Essays on Algorithmic Culture* (Minneapolis: University of Minnesota Press, 2006), 90–91.

52. Ibid., 106.

53. Carter Jernigan and Behram F. T. Mistree, "Gaydar: Facebook Friendships Expose Sexual Orientation," *First Monday* 14, no. 10 (2009), http://firstmonday.org.

54. Smith v. Maryland, 442 U.S. 735 (1979).

55. Jernigan and Mistree, "Gaydar."

56. Ibid.

57. Dean Spade, *Normal Life: Administrative Violence, Critical Trans Politics, and the Limits of Law* (Brooklyn, NY: South End, 2011).

58. The most well-known interpretation of this history is Michael Foucault, *The History of Sexuality, Volume 1: An Introduction* (New York: Vintage, 1990).

59. Michael Foucault, *The Order of Things: An Archaeology of the Human Sciences* (New York: Vintage, 1994); Eve Kosofsky Sedgwick, *Epistemology of the Closet* (Berkeley: University of California Press, 2008).

60. Roderick A. Ferguson, *Aberrations in Black: Toward a Queer of Color Critique* (Minneapolis: University of Minnesota Press, 2004); José Esteban Muñoz, *Disidentifications: Queers of Color and the Performance of Politics* (Minneapolis: University of Minnesota Press, 1999).

61. Identities like gay or lesbian are increasingly used as indices for marketing profiles. These categories remain largely disconnected from questions of oppression and lived experience. See Megan Sapnar Ankerson and Sarah Murray, "Lez Takes Time: Designing Lesbian Contact in Geosocial Networking Apps," *Critical Studies in Media Communication* 33, no. 1 (2016): 53–69.

62. Walter Scott, *Tales of the Crusaders* (London: Hurst, Robinson, 1825), Walter Scott Digital Archive, www.walterscott.lib.ed.ac.uk.

63. Omer Tene and Jules Polonetsky, "Big Data for All: Privacy and User Control in the Age of Analytics," *Northwestern Journal of Technology and Intellectual Property* 11 (2012): 239–273; Omer Tene and Jules Polonetsky, "Privacy in the Age of Big Data: A Time for Big Decisions," *Stanford Law Review Online* 64 (2013): 63–69.

64. This limited capacity comes from how many terms of service (TOS) agreements force users to accept conditions that disallow ownership or decision about how user data gets used.

65. Loren Baker, "Google May Change Gmail Advertising Model Due to Complaints," *Search Engine Journal*, April 14, 2004, www.searchenginejournal.com.

66. Truth Leem, "Google's Gmail-Reading Ad Service Faces Russian Privacy Probe," *Russia Today*, March 12, 2013, http://rt.com.

67. Kate Crawford and Jason Schultz, "Big Data and Due Process: Toward a Framework to Redress Predictive Privacy Harms," *Boston College Law Review* 55, no. 1 (2014): 106.

68. Ibid., 109.

69. Laurence H. Tribe, "The Puzzling Persistence of Process-Based Constitutional Theories," *Yale Law Journal* 89, no. 6 (1980): 1070.

70. Matthew Fuller, *Media Ecology: Materialist Energies in Art and Technoculture* (Cambridge, MA: MIT Press, 2005), 149.

71. Joseph Kupfer, "Privacy, Autonomy and Self-Concept," *American Philosophical Quarterly* 24, no. 1 (1987): 82.

72. Charles Taylor, "Responsibility for Self," in *The Identities of Persons*, ed. Amelie Oksenberg Rorty (Berkeley: University of California Press, 1976), 281.

73. Alexander Galloway, *The Interface Effect* (Cambridge, MA: Polity, 2012), 137.

74. Alan Westin, *Privacy and Freedom* (New York: Atheneum, 1967), 25.

75. Irwin Altman, *The Environment and Social Behavior: Privacy, Personal Space, Territory, and Crowding* (Monterey, CA: Brooks/Cole, 1975), 18; see also Irwin Altman, "Privacy Regulation: Culturally Universal or Culturally Specific?," *Journal of Social Issues* 33, no. 3 (1977): 66–84; Leysia Palen and Paul Dourish, "Unpacking 'Privacy' for a Networked World," *Proceedings of the SIGCHI Conference on Human Factors in Computing Systems*, 2003, 129.

76. Palen and Dourish, "Unpacking 'Privacy,'" 132.

77. Ibid., 131

78. Jonathan Grudin, "Desituating Action: Digital Representation of Context," Microsoft Research, 1991, http://research.microsoft.com.

79. Steven Levy, "Crypto Rebels," *Wired*, May–June 1993, http://archive.wired.com.

80. Google, "Google's Mission Is to Organize the World's Information and Make It Universally Accessible and Useful," 2015, www.google.com.

81. Brunton and Nissenbaum, "Vernacular Resistance."

82. Daniel Howe, Helen Nissenbaum, and Vincent Toubiana, "TrackMeNot," 2015, https://cs.nyu.edu.

83. Brunton and Nissenbaum, *Obfuscation*, 15.

84. José van Dijck, "Datafication, Dataism and Dataveillance: Big Data between Scientific Paradigm and Ideology," *Surveillance & Society* 12, no. 2 (2014): 198.

85. Paul Bogan and Andrew Roberts, *Identification: Investigation, Trial and Scientific Evidence* (Bristol, UK: Jordan, 2011).

86. United States Department of Homeland Security, "Per Country Limit | USCIS," United States Citizenship and Immigration Services, 2015, www.uscis.gov.

87. Nissenbaum, "Privacy as Contextual Integrity."

88. Jeff Weintraub, "The Theory and Politics of the Public/Private Distinction," in *Public and Private in Thought and Practice: Perspectives on a Grand Dichotomy*, ed. Jeff Weintraub and Krishan Kumar (Chicago: University of Chicago Press, 1997), 3.

89. Paul Schwartz, "Privacy and Democracy in Cyberspace," *Vanderbilt Law Review* 52 (1999): 1607–1702.
90. Julie E. Cohen, *Configuring the Networked Self: Law, Code, and the Play of Everyday Practice* (New Haven, CT: Yale University Press, 2012).
91. Ibid., 114.
92. Evgeny Morozov, "The Tyranny of Algorithms," *Wall Street Journal*, September 20, 2012, www.wsj.com.
93. Richard W. Severson, *The Principles of Information Ethics* (Armonk, NY: M. E. Sharpe, 1997), 67–68.
94. Galloway, *Interface Effect*, 143.
95. National Security Agency, "Types of IAT—Advanced Open Source Multi-Hop," 2012, https://www.aclu.org.
96. Bob Woodward, "How Mark Felt Became 'Deep Throat,'" *Washington Post*, June 20, 2005, www.washingtonpost.com.
97. Dune Lawrence, "The Inside Story of Tor, the Best Internet Anonymity Tool the Government Ever Built," Bloomberg, January 23, 2014, www.bloomberg.com.
98. As cited in the *Washington Post*, "Since 2006, according to a 49-page research paper titled simply 'Tor,' the agency has worked on several methods that, if successful, would allow the NSA to uncloak anonymous traffic on a 'wide scale'—effectively by watching communications as they enter and exit the Tor system, rather than trying to follow them inside. One type of attack, for example, would identify users by minute differences in the clock times on their computers." See Barton Gellman, Craig Timberg, and Steven Rich, "Secret NSA Documents Show Campaign against Tor Encrypted Network," *Washington Post*, October 4, 2013, http://www.washingtonpost.com/world/national-security/secret-nsa-documents-show-campaign-against-tor-encrypted-network/2013/10/04/610f08b6–2d05–11e3–8ade-a1f23cda135e_story.html.
99. Alexis Madrigal, "How Netflix Reverse Engineered Hollywood," *Atlantic*, January 2, 2014, www.theatlantic.com.
100. Julia Angwin, *Dragnet Nation: A Quest for Privacy, Security, and Freedom in a World of Relentless Surveillance* (New York: Times Books, 2014).
101. Facebook, "Terms of Service," last modified January 30, 2015, www.facebook.com.
102. David Shenk, *Data Smog: Surviving the Information Glut* (San Francisco: HarperOne, 1998).

CONCLUSION

1. Microsoft, "Microsoft Potential (Inside Us All, There Is a Code . . .)," YouTube, 2000, www.youtube.com.
2. Martin Heidegger, *The Question Concerning Technology and Other Essays* (New York: Garland, 1977), 17.
3. George Orwell, *1984* (Boston: Houghton Mifflin Harcourt, 1987), 88.
4. Zadie Smith, "Generation Why?," *New York Review of Books*, November 25, 2010, www.nybooks.com.

5. Cade Metz, "Facebook Envisions AI That Keeps You from Uploading Embarrassing Pics," *Wired*, December 9, 2014, www.wired.com.

6. Algorithmic specifics are kept secret within each company's proprietary walls precisely because each company doesn't copyright, and thus isn't required to publicly disclose, them.

7. Back in the 1990s and early 2000s, AOL's content ecosystem was seen as a "walled garden." It was a closed platform that disallowed the presumed dangers of the Internet from breaching AOL's walls (spam, pornography, viruses), while letting users enjoy news articles and forums curated by AOL engineers.

8. Margaret Jean Radin, "Regulation by Contract, Regulation by Machine," *Journal of Institutional and Theoretical Economics* 160, no. 1 (2014): 142–156; Hector Postigo, "Emerging Sources of Labor on the Internet: The Case of America Online Volunteers," *International Review of Social History* 48 (2003): 205–223.

9. Ethan Zuckerman, "The Internet's Original Sin," *Atlantic*, August 14, 2014, www.theatlantic.com.

10. Christian Fuchs, "The Political Economy of Privacy on Facebook," *Television & New Media* 13, no. 2 (2012): 139–159.

11. Alex Hern, "Sir Tim Berners-Lee Speaks Out on Data Ownership," *Guardian*, October 8, 2014, www.theguardian.com.

12. Jaron Lanier, *Who Owns the Future?* (New York: Simon and Schuster, 2014).

13. Tiziana Terranova, *Network Culture: Politics for the Information Age* (London: Pluto, 2004); Trebor Scholz, ed., *Digital Labor: The Internet as Playground and Factory* (New York: Routledge, 2012).

14. Mario Tronti, "Capitale Sociale," *Telos* 17 (1973): 98–121; David Palazzo, "The 'Social Factory' in Postwar Italian Radical Thought from Operaismo to Autonomia," Ph.D. diss., Graduate Center, CUNY, 2014; Rosalind Gill and Andy Pratt, "In the Social Factory? Immaterial Labour, Precariousness and Cultural Work," *Theory, Culture & Society* 25, nos. 7–8 (2008): 1–30.

15. Gilbert Ryle, *The Concept of Mind* (Chicago: University of Chicago Press, 2000).

16. David Golumbia, *The Cultural Logic of Computation* (Cambridge, MA: Harvard University Press, 2009).

17. Susana Rotker, *Captive Women: Oblivion and Memory in Argentina* (Minneapolis: University of Minnesota Press, 2002), 3.

18. Avery Gordon, *Ghostly Matters: Haunting and the Sociological Imagination* (Minneapolis: University of Minnesota Press, 2008), 63.

19. XBox, "Forza Horizon 2: What's a Drivatar, and Why Should I Care?," September 2014, news.xbox.com.

20. Herman Gray and Macarena Gómez-Barris, *Toward a Sociology of the Trace* (Minneapolis: University of Minnesota Press, 2010).

21. Minerva Initiative, "Program History & Overview," U.S. Department of Defense, 2015, http://minerva.dtic.mil.

22. Ibid. (emphasis added).

23. Ibid.

24. Ray Kurzweil, *The Singularity Is Near: When Humans Transcend Biology* (New York: Penguin, 2006); Amnon Eden, James H. Moor, Johnny H. Søraker, and Eric Steinhart, eds., *Singularity Hypotheses: A Scientific and Philosophical Assessment* (Berlin: Springer-Verlag, 2012).

25. N. Katherine Hayles, *How We Became Posthuman: Virtual Bodies in Cybernetics, Literature, and Informatics* (Chicago: University of Chicago Press, 1999); Hans Moravec, *Mind Children: The Future of Robot and Human Intelligence* (Cambridge, MA: Harvard University Press, 1990).

26. Nick Bostrom, "How Long before Superintelligence," *Linguistic and Philosophical Investigations* 5, no. 1 (2006): 11–30.

Index

Bold page numbers refer to figures

About the Author

John Cheney-Lippold is Assistant Professor of American Culture at the University of Michigan.